DUST THAT NEVER SETTLES

Stanford Studies in Middle Eastern and
Islamic Societies and Cultures

DUST THAT NEVER SETTLES

Literary Afterlives of the Iran-Iraq War

Amir Moosavi

STANFORD UNIVERSITY PRESS
Stanford, California

Stanford University Press
Stanford, California

© 2025 by Amir Abraham Moosavi. All rights reserved.

No part of this book may be reproduced or transmitted in any form or by any means, electronic or mechanical, including photocopying and recording, or in any information storage or retrieval system, without the prior written permission of Stanford University Press.

Printed in the United States of America on acid-free, archival-quality paper

Library of Congress Cataloging-in-Publication Data

Names: Moosavi, Amir, author.
Title: Dust that never settles : literary afterlives of the Iran-Iraq war / Amir Moosavi.
Description: Stanford : Stanford University Press, 2025. | Includes bibliographical references and index.
Identifiers: LCCN 2024047256 (print) | LCCN 2024047257 (ebook) | ISBN 9781503642140 (cloth) | ISBN 9781503642959 (paperback) | ISBN 9781503642966 (ebook)
Subjects: LCSH: Iran-Iraq War, 1980–1988—Literature and the war. | Persian fiction—Iran—History and criticism. | Arabic fiction—Iraq—History and criticism. | Comparative literature—Persian and Arabic. | Comparative literature—Arabic and Persian.
Classification: LCC PK6412.I73 M67 2025 (print) | LCC PK6412.I73 (ebook) | DDC 891/.5509358550542—dc23/eng/20241022
LC record available at https://lccn.loc.gov/2024047256
LC ebook record available at https://lccn.loc.gov/2024047257

Cover design: Michele Wetherbee
Cover art: Shiva Ahmadi, *Firecracker*, 2022. Watercolor and silkscreen print on paper, 40 × 60 in.
Typeset by Newgen in 10.5/14.4 Brill

The authorized representative in the EU for product safety and compliance is: Mare Nostrum Group B.V. | Mauritskade 21D | 1091 GC Amsterdam | The Netherlands | Email address: gpsr@mare-nostrum.co.uk | KVK chamber of commerce number: 96249943

Contents

	A Note on Translations and Transliterations	vii
	Map of Iran, Iraq, and the Surrounding Region	ix
Introduction	War, Writing, and Comparison	1
1	Mobilizing Literature	30
2	Representations of Survival and Loss	62
3	War Front Apocrypha	92
4	Writers' Home Front Wars	124
5	Ghosts of a Violent Past	154
Conclusion	Cultural Afterlives of 1979	181
	Acknowledgments	193
	Notes	197
	Bibliography	229
	Index	249

A Note on Translations and Transliterations

Unless otherwise noted, the translations in the following pages are my own. After referring to a title once in the Arabic or Persian original, I refer to it using the English translation. When referencing Arabic or Persian texts that have been published in English translation, I quote the published translation whenever possible and cite the page numbers for the translation and the original in the endnotes, using "(A)" for Arabic, "(P)" for Persian, and "(T)" for the English translation.

This book uses two transliteration systems for Persian and Arabic words. For words appearing in Arabic language contexts without common English equivalents, I have used the transliteration system of the *International Journal of Middle Eastern Studies*. For words appearing in Persian language contexts, I have used the transliteration scheme suggested by the journal *Iranian Studies*. The capitalization scheme of both follows English grammatical rules. Occasionally, using two distinct transliteration systems results in the same name spelled two different ways based on linguistic context (i.e., the proper name spelled as "Mohsen" in a Persian language context and "Muhsin" in an Arabic language context; "Mohammad" or "Naser" in Persian and "Muhammad" or "Nasir" in Arabic, etc.). Whenever possible, I have used conventional, anglicized forms of words (i.e., Khomeini, Saddam Hussein, Khuzestan). In the case of authors who have at least one work published in English, I have used the spelling that appears on their publication without altering the spelling of their names to force them to adhere to the conventions of the Anglophone academy (e.g., Antoon, Khoury, Betool, Marashi). Words and titles written in Arabic or Persian contain diacritical markings signifying short or long vowels, emphatic sounds, etc. Names of individuals do not contain diacritical markings unless the English spellings could result in an incorrect pronunciation, in which case a transliterated version of the name is provided on its first use.

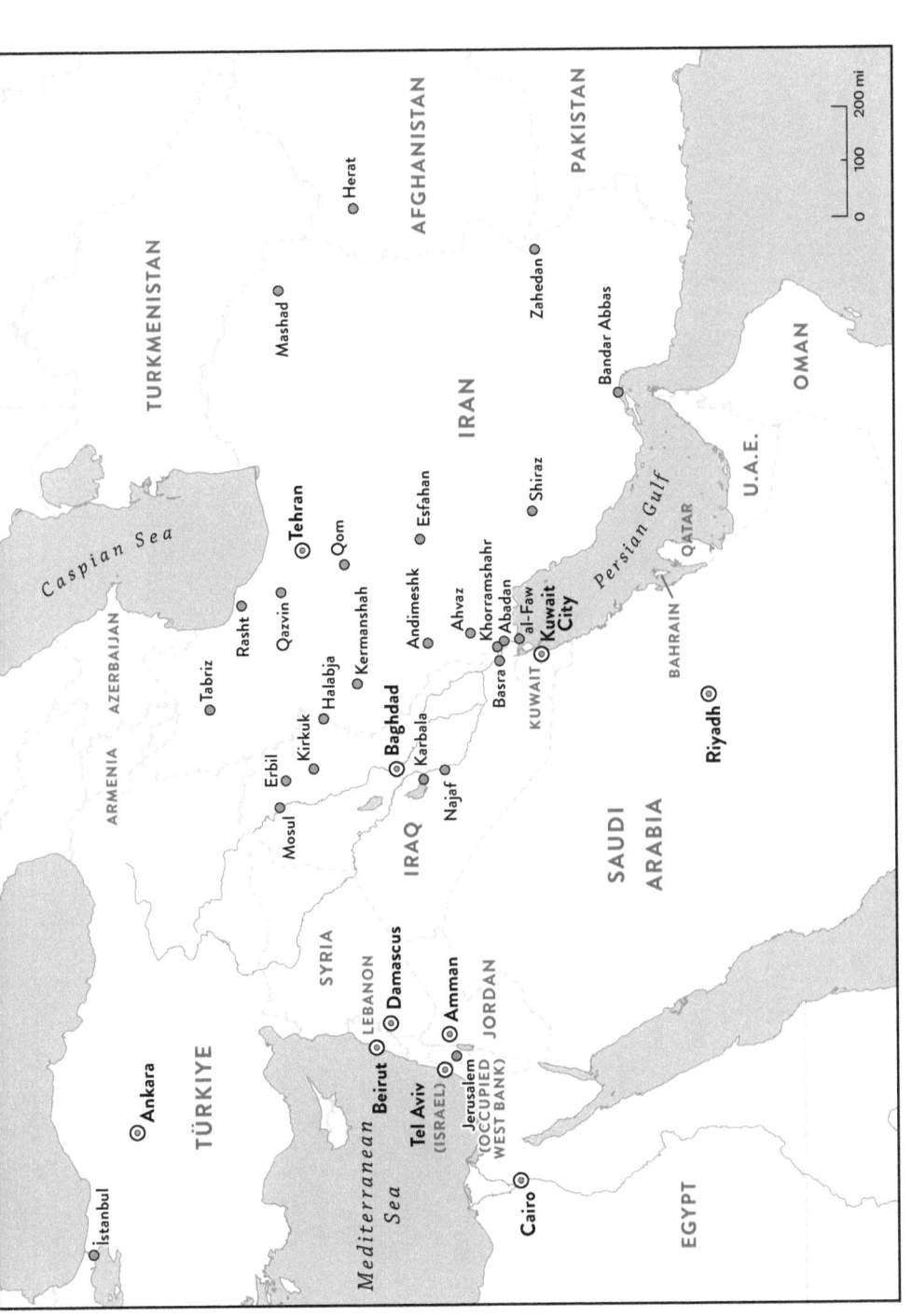

Map of Iran, Iraq, and the Surrounding Region

Introduction
WAR, WRITING, AND COMPARISON

In August of 1990, almost three and a half years after Ammoury's death, Saddam invaded Kuwait. To secure the eastern front with Iran and withdraw troops from there to Kuwait, he agreed to all the Iranian conditions and relinquished all the demands for which he'd waged the war in the first place. Father punched the table and shouted: "Why the hell did we fight for eight years then and what in hell did Ammoury die for?"

—*Sinan Antoon*, Waḥdahā Shajarat al-Rummān (The Corpse Washer, 2010)[1]

"And what about you? You think I've gotten used to the worthless army salary, or that I'm here to fight for my flag, or I don't know, my country? . . . No! I didn't bury two of my own for nothing, even if it's all gone to hell here. . . I lost two people, and I'll take two people . . . with this bayonet. And if not, then with this!"

And he pointed to the rifle on his shoulder.

"Your mother died, too!" I said.

"All mothers die of sorrow."

At night, we would look out at the horizon that was brighter than all the earthworks around us. Far away, it was all flaming red, with a yellow blaze that seemed to flicker on and off. It was only when the sound of exploding mortar shells and missiles stopped for a moment that we would realize what a racket they created. Rahman would say, "Poor Naft-Shahr." I would say, "Well the other side could say the same thing." And he would reply, "They're right, too."

—*Hossein Mortezaeian Abkenar*, "Dāstān-e Rahmān" ("Rahman's Story," 1999)[2]

In 1988, after eight years of war and over one million people killed or injured, the Iran-Iraq War ended. For a moment, people on both sides celebrated; the carnage had finally stopped. As Jawad, the protagonist of Sinan Antoon's acclaimed novel *The Corpse Washer* recalls, the war's reach went much further than the war front.[3] The bodies of all those soldiers killed in action—whenever they were recoverable—had to be returned to their families from the killing fields in the borderlands between Iran and Iraq. Their corpses were delivered by army officers to surviving family members across Iraq. For Jawad, the moment when his older brother, Amir, is "transformed from 'Doctor' to 'Martyr'" is seared into his memory when a taxi carrying a flag-draped coffin arrives in front of his family home.[4] In Iraq, as in Iran, the families of these martyrs were supposed to balance the pain of eternal loss with a state-imposed pride in their sons and husbands for attaining martyrdom. After living through eight years of war, though, the families of martyrs, veterans, and civilians, many of whom had their homes and livelihoods destroyed, were left wondering what all this sacrifice was for. With both wartime governments still in power, borders unchanged, and hundreds of thousands of dead, there was nothing to show for the "victory" the governments proclaimed.

In the years since the war ended, historians have repeatedly dived into the reasons for its protracted length. Among the Iran-Iraq War's many slogans was one repeated by both Ayatollah Khomeini and Saddam Hussein: "war until victory" (Persian: *jang tā piruzi*; Arabic: *al-qitāl ḥattā naṣr*). "Rahman's Story" by Iranian writer Hossein Mortezaeian Abkenar exposes what that slogan entailed for the soldiers who did the actual fighting, through a conversation that the author stages between two Iraqi soldiers. One of them, Rahman, whose back was once full of shrapnel from combat, has willingly stayed at the front for more than five years. His motives for being there are purely personal. Iranian airstrikes against his town killed his brothers, and after their mother buried them, grief chased her into the grave too. Rahman is at the war front for no other reason than to avenge their deaths. While listening to Rahman's story, the second soldier remembers an earlier moment when, likely peering out from their trench, they could see the bombing of the Iranian border village Naft-Shahr. The sight prompts a sense of parity between the situations in which Iraqi and Iranian soldiers found themselves. Soldiers on both sides had lost all sense of what they were fighting for in a seemingly endless cycle of violence and vengeance.

Both cases highlight how the Iran-Iraq War has lived on in fiction far after the war ended. Since 1988, Iraqi and Iranian writers have persistently taken up the war's various afterlives, including its legacies of death, destruction, and loss. In doing so, they have rewritten the narratives of the war put forth by the two states that fueled the conflict for nearly a decade. While the Iraqi wartime government no longer exists, the Islamic Republic of Iran remains invested in maintaining the primacy of its narrative in Iranian society, tethering it to the foundational pillars of its very existence. In this book, I take up the twin literary legacies of the war and offer a comparative study of its reflections in Arabic and Persian fiction. I argue for the expansion of comparative literary studies between these two languages based on shared experiences of the war, the ways it has been written, and the politics of publishing fiction about this recent, violent past in the Islamic Republic of Iran and Ba'thist and post-Ba'thist Iraq. This comparison demonstrates how Iraqi and Iranian writers have constantly wrestled with the political contentiousness of representing the Iran-Iraq War and its legacy from wartime until the present day, by showing how writers from both countries have transformed once militarized, officially sanctioned, and propagandistic war literatures into literatures of mourning and loss. With time, these narratives have been transformed into vehicles of protest with powerful counternarratives to official state narratives of the war first developed in the 1980s.

Dust That Never Settles has three primary aims. Firstly, it introduces readers of English to the central role that the Iran-Iraq War has played in contemporary Persian and Arabic literatures. Secondly, it highlights how contemporary fiction contributes to robust social and political debates about the recent past in Iran and Iraq. Finally, it proposes the war and its afterlives as one entryway to the comparative study of modern and contemporary Arabic and Persian literatures, adding to the growing body of South-South cultural studies and comparative literary scholarship. The book examines Arabic and Persian fiction from 1980 to 2018 to show how literature has emerged as a vociferous site of struggle among competing narratives of the war in Iran and Iraq, playing distinct but comparable roles for writers from each country. The texts under analysis have received significant critical recognition in their home countries and in some cases have been translated into English and other languages, at times to much acclaim. This book does not attempt to be a complete survey of the literature of the Iran-Iraq War—something that would constitute several volumes. Instead, it offers a comparative approach using prominent works of prose fiction that exhibit overlapping thematic similarities, are formalistically comparable, and are emblematic of trends in contemporary Arabic and Persian fiction. My goal is not to flatten the important differences between the Arabic and Persian literatures of this war, but to expose how they shed light on the various ways that Iranian and Iraqi writers have dealt with their entangled histories of wars, modern dictatorships, parallel twentieth-century literary developments, common religious heritage, and shared natural environments.

As a comparative study of two literatures from the Global South, this book seeks to break free of the "North-South" models of comparison that have perpetuated Eurocentric paradigms in the study of non-European literatures.[5] Within studies of "Middle Eastern" literatures and cultures, it asks readers to think across the national and linguistic silos that often divide studies of this region.[6] My approach borrows from Shu-mei Shih's proposal of "relational comparison," to avoid privileging analysis of one literature over the other, or creating a hierarchy between Arabic and Persian literary traditions.[7] By using literary texts from Iran and Iraq to think through the entanglements of the historical circumstances of the eight-year war between the countries and its various afterlives, this book excavates and activates a historically specific sets of relationalities between the literatures of Iran and Iraq, rooted in historical and sociopolitical contexts, strategies of narrative, and aesthetic choices.[8]

The remainder of this introduction offers a general history of the Iran-Iraq War and discussion of modern and contemporary Persian and Arabic literatures. While I do not directly address the war's political or military history, or its ramifications for other parts of the Iranian and Iraqi cultural spheres (e.g., the cinema, music, or visual art), numerous references in the book's bibliography do.

A WAR NOT FORGOTTEN

Lasting from September 1980 to August 1988, the Iran-Iraq War was the longest conventional war fought between two states in the twentieth century. For the better part of a decade, the war was front and center for both warring governments and most of each country's population, and constantly in the background for the rest of the world. It marked a period that began just after a revolutionary government in Iran declared itself an Islamic Republic and

Saddam Hussein consolidated power in Iraq. The war became another event in a region that was increasingly tumultuous throughout the 1970s, rocked by violence, wars, and political shocks that culminated in 1979. In the span of a year, the world witnessed dramatic political and social transformations in Iran and Iraq, the Soviet invasion of Afghanistan and the beginning of the Soviet-Afghan War, Egypt's peace treaty with Israel and its withdrawal from the "resistance camp," the dramatic siege of the Grand Mosque in Mecca, and the continued mayhem of the Lebanese Civil War.[9]

The Iran-Iraq War started after Saddam Hussein invaded Iranian territory on September 22, 1980. Despite months of tensions around the border, the Iraqi military caught the newly founded Islamic Republic off guard by simultaneously launching airstrikes throughout Iran, and commencing a massive land invasion that overran Iranian ground defenses from dozens of points along the countries' shared border of 1,600 kilometers. From that day until late May 1982, the Iraqi military occupied parts of Iran's southwest, with Khorramshahr being the most significant town to be under full occupation, while the nearby major oil-producing city of Abadan fell under a complete siege. Saddam had hoped to break the back of a population fresh out of a revolution, and turn Iran's local Arab population—who are heavily concentrated in the border province of Khuzestan and who share a geography, dialect, religion, and customs with the peoples of southern Iraq—against the new, post-revolutionary Islamic government. Instead, the invasion and occupation proved to be an enormous nationalist rallying cry across Iran, including among the Khuzestani Arab population.[10] Thousands volunteered to join the fight for the liberation of Iranian territory, both by joining the regular armed forces, and the newly established Revolutionary Guard Corps (IRGC) known in Persian as *Sepāh-e Pāsdārān*. By late May 1982, Iranian forces successfully pushed the Iraqi military out of most of the country, liberated Khorramshahr, and then began launching their own offensives into Iraq.

During the spring of 1982, the Organization of Islamic States, the Arab League, and the United Nations, each attempted to negotiate a ceasefire. Although diplomats believed they were close to a breakthrough, Ayatollah Khomeini made a ceasefire contingent on some major demands—including Saddam Hussein's removal from power, official Iraqi recognition of its responsibility for the initial outbreak of hostilities, and the payment by Iraq of $150 billion in reparations. Khomeini's demands also included free passage of Iranian troops through Iraqi territory to fight Israel (which had recently invaded southern Lebanon), and the repatriation of Iraqi Shi'a that Saddam's Ba'thist government had expelled to Iran prior to and throughout the first year and half of the war and who at that point already numbered over 100,000.[11] In June 1982, Saddam responded, saying that he would accept responsibility for starting a war that was "imposed" on Iraq, allow the Iranians to pass through the country to fight the Israelis, and accept the internationally recognized border between the two countries, but he would never accept the other demands. Thus, the war went on.[12]

For the next six years, the two militaries slaughtered each other, largely along the border between the two countries, while each country's air force also bombed the other's major civilian centers in a phase of the war that came to be known as the "War of the Cities." The images that emerged from the war front were especially horrific. Trench warfare, the Iraqi military's use of chemical weapons (both against Iranians and Iraqi Kurds), the Iranian regime's widespread use of child soldiers, and piles of corpses left in the aftermath of battles, prompted observers worldwide to draw comparisons with the First World War. Added to that was the complete mobilization of the home front and the development of two distinct, all-encompassing war cultures that utilized each country's media and culture to promote the war effort. Sites across each country were hit by rockets and bombs, which led to widespread destruction, and civilian deaths and injuries. The cities and landscapes of Iran's southwest and southern Iraq bore the brunt of the war, particularly the Iraqi province of Basra and the Iranian province of Khuzestan. Basra and its surroundings, especially the region between the Shatt al-Arab/Arvand Rud south to the oil-producing Faw Peninsula, and the Khuzestani cities of Abadan, Ahvaz, and Khorramshahr, appear repeatedly in literature of the Iran-Iraq War.[13]

For Iran and Iraq, their war consumed the 1980s and concluded just before the end of the brutal civil war in Lebanon and the Soviet-Afghan War. The war also heralded the beginning of a new, post-1979 era, where, in this part of the world, the political left found itself increasingly sidelined in the face of political Islam, a singular American superpower, and a regional and global onslaught of neoliberal economic policies. Globally, not long after the two governments signed a peace treaty, the Berlin Wall fell, and the Soviet Union began to crumble. The war was not a "Cold War conflict," but it was the last major war of the Cold War era, and it took place in a global Cold War dynamic that partly contributed to increasingly direct U.S. involvement in the war's later years.

Despite its significance, American media often refers to the Iran-Iraq War as a "forgotten war." Although it should not be, for Americans (as well as many people living outside Iran and Iraq), it mostly is. The war has never captured the imagination of Hollywood or become the subject of a hit television series or a work of popular literature in English or other European languages. Outside of Iran and Iraq, there are no monuments or days on the calendar to commemorate this war's numerous dead. Instead, American cultural memory overlooks the Iran-Iraq War to instead focus on images of the 1979 Iranian Revolution, the Iran Hostage Crisis (November 4, 1979-January 20, 1981), and the overwhelming U.S.-led response to Saddam Hussein's 1990 invasion and occupation of Kuwait known as "Operation Desert Storm" (January 17-February 28, 1991).

The near nonexistence of the Iran-Iraq War in American cultural memory can partly be explained by the absence of American or European soldiers in the war. For nearly a decade, Iran and Iraq did the fighting themselves without significant support of foreign troops.[14] Still, regional and world powers were involved. They armed, provided military intelligence, and financed the two belligerent states from the beginning, many while either ignoring the atrocities taking place or spectating at the seemingly interminable and incredibly violent conflict that killed at least 500,000, and perhaps up to 1,000,000 people.[15] In comments about the war, the late Henry Kissinger, a leading architect of U.S. foreign policy and advisor to the Reagan administration, is widely rumored to have quipped that "it's a pity they can't both lose." Considering the war's length and the general disdain that much of the contemporary diplomatic world had for both states, it is fair to assume he was not the only diplomat or commentator to feel that way.[16]

It is now well-known that the U.S. armed both sides over the course of the eight-year bloodbath, most memorably during the Iran-Contra scandal (1985–1987), which saw the U.S. go against its own embargo and sell weapons to the Iranian government. Officially, this was to build goodwill with elements of the Iranian government and free U.S. hostages in Lebanon held by Iranian-backed militants in Hizballah. Unofficially, the U.S. used the proceeds to fund the CIA-backed militias known as the Contras in Nicaragua.[17] Somewhat less remembered, is how the U.S. sided with Saddam Hussein early in the war by quietly de-classifying the country as a state-supporter of terrorism in order to provide his government with military intelligence and technology. Doing so gave the Iraqi military an important advantage on the battlefield. Then, from 1984 to 1988, during another phase of the conflict now known as the "Tanker War," the American Navy played a major role in the Persian Gulf, actively engaging with Iranian naval forces.[18] Their presence eventually led to the accidental shooting down of a passenger plane, Iran Air Flight 655, killing 290 Iranian civilian passengers along with the plane's crew. The incident contributed to Iran's decision to finally agree to a peace treaty and was seared into Iranians' collective memory of the period.[19] Despite its support for Saddam Hussein throughout the war, by 1990 the U.S. did an about-face and American media utterly vilified the Iraqi dictator until he was removed from power in 2003. The demonization of Saddam helped drum up support among the American population for massive military engagements with Iraq in 1991, and a sustained bombing and brutal sanctions campaign that lasted until the 2003 invasion.[20]

As for Iran and Iraq, their war officially ended on August 8, 1988, with the implementation of U.N. Treaty 598. Neither side emerged triumphant, but both eventually claimed victory in one form or another. Saddam's government did so immediately after agreeing to a ceasefire, which Khomeini described as "drinking from a poisoned chalice." For the 86-year-old cleric, in a sense, it was. Less than a year after the war ended, on June 3, 1989, he died. There were no territorial gains for either side. Both countries suffered staggering losses of life and the mass destruction of infrastructure, and also incurred tremendous financial losses. In the process, both Iraqi and Iranian military and political leadership badly miscalculated and repeatedly made grave mistakes on the battlefield that led to high numbers of casualties and widespread injuries among combatants. Each country's political leadership dismissed the advice of seasoned military officers in favor of politicians and military apparatchiks, who told them what they wanted to hear and falsely imagined assistance that never materialized from fifth columns among the enemy populations. With very few exceptions, Iran's Arab population remained loyal to Iran and Iraqi Shi'a sided with Iraq.

Official proclamations of victory or acceptance aside, Saddam Hussein's Ba'thist regime and Khomeini's Islamic Republic were the two clear winners of this war. At war's end, "the Iranian Republic had become unambiguously 'Islamic' and Saddam Hussein's rule was there to stay, only to be dislodged by the might of the world's sole superpower."[21] The persistence of each wartime government—at least in the short-term in the Iraqi case—guaranteed an afterlife for official war narratives after 1988. Thus, in Iran, the war is still referred to by the state and its supporters as the "Sacred Defense" (*Defā'-e Moqaddas*) or the "Imposed War" (*Jang-e Tahmili*), and has become a bedrock in the foundational myth of the regime that has ruled the country since the 1979 Revolution. In Iraq, the war with Iran is now recognized as the beginning of that country's decades-long experience with warfare and violent instability from which it has only recently and fragilely emerged.

The Iranian regime has never let its population forget the sacrifices it made and still considers the war with Iraq its most defiant and successful act of "resistance" (*moqāvemat*) against the conglomerate of powers that has been seeking to overthrow it since 1979, chief among them the U.S., Israel, and Saudi Arabia.[22] In Iraq, the heavy propaganda effort to build a discourse of victory around the war and frame it as "Saddam's Qadisiyya"—a reference to the Arab-Islamic conquest of Iran in the seventh century CE—was quickly overshadowed by the "Mother of All Battles" (*Umm al-Ma'ārik*), the government's epithet for its standoff with the U.S.-led coalition following the Iraqi invasion of Kuwait in August 1990. Iraqis now tend to conflate the Iran-Iraq War with the peak of Saddam's personality cult and see it as the first episode of violence in a decades-long period dominated by war and sanctions that outlived Saddam Hussein himself and lasted well into the 2010s. Today, more than anything else, this war makes clear how easy it is for wartime and postwar regimes to make jingoist claims of victory and resistance, but those claims are undoubtedly more difficult to accept for those who were killed, injured, or forced to continue living without their loved ones, still upheld as "martyrs" by both states.

MAKING THE WAR STORY

In crafting their war narratives, the architects of each official war culture drew upon elements of national and religious history to frame the war. Essential to both state war narratives were two seventh-century war stories from the foundational years of Islam. In and of itself, this type of action is not unique. Modern governments undergoing challenges and states of crisis, including revolution, war, and imperial expansion, have mobilized their populations by drawing from earlier historical events or traditions.[23] In Iran, government officials and cultural producers working in support of the state used the martyrdom of the third Shi'i Imam, Hussein, at the Battle of Karbala to frame the war, while the Iraqi government turned to the Battle of Qadisiyya, which paved the way for the Arab-Islamic invasion of Iran. In the dramatic accounts of both battles, the details of which have been passed down through historical and literary sources, heroic acts during war, and martyrdom on the battlefield, lead to distinct forms of righteous victory of true Muslims over non-believing or misled enemies. For both states, connecting this era of Islamic history to the war not only imparted the sense of inevitable triumph contained in the early epic battle stories to the contemporary stories of "Saddam's Qadisiyya" or the "Sacred Defense," but it also advanced an ideological understanding of the present firmly rooted in an Islamic past.

In using the Battle of Karbala as a main point of reference, the Iranian government framed the war in terms of the Shi'i story of martyrdom par excellence. Like other well-known historical events with religious significance, "the tale of Karbala has been told and retold over the centuries without a single authoritative version emerging to supplant completely all others."[24] Several historical and literary accounts of the battle have been written since the event. Some of these accounts claim historical accuracy, while others are clearly more invested in attending to the sentiments of Shi'i Muslims who want to ensure the "correct" representation of the event.

Although details differ, the basic contours of the Karbala story are as follows: in the first days of the Islamic calendar month of Muharram, year 61 on the Islamic calendar (October 10, 680 CE), Hussein bin 'Ali, the grandson of the Prophet Mohammad, was leading a party of seventy-two followers, consisting of men, women, and children from Medina to Kufa, where a group of like-minded people had called upon him to lead an uprising against the Umayyad Caliphate, which ruled over the lands conquered by Muslim armies from 661–750 CE. In the plains outside of the city of Karbala, located in present-day central Iraq, they were intercepted by an overwhelmingly large Umayyad battalion of thousands of soldiers, who demanded that Hussein pledge allegiance to their Caliph, Yazid ibn Mu'awiya. Hussein refused. His group, stranded in the desert and cut off from water, was drawn into a grossly uneven battle between the two sides on the tenth day of the month, which, in the Shi'i tradition, has come to be known as Ashura (*'Āshūrā'*). According to the story, Hussein and all of his adult male companions were massacred, with Hussein the last to be killed at the hands of an opposing military commander, Shimr. The Umayyad army decapitated the bodies of the dead, looted the camp, and took women and children as slaves and prisoners, including Hussein's son, who would later become the next Shi'i Imam. The men's decapitated heads were taken to Damascus and presented as trophies to Yazid. Since its passing, the tragedy of Karbala has become "the constitutive event of Shi'ism as a religion and the symbol of the victory of the oppressive majority over the righteous few."[25]

Historical and literary sources, such as al-Tabari's tenth-century history and Kashefi's sixteenth-century martyrology, *Rawzat al-Shohadā'* (*The Garden of the Martyrs*), provide details about the deaths of individuals, the speech, actions, and even the psyches of the heroes and their enemies, so much so, that today, many of the details about the Battle of Karbala and Hussein's martyrdom are "known" by believers and rehearsed annually during mourning processions and passion plays (*ta'ziyeh*) during Muharram.[26] These particulars form part of the emotionally-charged story of Hussein's sacrifice and call for justice, which is why the Karbala story was a useful point of reference for anti-Shah revolutionaries during the lead up to the 1979 Revolution, even before it came to be used by the new government in the war against Iraq. The Battle of Karbala became the allegorical model for the war, and Hussein became the most important figure for soldiers to emulate on the battlefield. It was the defining element that transformed the defense of the country into a "sacred" undertaking, imbuing Khomeini's cause against Saddam Hussein with a righteousness "rooted in [...] Imam Husayn's cause against the Umayyad caliph."[27] The war's "Karbala paradigm" inspired a slew of visual and literary iconography related to the war, including the frequently heard slogan that accompanied the Iranian push into Iraqi territory after 1982: "The path to Jerusalem passes through Karbala" (*rāh-e Qods az Karbalā migozarad*).²⁸

On the other side of the border, the Iraqi regime's use of the Battle of Qadisiyya, which took place in 636 CE shortly after the death of the Prophet Muhammad, was quickly deployed as the historical antecedent for Saddam Hussein's invasion of Iran. The Battle of Qadisiyya is seen as the definitive event that led to the fall of the Persian Sassanian Empire and paved the way for the Arab-Islamic conquest of Iran. Iraqi journals and newspapers were quick to incorporate references to the battle into their descriptions of the event, as demonstrated, for example, in the October issue of the cultural magazine *Āfāq 'Arabiyya* (*Arab Horizons*). Only a month into the war, images of Saddam were superimposed onto drawings of Muslim warriors on horseback charging into battle, alongside poems pledging allegiance to Saddam, and photos of the early days of the Iraqi invasion and occupation of Iranian towns. The photo that adorns the rear cover of the issue features the ruins of buildings supposedly located in the border town of Zayn al-Qaws, which was quickly overrun by the invading Iraqi army. Bold, Kufic print above the photo reads "Zayn al-Qaws. . .the Beginning of Saddam's Qadisiyya."²⁹

The use of the Battle of Qadisiyya as the historic inspiration for this war was meant to recall the bravery and valor of the first Muslim armies and their successful conquests of the surrounding non-Muslim lands. Popular imagination of the battle pits a severely outnumbered Muslim-Arab army against the army of an arrogant Persian empire. Despite scholarly doubts on this characterization of the battle, historical details matter very little in such circumstances, and it is undeniable that the Battle of Qadisiyya was of paramount importance in paving the way for the full conquest of the land encompassed by present-day Iran and Iraq by Muslim armies.³⁰ Critical to this story is the presumption that the Muslim army consisted predominantly of ethnic Arabs, not non-Arab converts or allies from recently conquered lands, and certainly not ethnic Persians. This version of the story harmonized with other forms of propaganda and official state discourse of the war that portrayed Iraqis as simultaneously having a strong pre-Islamic, Babylonian identity (i.e., distinctly non-Persian), and since the establishment of Islam, being part of a larger Arab-Muslim nation (*umma*). In this narrative, Iran is clearly characterized as a non-Arab, non-Muslim, Zoroastrian other.

THE BAʿTHFICATION AND ISLAMIZATION OF THE LITERARY SPHERES
The war put into place unprecedented processes of state control over the Iranian and Iraqi cultural spheres that were used in propagating state war discourses and building official war narratives. The projects of manufacturing state war culture and literature were possible partly because of the power-consolidating nature of the war that allowed each state to eliminate political opposition in a time of national emergency. They also owed a great deal to certain pre-existing dynamics in the two countries' cultural scenes that allowed both regimes to quickly capture and co-opt intellectual and cultural production. The ways that these processes played out in each country were not identical, but they did bear similarities. Their characteristics expose some of the ways in which the cultural trajectories of twentieth-century Iran and Iraq are not only entangled and overlap, but also diverge from each other.

The near-instantaneous transformation of all forms of media and cultural production in Iraq into propaganda outlets for the war in the fall of 1980, was enabled through the Baʿthification (*tabʿīth*) of Iraqi society that had initially begun in 1968 with the coup that brought the Baʿth Party to power. Baʿthfication was a "totalitarian strategy" aimed at indoctrinating "loyalty in the Iraqi populace by making the brand of Baʿthist ideology employed by the regime during Hussein's presidency [....] the primary basis for political and social order and the supreme source for individual and collective identity."[31] Government officials responsible for the implementation of Baʿthism—foremost among them Saddam Hussein—became more ambitious with their project after the nationalization of the oil sector in 1972, the swift rise in oil prices globally in the 1970s, and the transformation of Iraq into a rentier state. More precisely in this context, Baʿthification "was a set of policies and tactics designed to coerce and elicit support for Hussein's regime, and to eliminate alternatives to it."[32] As the state's financial power grew, so did its capability to gain the loyalty of the Iraqi population (at least superficially) and to police society.[33] Thus, throughout the 1970s, Baʿthification policies permitted the state to purge its political enemies from the cultural sphere, most notably those who were members of, or aligned with, the Iraqi Communist Party, which constituted the largest political threat to the Baʻth. At the same time, it also lured and coerced intellectuals, writers, and artists to join its ranks or face "death, prison, or exile," resulting in an exodus of writers and intellectuals by the late 1970s.[34] By 1979, a specifically *Husseini* Baʻthification was on display, best evidenced by Saddam Hussein's personality cult after his total assumption of power that year, which only intensified during the war with Iran.

The nascent Islamic Republic of Iran went through a different process of power consolidation after the 1979 Revolution and during the war. Throughout the 1970s, multiple oppositional factions accelerated toward revolution against the Pahlavi regime, which was losing hold of the country as massive demonstrations and strikes brought it down. On January 16, 1979, Mohammad Reza Pahlavi fled the country, and two weeks later Ayatollah Khomeini returned. On February 11, Radio Tehran made the historic announcement: "This is the voice of Iran, the voice of true Iran, and the voice of the Islamic Revolution."[35] On April 1, a referendum with widespread participation affirmed the establishment of an Islamic Republic. Barely a year and a half had passed from the revolution's successful establishment of a new regime when Iraq invaded.

When the war started, the new Islamic Republic had purged some 12,000 Iranian military personnel, many from the upper echelons of leadership, and the Iranian cultural sphere reflected the fractured, cacophonous nature of the early post-Revolutionary society.[36] But the new revolutionary regime in Iran did not start entirely from scratch. Instead, it purged, refilled, and expanded existing government institutions. Khomeini's leadership was increasingly galvanized through a growing cult of personality that drew its strongest institutional support from a network of clerics, and the newly established, ideologically committed Revolutionary Guards.[37] State institutions "became an arena in which various interest groups jockeyed for power" within the tightening limits of the Islamic Republic, reflected in the tumultuous power plays within ministries and cultural institutions between spring 1979 and late 1983.[38] Even before the Iraqi invasion, this was the context that Khomeini and his allies exploited to eliminate their political rivals on all sides, and more broadly launch the Cultural Revolution (*Enqelāb-e Farhangi*) aimed at Islamizing the country's press and all levels of education. Accompanying these radical changes was a generalized top-down attempt to Islamize society involving, among other things, renaming streets, buildings, and public spaces, implementing new censorship laws, rewriting school textbooks, establishing a number of quasi-governmental religiously-inspired foundations (*bonyād-hā*), and creating the Ministry of Islamic Guidance (later changed to the Ministry of Islamic Culture and Guidance). The latter implemented censorship regulations influenced by the new constitution that affected all published materials and films.[39]

NEW COMMITMENTS

Key to top-down attempts to culturally Baʻthify and Islamize Iraq and Iran, respectively, were new notions of political commitment (*iltzām* in Arabic and *taʻahhod* in Persian) among the two countries' writers. By the mid-twentieth century, the idea that literature should be in the service of political causes was widespread throughout Southwest Asia and North Africa.[40] Many writers and readers of Arabic and Persian had come to expect that literature should depict the reality of the masses, be the voice of the voiceless, and promote justice, equality, and overall social emancipation. The major events that heralded literary commitment in the Arab world and Iran, however, were not the same. And despite the transregional similarities in the popularization of the concept, committed literatures reached their apex at different times in the two linguistic zones due to the distinct political histories that coalesced around different moments of sociopolitical importance. In the Iranian case, the First Iranian Writers' Congress (*Nokhostin Kongereh-ye Nevisandegān-e Irān*), which was held at the Iran-U.S.S.R. Cultural House in Tehran in 1946, is often cited as the highest profile event that promoted the idea of literary commitment among Iran's contemporary writers.[41] Later, the 1953 coup that removed Mohammad Mosaddeq from power, combined with the Shah's foreign and domestic politics, gave Iranian writers particular reference points for their literary works. In Iran, "the term *taʻahhod* seems to have entered the lexicon of Persian literary discourse as a calque on Jean Paul Sartre's *engagement*," although as a principle the idea had taken root long before Sartre's translation gained much attention in the Persian-speaking world.⁴² In the Arabic-speaking world, the towering Egyptian intellectual, Taha Hussein, is credited with introducing the term *iltizām* (commitment) into Arabic in 1947, as a translation of Sartre's concept of "Littérature engagée," (also rendered more precisely as *al-adab al-multazim*). The Beirut-based literary journal *al-Ādāb* initially played a major role in popularizing and circulating the term widely among Arabic reading audiences, especially throughout the Levant, Egypt, and Iraq.⁴³ For their part, committed Arab writers rallied around pan-Arabism, the politics of the newly established post-colonial Arab states, and the Palestinian cause.

Neither in the Arab world nor in Iran was commitment conceived of as a singular idea. As the debates among Arab intellectuals and writers indicate, commitment became "the catchword for a wide range of political literary ideas," and literary styles in Arabic.⁴⁴ Hence divisions existed between the proponents of Satrean-inspired commitment in the pages of *al-Ādāb* and the partisans of socialist realism, notably promoted by Mahmud Amin al-'Alim and 'Abd al-'Azim Anis in their 1955 book, *Fī al-Thaqāfa al-Miṣriyya (On Egyptian Culture)*.⁴⁵ Among Arab writers, literary commitment reached its zenith in the late 1950s and early 1960s, but the Arab armies' loss in the 1967 Six Day War, known in Arabic as the *naksa* or setback, "forced writers to reevaluate the role of committed writing, which lost its former luster in the wake of the defeat."⁴⁶ That reevaluation did not lead to an abandonment of the idea of committed literatures after 1967, but rather prompted a shift in styles and subject matter within Arabic literature that gave way to "a new sensibility" (*al-ḥassāsiyya al-jadīda*) and political priorities for writers and poets.⁴⁷ This is what late Lebanese writer Elias Khoury calls a post-1967 "beyond *iltizām*," which represented "a combination of a critical attitude and an approach towards exploring new and freer ways of writing" among novelists and short-story writers beyond those of the first wave of committed writers, and especially among the proponents of socialist realism. This new sensibility featured a set of political priorities that were showcased most directly through the publication of Palestinian author Ghassan Kanafani's two studies on "resistance literature" (*adab al-muqāwama*) that centered Palestine and Palestinian literature under Israeli occupation as "shining examples of true *iltizām*."⁴⁸

Iraq was affected by the literary trends sweeping across the Arab world, but the country also had its own dynamics that distinguished how the commitment debates played out among its literati. Fatima Mohsen explains that in 1940s and 1950s Iraq, "the intellectual's affiliation with the Left was like a wave, characterized by freedom slogans directed against the monarchy."[49] Among those intellectuals were many of the country's writers and poets, the majority of whom belonged or sympathized with the Iraqi Communist Party (ICP), with a far smaller contingent identifying as Ba'thists. In the cultural sphere, this period witnessed fierce debates over poetic forms, but a relatively stable and harmonious scene of fiction writing dominated by Marxist modernists such as Fu'ad al-Takarli (1927–2008), Gha'ib Tu'ma Farman (1927–1990), and Mahdi 'Isa al-Saqr (1927–2006), who transformed Iraqi fiction by inaugurating "a new era of complex and nuanced social realism [. . .] from the 1960s onwards."[50] The 1950s and 1960s in the country constituted a politically tumultuous period that witnessed the July 1958 Revolution that ended the Iraqi Monarchy, and two Ba'thist coups (1963 and 1968). Specifically, the Iraqi context from the 1960s onward was driven by hegemonic struggles among Iraqi nationalists, Ba'thists, and Communists that played out over a backdrop of rising sectarian culture, disagreements over the role of diasporic Iraqi intellectuals within the domestic Iraqi cultural scene, and multiple levels of censorship that involved "a hierarchy of state, economy, media, and the reflective self."[51]

Despite the popularity of the ICP, the coups of the 1960s brought the Ba'th Party to power, and the 1968 Coup made possible the process of Ba'thification as the party placed its own intellectuals into government positions, while marginalizing and gradually crushing the political opposition. After 1968, the state became the sole sponsor of culture in Iraq. So much so, that Haidar Saeed notes that it was "the first state in the modern history of Iraq to position itself as the sole director, supervisor, and controller of the country's cultural process as defined by cultural institutions and public activities." The 1968 coup heralded an era of "an official state culture and an unofficial opposition culture, the former being propagated in media and school curricula" and the latter in coffee-houses, bars, and other places where intellectuals gathered."[52] Throughout the 1970s and into the Iran-Iraq War, the Ba'th Party attempted to channel what was left of the spirit of commitment into its own cause by co-opting the values of committed writers and tethering them to the regime.

The Iranian experience with literary commitment in the mid-twentieth century bears some similarities to the Iraqi one. Like the ICP, the Iranian Communist Tudeh Party (*Hezb-e Tudeh*, the "Party of the Masses") had an immense influence on the country's mid-century intellectuals and writers. Also, like its Iraqi counterpart, the party's "members and sympathizers were many of the country's intellectual luminaries." By way of example, just among the literati, it could count on the varied support from the likes of eminent prose writers Sadeq Hedayat (1903–1951), Bozorg Alavi (1904–1997), and Sadeq Chubak (1916–1998), as well as poets such as Ahmad Shamlu (1915–2000) and Nima Yushij (1895–1960). Like their Iraqi counterparts, these writers and poets were usually not lifelong, card-carrying members, but often allied themselves with causes championed by the Tudeh, especially in the period leading up to the Revolution.[53]

If the Iraqi revolutions between 1958 and 1968 caused social and cultural transformations with enormous ramifications for the Iraqi literary sphere, the comparable moment in Iran is the 1953 CIA-backed coup against Prime Minister Mohammad Mosaddeq, who famously nationalized Iranian oil. In the literary sphere, Alavi identifies the coup as setting off two successive prevailing sentiments within committed poetry: one immediately following the coup that expressed "defeat and hopelessness," followed by another "period of intense creativity towards rethinking both resistance and poetic commitment" primarily in the 1960s, giving rise to even more radical commitments to political change in the 1970s.[54] Iranian writers' rethinking of the role of literature vis-à-vis social change in the 1960s and 1970s encompassed various strands of Marxism under the influence of guerilla groups fighting against the Pahlavi Regime, such as the Fedaian (*Fedā'iān-e Khalq-e Irān*) and the People's Mojahedin Organization of Iran (*Mojāhedin-e Khalq-e Irān*, variously abbreviated as PMOI, MKO, or MEK in English), and rising Islamist trends that increased throughout the 1970s. Writers of fiction conveyed their notions of commitment through social and socialist realism during these decades, best exemplified in the novels of Ahmad Mahmud (1931–2002) and Mahmud Dowlatabadi (b. 1940).[55]

The victory of the 1979 Revolution, the establishment of the Islamic Republic and, more than anything else, the war with Iraq, transformed understandings of political commitment among Iranian writers and readers of Persian. As in Iraq, after the Iranian revolution, "commitment" came to "signify the conformity of the author with the ruling regime." Especially in the early 1980s, when the new state redefined committed writers as pious Muslims ready to put their art at its service. Fatemeh Shams notes that "in almost all aspects of social life, *ta'ahhod* (commitment) superseded *takhassos* (professionalism), and the political loyalty of people to the revolutionary ideology became the main state criteria by which the truthful commitment of an artist to the revolutionary system was judged."[56]

LITERATURE AS A SITE OF STRUGGLE

Both the novel and the short story have been popular in Iran and Iraq since the mid-twentieth century, with the novel arguably the most popular literary form in recent decades. My choice to limit my focus to fiction from the war, and exclude other forms of literature such as poetry, memoir, or even film, is because of the importance that writers of both Persian and Arabic fiction have placed on the war from wartime until the present day. Debates around the war and its representation have a signal importance in the fictional literature of both countries that do not exist in other forms of cultural production. Prominent references to the Iran-Iraq War have appeared in fiction as much as, if not more than, in poetry in both languages. War memoirs frequently appear in Persian (almost exclusively published by state-sponsored publishing houses in Iran), but they are not as prevalent in the Iraqi context, which has seen its own recent proliferation of memoirs and autobiographies, but without a primary focus on the war or even the 1980s.[57] Similarly, while Iranian cinema showcases a plethora of feature-length films dealing with the Iran-Iraq War that began to appear during wartime and continue to be made today, Iraqi cinema has no equivalent due to, among other things, the near total destruction of all that was left of its film industry after 2003, from which the country has only recently started to emerge.

My use of prose fiction points to how I view not only war and literature, but the relationship between literature and politics more generally. Plainly stated: I read the literature of the Iran-Iraq War as a site of struggle between multiple ideological discourses that constitute different, sometimes conflicting, war narratives. As indicated earlier, the Iranian and Iraqi states developed war narratives with distinct reference points. Despite those differences, they similarly deployed them to suppress narratives of the war that did not harmonize with their own, setting the stage for culture to become a battlefield. More than any other moment, during the war, each state sought to make their own narrative of the conflict the supremely dominant one by first suppressing and then denying the very existence of alternative narratives. By the start of the war in Iraq and by mid-1982 in Iran, they had each largely succeeded. The stories of Saddam's Qadisiyya and the Sacred Defense were built on "linearity, logic, stability, clarity, and order" and they "reject[ed] ambivalence and ambiguity, and strive[d] to maintain a strict hierarchy of values."[58] Having achieved this position of domination, each state's dominant war discourse enjoyed "the structural privilege of appearing to be unaware of the very questions of its own legitimacy" and could rely on a presumed "social impossibility of their absence."[59]

In the late 1980s, challenges to the states' war stories began to emerge in both Iranian and Iraqi contexts and only increased in the postwar period. By the 1990s, literature became a clear site of struggle between various counter-discursive writings that challenged the states' war narratives. These challenges to both states' framings of the war have taken a variety of forms, ranging from formally experimental representations of the home front that spotlight the war's victims who are often ignored by official discourses, to depictions of the war front that contradict state-sanctioned portrayals of soldiers, the battlefield, and what it means to die as a martyr. I read these literary challenges to the states' war narratives against the complex and uneven ways in which the material and intellectual conditions for writing in Iran and Iraq have changed in the three decades following the August 1988 ceasefire. Despite the distinct temporal challenges that these writers have had (e.g., in Iraq, the 1990-91 Gulf War, followed by twelve years of crippling sanctions, and the chaos unleashed by the 2003 U.S.-led invasion. In Iran, a state that increasingly tethered its foundational story and proclaimed policies of "resistance" to its narrative of the war against Iraq), they have continually returned to this conflict and write about it in ways that demonstrate its unsettled nature until today.

At this point, many readers will notice gestures to well-known writings of Antonio Gramsci and Michel Foucault around conflicts over power and the struggles for hegemony. The dynamics that surround my understanding of literature as a site of struggle come primarily from these two theorists, and my localized approach is informed by scholars of Iran and Iraq such as Eric Davis, Yasmeen Hanoosh, and M.M. Khorrami, who have each written about how cultural production in Iraq or Iran has become an important "domain of struggle," especially since 1979.[60] Narrowing in on literary production, Hanoosh builds on Davis's claim vis-à-vis Iraq to expose the "tradition of literary diatribes" in that country, which continues today between the perceived state and "street" (non-state) literati. She demonstrates how, in the mid-twentieth century, the post-1980 era, and the post-2003 era, debates between Iraqi writers and intellectuals indicate that "the state was never able to achieve full cultural hegemony, nor was the Iraqi intellectual able to fully assume the role of the 'organic intellectual' [via Gramsci] in the face of the dictates of state agenda."[61] In the post-Revolution Iranian literary context, Khorrami also identifies "the field of culture, in its broadest sense" as one of many "fronts" that the Islamic Republic has opened in its "continuous war with the enemies of the revolution, be they individuals, other governments, opposition entities, or other religions"[62] As an essential part of the "field of culture," literature is a target in the Islamic Republic's quest for Gramscian hegemony, and as Khorrami and others demonstrate, that regime has made literature one of its prime targets for symbolic domination.

These struggles over the war's narrative in literary fiction are highlighted throughout this book. While Chapter 1 exposes how the two wartime states captured the literary spheres, Chapters 2-5 focus on Iranian and Iraqi writers' confrontations with the hegemonic state narratives of the Iran-Iraq War, highlighting literature's contentiousness and political relevance in these countries. Some of these confrontations can be understood as explicit acts of "writing back" against the state's war narratives, while at other times they are better seen as writing differently. Used in this context, "writing back" conjures the "dualities of counter-discursive practices articulated by first-wave postcolonial theorists."[63] In this way, some of the texts I analyze in this book should be read as sharp rebukes of the states' framings of the war, such Jinan Jasim Hillawi's *Layl al-Bilad* (*Night of the Country*) or Hossein Mortezaeian

Abkenar's *'Aqrab* (*The Scorpion*), each covered in Chapter 3. These oppositional texts' portrayals of the war contradict those of the Iraqi and Iranian states. To read them as "writing back" against the state-sponsored literatures also evokes the relationship of writers to empire. This time, however, empire refers not to the European colonizer but rather the relatively new authoritarian, "revolutionary" state.[64] Thus, these writers transform the assumed geographic and power relations inherent in the notion of "writing back," and complicate some of the assumptions of postcolonial literary criticism. Other texts, like the short stories of Lu'ay Hamza 'Abbas or Amir Hasan Cheheltan that appear in Chapter 2, are not so confrontational in the ways they treat the war. They largely ignore, rather than engage and grapple with, official state narratives. In doing so they open spaces to engage with other social phenomena connected to the war, such as mental illness or the grief of parents who lost their sons at the front.

In nearly all the cases I cite throughout Chapters 2-5, the writers who contest state-sponsored war narratives do so through both form and content. In both the Iranian and Iraqi cases, these postwar writers often employed techniques that were associated with modernist literary fiction in each country. While this is not a place for a detailed literary history of Arabic and Persian modernist fiction (or the debates surrounding what exactly it is), a few words about what I am referring to and how I use the term are in order.

Within fiction, the literary techniques that I refer to in the following chapters under the rubric of modernism generally developed in the mid-twentieth century in the Arabic- and Persian-speaking contexts. In the broader Arabic literary context, its origins can be found in 1960s Egypt and the Levant, in reaction to the 1952 Revolution in the former, and events in Palestine in the latter, as well as the contemporary dominance of social and socialist realisms. Early modernist Arabic fiction is now associated with very well-known writers such as Sonallah Ibrahim (b. 1937), Ghassan Kanafani (1936–1972), Edwar al-Kharrat (1926–2015,) and even the later (post-Trilogy) works of Naguib Mahfouz (1911–2006).[65] Specifically related to Iraq, Gha'ib Tu'ma Farman (1927–1990) is generally recognized as the main innovator of modernist fiction with the publication of his 1967 novel *Khamsat Aṣwāt* (*Five Voices*). The novel features a shifting Faulkner-esque narrative technique that is also found in Kanafani's *Rijāl fī al-Shams* (*Men in the Sun*, 1962) and

Naguib Mahfouz's *Mīrāmār (Miramar*, 1967).[66] In the Iranian-Persian context, the emergence of modernist fiction is usually traced to Sadeq Hedayat (1903–1951) and especially the 1941 publication of the landmark novel *Buf-e Kur (The Blind Owl)*. Later, Bahram Sadeqi (1937–1985) and Hushang Golshiri (1938–2000) are writers whose names are linked to Persian modernist fiction.[67]

What modernism practically means for Arabic and Persian fiction is an array of literary styles and outlooks that frequently reject many of the tenets associated with realism. It often encompasses artistic self-consciousness, ambivalence toward modernity, and complex and fragmentary literary forms that break free from the determination of plot.[68] In neither of these linguistic contexts is modernist fiction entirely separate from conversations of literary modernism across the globe, but there are also internal dynamics that are often connected to localized avant-garde poetics and experimentalism. Concerning the Iran-Iraq War, the detractors of state culture often produce formally innovative and/or experimental literary texts that reject the ideological and aesthetic prescriptions of wartime Iranian and Iraqi official literatures, which, for their parts, drew from more recent legacies of socialist realism. These challengers confront the authority of literature that supports the dominant, state-sponsored narratives of the war. More than simply dissent on the level of content, these texts often prioritize personal, individualistic narratives that defy the collective sonic boom promoted by the state, resist heroization, and shed light upon aspects of the war that the official narratives suppress or ignore.

WAR AND LITERATURE

The Arabic and Persian literatures of the Iran-Iraq War began to appear shortly after the war started. As previously indicated, they were born into environments where literature and the literati were already highly politicized and with the outbreak of the war, subjected to broader, state-led projects of capturing and co-opting cultural production. That context, combined with each state's quest to dominate literary discourse during wartime, and the ways in which writers from the two countries have continually returned to the war to revisit its ever-unfolding consequences, invites comparison between these Iranian and Iraqi literatures. It should be noted from the start, though, that this book is better understood to be about "war and literature" rather than strictly "war literature." What critics writing about both the Arabic and Persian literature of this war have tended to qualify as "war literature" has predominantly been the stories of soldiers' experiences of combat or their postwar readjustment to civilian life. This view marginalizes the experiences of non-combatant civilians—whether in the face of enemy bombing, interactions with combatants on the home front, or ways of dealing with physical environments transformed by conflict, to mention only a few of the myriad examples.[69] This is especially true regarding literary criticism published during the war or in the decade and a half that followed. Literary critics on both sides throughout those years stressed the experiences of soldiers as the most important manifestation of war literature.

Since 1980, the primary elements that dictate the terminology used to describe the literature of the Iran-Iraq War have been determined, on the one hand, by shifting sociopolitical circumstances in Iran, Iraq, and their ever-expanding diasporic and exilic communities, and on the other, the various ideological standpoints of writers and critics. Iraqi literary critics writing from a Baʿthist perspective referred to the literature of the war firstly as "*adab Qadisiyyat Saddam*" (the literature of Saddam's Qadisiyya), and secondarily as "*adab al-ḥarb*" (war literature). That framing underscores the ways in which critics approach texts, with the former term offering a predictable set of criteria for judging them. Calling the war's literature "the literature of Saddam's Qadisiyya" happened most during wartime and started nearly as soon as these writings began to appear. Similarly, in studies of Persian literature, critics ideologically aligned with the Islamic Republic generally use the term "*adabiyāt-e Defāʿ-e Moqaddas*" (the literature of the Sacred Defense) to refer to the literature of the war. Other terms that point to a similar perspective are "*adabiyāt-e paydāri*" (the literature of resistance) and "*adabiyāt-e jang-e taḥmili*" (the literature of the Imposed War). By contrast, critics who are independent of the government or who wish to include non-combatant narratives of the war, like their Iraqi counterparts, usually speak of "*adabiyāt-e jang*" (war literature).[70] While the production of Saddam's Qadisiyya literature effectively ceased in Iraq with the end of the Iran-Iraq War, Sacred Defense literature has continued until the present day in Iran.

My approach in this book takes a broad look at the ways in which a wide range of writers have written about this war, inclusive of the diverse perspectives of combatants and civilians, both during wartime and in the postwar years, published in Iran, Iraq, and elsewhere. Aside from "war literature" I do not use the previously mentioned terms except when citing other critics or speaking specifically about state-sponsored literature. My inclusion of texts that reference the war but do not directly engage with its violence is not to suggest that all literature that merely mentions war be considered "war literature." Rather, I insist that a more inclusive understanding of war and the experiences it creates should be considered when examining its literary reflections. In this way, I take a cue from writer and critic Viet Thanh Nguyen, who critiques the understanding of war literature as that which primarily revolves around the experiences of soldiers. Instead, he posits:

> A true war story should also tell of the civilian, the refugee, the enemy, and, most importantly, the war machine that encompasses them all. But when war stories deal with the mundane aspects of war, some may see them as "boring" or simply not even about "war." These conventional perceptions of war stories blind us to war's extensive nature, for these perceptions divide the heroic soldiers who seem to be the primary agents of war from the citizens who actually make war happen and who suffer its consequences.[71]

Although this book is not about determining what is or is not a "true war story" within the fiction of the Iran-Iraq War, Nguyen's call to go beyond "conventional perceptions of war stories" is one that I heed. His quotation comes from a chapter of his book titled "On True War Stories," which is partly a retort to American author Tim O'Brien, whose now classic book of American Vietnam War literature, *The Things They Carried*, contains his famous short story titled "How to Tell a True War Story." Nguyen notes that the definition of war literature offered by O'Brien's narrator falls short in many ways. In "How to Tell a True War Story," O'Brien writes,

> War is hell, but that's not the half of it, because war is mystery and terror and adventure and courage and discovery and holiness and pity and

despair and longing and love. War is nasty; war is fun. War is thrilling; war is drudgery. War makes you a man; war makes you dead. The truths are contradictory.[72]

In Nguyen's critique, O'Brien's story and others like it are limited to the experiences of soldiers in combat that can be neatly packaged into a narrative that is simultaneously thrilling while "communicat[ing] the obligatory sentiment that war is hell."[73] He aptly notes that "Children playing soldier may fantasize about glorious death, but probably not dismemberment, amputation, shellshock, inexplicable and debilitating illness, homelessness, psychosis, or suicide, all of which are not unusual experiences for soldiers and veterans."[74] However, such stories overlook war's profitability and ignore its terrifying disruptions to civilian life, and its horrors of displacement, physical and mental injury, and rape.

Like Nguyen, I believe that criticism of war literature "requires the right kind of panoramic optics, an ethical one and an aesthetic one that allows us to see everyone and everything involved in war."[75] Doing so allows us to recognize the diverse ways that writers have dealt with the war at a distance, or used the war as a starting point to launch into narratives distinct from but entangled with the broader experiences of war. The chapters that follow include stories of soldiers and civilians alike and demonstrate how the two categories are not mutually exclusive. Thus, my readings of war and fiction incorporate narratives of soldiers on the front and their uneasy return to civilian life, as well as those of deserters, civilians, and children affected by the war.

LITERARY AFTERLIVES OF THE IRAN-IRAQ WAR

The Iran-Iraq War remains a major thematic preoccupation for writers from both countries. By invoking "afterlives" I refer to the physical and mental consequences of the Iran-Iraq War, as well as its ongoing political effects, its traces left in and on the earth, and writers' ongoing engagements with it. The literary afterlives that I treat in this book demonstrate how fiction dealing with the Iran-Iraq War transformed in the decades following the conflict, as writers from both countries forged literatures of mourning, loss, and protest that have put forth powerful counternarratives to official state representations of the war. Until today, whenever writers from either country have attempted to write about the war and its consequences, directly or indirectly, they inevitably contend with the residual discourse from the official narrative of each regime. This, I believe, is the case even if the official narrative is no longer being produced on a massive scale by government-sponsored cultural institutions as in Iraq; or if it has taken on a life of its own, with multiple government-sponsored institutions creating cultural productions to sustain it, as in Iran.

Each of the following chapters deals with a limited period between 1980 and 2018, and in most cases, each one treats four writers—two Iranian and two Iraqi. In each chapter, I show how writers from two sides of formerly warring states grapple with the ideologically-charged, state-sponsored discursive debris from the war. The chapters progress chronologically, highlighting how, in both cases, the passage of time leads to more critical portrayals of the war. Each chapter sheds light on how these writers have thematic overlaps in their treatment of the conflict, but also how their mutual entanglement with the war and its consequences have produced aesthetic intersections and departures across the two literatures.

Chapter 1, "Mobilizing Literature," lays out the grounds for comparison between Iranian and Iraqi war literatures. It begins with a comparative assessment of Iranian and Iraqi wartime literary production and state-sponsored war cultures by juxtaposing the "literature of the Sacred Defense" (*adabiyāt-e Defā'-e Moqaddas*) with the Iraqi state-sponsored "literature of Saddam Hussein's Qadisiyya" (*adab Qādisiyyat Ṣaddām*). It examines how a particular aesthetic overwhelmed the content and form of each country's wartime fiction and how certain formal features shaped the discursive landscape with which future writers wishing to treat this war would inevitably have to contend. The chapter shows how each state flooded the literary sphere by encouraging the production of fiction that enchanted war front heroism, praised martyrdom, and claimed to speak the sole truth.

Chapter 2, "Representations of Survival and Loss," examines how the home front has been used in different ways to produce narratives of loss published primarily in the early 1990s in the writings of Muhammad Khudayyir, Lu'ay Hamza 'Abbas, Shahriar Mandanipour, and Amir Hasan Cheheltan. As state priorities in the cultural sphere changed, writers from both sides had more freedom of expression. This chapter examines how writers resorted to modernist-oriented aesthetics within this transformative context to produce powerful narratives of survival and loss during and shortly after the war. The chapter argues that these war narratives exhibit restraint in their criticism of the Iran-Iraq War and wartime regimes, while also undercutting the binary nature of the official war narrative of each state.

Chapter 3 returns to the war front and deals with the representations of martyrdom, soldiering, and desertion in novels by Ahmad Dehqan, Hossein Mortezaeian Abkenar, Jinan Jassim Hillawi, and Muhsin al-Ramli. Titled "War Front Apocrypha," this chapter treats subversive depictions of the war front in novels written in the 1990s and early 2000s. It specifically examines how writers recast common tropes in state-sponsored literatures to write transgressive narratives of the war front experience in the early postwar period. The first half of the chapter compares literary representations of battlefront death and the concept of martyrdom. It demonstrates how alternative depictions of martyrdom become powerful tools that disenchant the official war narratives of each state, turning martyrdom into a polyvalent signifier and flashpoint around which counternarratives of the war are formed. The second half of the chapter turns the spotlight on how Iraqi and Iranian authors have disenchanted the war through destabilizing representations of other elements of the war front. In doing so, they also reveal aspects of the war that are unacknowledged by official state narratives. It identifies portrayals of cowardice, cruel leaders, soldierly disobedience, and dystopic accounts of trench life and combat as overlapping themes that Iraqi and Iranian writers have used to write the state war narratives anew.

The fourth chapter, "Writers' Home Front Wars," returns to the home front to show how writers between the late 1990s and 2015 have treated issues related to language and debated the power and/or futility of literature during the war in novels by Betool Khedairi, Sinan Antoon, Hushang Golshiri, and Alireza Gholami. These writers' novels and short stories transformed the narrative of the Iran-Iraq War by focusing solely on the experience of the war from the viewpoint of civilians whose view of the official discourses ranged from quietist to dissident. Their writings demonstrate the sustained interest of postwar-era authors in reexamining and giving voice to silenced non-combatants' view of the conflict. Moreover, these counternarratives of the Iran-Iraq War highlight the frustrations and struggles of writers themselves to produce literature during wartime outside the framework of the states' narratives. They also reveal the ways in which Iraqi and Iranian writers have returned to that moment to shed light on their internal battles in writing the story of this conflict.

The fifth and final chapter, "Ghosts of a Violent Past," examines fiction published between 2008 and 2018 by a handful of writers who have recently become very well-known globally—Ahmed Saadawi, Hasan Blasim, and Diaa Jubaili from Iraq, and Nasim Marashi from Iran—and their methods of incorporating undead ghost-like figures that haunt postwar life, as well as environmental commentary about war. In both Arabic and Persian, recent writings portray the Iran-Iraq War as but one of many episodes of violence in the contemporary history of the region. The afterlives of the war, as novels and short stories by these writers demonstrate, include two more major wars in Iraq, a state that bases its legitimacy on the eight years of "Sacred Defense" in Iran, and the slow violence of postwar environmental ruin in the border zone between the two countries.

This is not the first book written about the literature of this war and it will not be the last. It is, however, the first to comparatively examine the simultaneous developments in Arabic and Persian literature of this war, largely from a postwar perspective. I hope it prompts others to investigate the relations between these literatures to further this line of inquiry or open another.

One
MOBILIZING LITERATURE

MOST WAR STORIES PUBLISHED DURING THE IRAN-IRAQ WAR ARE NO longer read with interest by readers of Persian or Arabic fiction. In Iran, critics of all ideological persuasions have dismissed this decade of literary production as largely fruitless. By way of example, in a 1994 issue of *Adabiyāt-e Dāstāni,* a journal published by the Ministry of Culture and Islamic Guidance's Center for Islamic Art and Thought, known as the "Howzeh-ye Honari," late writer and literary critic of Sacred Defense fiction, Kaveh Bahman, explained, "Writers who have promoted the literary fiction of the Imposed War have been unsuccessful in writing good, or even mediocre, war stories because their way of seeing the issue and their passion for the topic and characters [of the war] prevents them from putting aside their own biases, even temporarily, and prevents the tension needed to create successful fiction."[1] Similarly, just after the war ended, several well-known Iraqi critics who were active in both writing literature and literary criticism in Iraq reassessed the literature of Saddam's Qadisiyya, restating how necessary it was for mobilizing the population during the war, even if it lacked the "artistic and aesthetic qualities" of good literature.[2] Iraqi critics writing from outside the country have been far more derisive in their critiques of wartime state-sponsored literature. Paris-based poet and critic Kadhim Jihad Hasan, for example, characterizes this literature as "propaganda [...] an obscenity unparalleled in the history of the world [. . .] a 'literature of violence' [. . .] a 'literature of shame.'"³ Salam 'Abbud, another critic writing from Europe, is scathing in his critiques of literature produced under Saddam Hussein and especially during the war with Iran, which he describes as "totalitarian" and "written in a fake language [. . .] with no connection to reality, the war, or the country."⁴

These critics rightly identified the problems with the early literature of the Iran-Iraq War, which primarily served as propaganda for each side's government. But despite its literary shortcomings, officially sanctioned writing about the war—which was produced in vast quantities and with the financial support of cultural institutions directly linked to each state—did succeed, along with other forms of cultural media, in reinforcing each state's narrative of the Iran-Iraq War as the dominant one. For both readers and writers, it also tethered certain aesthetic expectations to the literature of the war. The literature of Saddam's Qadisiyya and the literature of the Sacred Defense were responsible for establishing the representational limits of fiction dealing with the conflict. Combined with the heavy hand of governmental censors in each country, these two bodies of war literature drowned out the voices that did not comply with the official discourses of the eight-year conflict. The result was nearly a decade of "bad literature," hundreds of works of fiction that, with very few exceptions, are largely dismissed as propaganda and not read by anyone except for literary critics and historians who wish either to make this very argument or laboriously point out the few exceptions that existed in each country.

OFFICIAL WAR CULTURES

From the outset of the war, the Iranian and Iraqi governments sought to control the entire field of cultural production in their countries to promote the war effort. While these processes were distinct in each country, by the second half of the war (1984–1988) and into the early postwar years (1988–1990), they bore a strong resemblance to each other. The differences between the two countries during the first half of the war were mainly due to the unequal footing of both governments when hostilities began. At their peaks, the ways in which both governments sought to dominate the entire cultural landscape of their countries to promote the war effort resembled earlier attempts by other states during other twentieth-century wars. I use the term "war culture" to refer to the state's attempt to dominate the war narrative through all forms of media and the arts, including literature, and draw from a definition of the concept put forth by Patrick Deer in his study of British war culture during the First and Second World Wars. Deer's definition of war culture refers to "work and practices produced during wartime and those that actively constitute part of the war effort." Modern war cultures, he writes:

> [A]re defined by their drive to normalize the state of conflict and a process of war-making, by their struggle to colonize and militarize the cultural field, and by their claim to monopolize representations and interpretations of the conflict. War cultures are shaped by the official effort to impose a dominant vision of war through propaganda, censorship, film, speeches, press and radio statements, recruiting materials and training manuals, as well as the work of officially sponsored war artists and writers.[5]

This definition of war culture as a top-down process of the state's attempt to control the representation of a conflict broadly captures the dynamic between writers and the Iranian and Iraqi states during the Iran-Iraq War. Each state sought to dominate the cultural field through financially incentivizing new writers, doling out prizes and awards, and censoring dissenting representations of the war. Cultural organizations with direct financial ties to each state employed all media at their disposal to disseminate the state's official narrative. Between 1980 and 1988, the war cultures of Iran and Iraq included speeches, press and radio statements, pamphlets, posters, murals, songs, films, television programs, and literary works of various genres. The war cultures of Saddam's Qadisiyya and the Sacred Defense instilled the bellicose aims of wartime governments into literature, film, music, and visual art, which, although aesthetically distinct in Iran and Iraq, served parallel aims of mobilizing the nation, demonizing the enemy, and dominating the war narrative.

The two war cultures gave the conflict a ubiquitous presence that attempted to engulf the two populations, including civilians and combatants. On the home fronts, they entered the everyday life of civilians through constant reminders of the war front soldiers' sacrifices. Iraqi and Iranian civilian populations were not only targeted by bombs but were also sonically and visually bombarded by continuous television and radio broadcasts about the war.⁶ In Iran, some of the most memorable of these included the dirges (*nowheh-hā*) of Sadeq Ahangaran, and the images and dramatic voiceovers of the seventy television episodes of Morteza Avini's the *Chronicles of Victory* (*Revāyat-e Fath*). In Iraq, the nightly television broadcast of *Images from the Battlefield* (*Ṣuwar min al-Maʿrika*), or the militant, nationalist pop songs now referred to as "the songs of Saddam's Qadisiyya," remain instantly recallable by soldiers and citizens who lived through the era.⁷ Alongside these broadcasts of war songs and images, several war films were made in both countries during the conflict that presented the virtues of each government's cause to Arabic or Persian-speaking audiences, some of which found massive viewership both domestically and abroad.⁸ As twenty-first-century readers, we ought to remind ourselves that the technology of the 1980s, compared to today's seemingly endless entertainment choices, was severely limited. One could not necessarily change the television channel or turn the radio dial to avoid government-sanctioned war rhetoric. The omnipresence of such films, television shows, and music was part of normalizing the state of conflict in both countries.⁹

At the same time, monuments, murals, street names, and posters, many of which are still visible today, were also utilized by both governments to visualize the Iran-Iraq War. In Iraq, for example, the Martyr's Monument (*Nuṣb al-Shahīd*) and the Victory Arch (*Qaws al-Naṣr*) still stand as major landmarks in Baghdad.¹⁰ In a more militaristic fashion, until shortly after the 2003 invasion of the country, the statues of one hundred Iraqi sergeants in Basra pointed accusingly at Iran over the banks of the Shatt al-Arab waterway.¹¹ The high rate of casualties that occurred on the Iranian side gave birth to an industry of murals and posters commemorating the martyrdoms of Iranian soldiers who died at the front, while their names provided an entirely new nomenclature for streets and alleyways in Iranian cities and towns.¹² Decades after the war ended, new murals commemorate the Iran-Iraq War by drawing a connection between it and other battles with which Iranian society and armed forces (or Iran-sponsored militias) have been engaged, such as the civil war in Syria or the Coronavirus Pandemic.¹³ Many of the commemorative sites created during or shortly after the war still stand and, occasionally, similar sites are produced today, with the most recent, prominent example of a large-scale site of remembrance in Iran being the Sacred Defense Garden Museum, which opened in Tehran in 2013.[14] Collectively, the physical presence of monuments and murals were and are visual embodiments of state-sponsored war culture. During the war and the postwar period that saw both wartime regimes in power (1988-2003), they reinforced the state's ideology and reminded viewers of its overwhelming power to wield force against its external and internal enemies. While that power has faded away in Iraq, it remains today in Iran.

LITERATURE AND THE STATE

State-sponsored war cultures were the midwives of two distinct literatures of modern warfare, each overdetermined by the wartime ideologies of the Iraqi Baʻthist State and the Islamic Republic of Iran. The governments of both countries harnessed the literary sphere. They exploited it for maximum benefit during wartime by offering moral and financial support for cultural projects that backed the war and praised each country's government. With very few exceptions, the message of most Iranian and Iraqi literary works during the war (including prose, poetry, and memoir) harmonized with the message of other forms of cultural production, demonstrating the comprehensive reach of each state's discourse over the entire cultural sphere.

Literature was central in propagating each state's war story, even if it was not the most visible aspect of Iranian or Iraqi war cultures. For several reasons and by its very nature, the literary field is more selective than other areas of culture. Both readers and writers often have higher levels of education; they must not only be literate but also have time and space, the privilege, in other words, to read. Rightly or wrongly, the creators of literature—writers, poets, journalists, etc.—often present themselves as intellectuals and purveyors of a more refined taste. Moreover, the act of reading itself is distinct from hearing a song on the radio or seeing an image on television. In most cases, one must actively separate oneself from other activities to engage with a written text. Thus, readers wield a degree of agency in their consumption of literary texts that often does not exist for the consumers of images or sounds of audiovisual media. These other artistic forms can attract the attention of anyone casually passing by. This point is even more valid in the choice to read novels and short stories rather than poems. Although wartime poetry was popular and perhaps produced in an even larger quantity than fiction, it was generally short and lent itself to slogans and music, where many more people would encounter and consume it, actively or passively.[15] Reading prose fiction, on the other hand, demands more attention and time. It also arguably provides writers more opportunities to develop more complicated and multivocal narratives.

Wartime support for the production of literature was part of each government's attempt at total societal war mobilization. Most works of Arabic and Persian wartime fiction glorified war front heroism, romanticized martyrdom, and demonized the enemy. During the war, literary critics generally read this literature positively by default and often spoke about literature's obligation to represent the war this way, in a prescriptive manner that stressed literature's importance in mobilizing the nation. In referring to the importance of this literature, Iranian critics tended to prescribe the term "*tahyij*" (encouragement, excitement, or incitement), while in Iraq critics used the Arabic word "*ta'bi'a*" (to mobilize or call to arms). In this sense, mobilization meant promoting various forms of home-front volunteerism (donations, participation in rallies and parades, etc.), encouraging enlistment in the military, and preparing soldiers and their loved ones for the ultimate sacrifice of martyrdom. Thus, wartime literature from both countries sought to build support among readers for the war effort by painting it as an admirable and just cause. It was never portrayed as a war of aggression, and was always framed as "imposed" on the nation. This was despite the official war rhetoric in Iraq that drew from the Arab-Islamic invasion of the Persian empire, or the frequently heard slogan that accompanied the Iranian push into Iraqi territory after 1982: "the path to Jerusalem passes through Karbala" (*rāh-e Qods az Karbalā migozarad*). In Iran, the war was called "the Imposed War" (*Jang-e Tahmili*) from the start and the term was (and is) used as an epithet for the war by Iranians from across the political spectrum. The equivalent Arabic phrase (*al-Ḥarb al-Mafrūḍa*) was not employed as frequently in Iraq but did appear in newspapers, magazines, speeches, and internal governmental memos throughout the war. In Iran, a major shift in wartime nomenclature came on the third anniversary of the

Islamic Revolution, when for the first time Khomeini used the term *Defāʿ-e Moqaddas* (the Sacred Defense) to refer to the war. It quickly gained traction and continues to be used today alongside other terms.[16]

Perhaps most importantly, war fiction was meant to demonstrate that the country's educated, artistic, and intellectual classes supported the war effort. By the time the war began, writers throughout the Middle East and North Africa often had reputations as rebellious and outspoken figures who frequently found themselves at odds or in outright confrontation with those in power, and neither Iranian nor Iraqi writers were exceptional in this regard.[17] In commandeering the literary sphere, the two governments harnessed an expectation of a specific type of political activism that already existed in the literary field. They absorbed into the official war rhetoric the language and causes of committed literature and cannibalized the work of leftwing activist-artists, who were often simultaneously silenced or coopted into each state's war effort. It mattered little whether the political leaders in Baghdad or Tehran or even the soldiers fighting on the front believed in the causes promoted in committed literatures. On a discursive level, they were incorporated into the official war narratives. Ironically, this pitted two states against each other that claimed to be fighting for the same greater causes, including a "Revolution" against the imperialistic agendas of the United States and Israel, the liberation of Palestine, and a war waged in the name of the true and just interpretation of Islam.[18] By dominating the literary field, each government could now claim that it stood for the causes that rebellious writers had previously championed. One could certainly speculate that the pervasiveness of the notion of commitment among the Iranian and Iraqi literati before 1980 assisted the governments of Iran and Iraq in quickly incorporating the literary field into the war effort. Throughout the war, both states valorized political allegory and promoted their own ruling ideologies, while censoring critical representation of the government and the war. To this end, throughout the war, writers who became committed to the causes of each state exploited preexisting notions of legitimacy in the literary sphere to stress notions of heroism and victimhood, and manipulate Iranian and Iraqi national and religious symbols and identities to fulfill the goals of the wartime state.

In some cases during the war, some of those previously rebellious, committed writers and poets wrote under the banner of the Iranian or Iraqi state.

In neither country, however, were the numbers of established literati willing to write for the state great enough to truly dominate the literary sphere. To fill what could have been perceived as a silent void among writers in producing works supportive of the official narratives, both states also created a cadre of new, young writers whose names would become synonymous with the literature of the war. Their participation in the literary war machine was encouraged through publication in state-funded journals and books, financial compensation, and the name recognition that came with state-funded awards. In coopting and building new cadres of writers, each state efficiently utilized governing notions of legitimacy in the literary sphere and repurposed them for their own goals.

Iranian and Iraqi ministries of culture censored texts that contained representations of the war that contradicted the official state narrative. This discouraged many writers who were not willing to promote the official war story from even attempting to write about the conflict, since they knew they had little to no chance of publication. The same writers also risked retribution from governments that rarely hesitated to mete out violence against dissenters. Some more established writers were coopted by (or perhaps sincerely believed in) the governments' war causes and produced works of fiction that affirmed the states' war narratives.[19] In Iraq, the state was even able to control the existence of oppositional discourses by permitting what Muhammad Ghazi al-Akhras calls "formal antonyms" (aḍādd naw'iyya) that gave the appearance of an oppositional literary culture in the country but were in fact entirely regulated by the state.[20] The writers and poets who represented this toothless and controlled "opposition" were largely drawn from "representatives of modernist [poetic] trends, such as Khazal al-Majidi, Salam Kazim, and others, who were staged as a threat to the official cultural discourse." Their publications were largely concerned with "linguistic and structuralist textual debates of considerable complexity and ambiguity without attempting to contextualize them within the sociopolitical scene of the times."[21] These "seemingly contradictory discourses of official and marginal intellectuals in fact worked synergistically to form a collective culture [. . .] that did not correspond with reality, did not represent anyone, and did not engage a real adult audience."[22]

THE BEGINNINGS OF WAR LITERATURE IN IRAN

The Journal of the Iranian Writers' Association

Revived in 1977, the Iranian Writers' Association participated in the Iranian Revolution, most notably from October 10–19 of that year, during a series of poetry readings and speeches held at the German Goethe Institute in Tehran that became known as the Ten Nights (*Dah Shab*).[23] The emotionally and politically charged readings were an early landmark moment in the Revolution, which allowed "young literate Iranians to see and hear in-person and for the first time [. . .] writers and poets who had for years remained wrapped in a reverential halo of intellectual opposition to a repressive regime."[24] Perhaps most importantly, for many, it cracked the wall of fear that the Pahlavi regime built around the idea of peaceful protest.

From March 1979 to June 1981, the Iranian Writers' Association was very active. Several of its members' previously censored works appeared in print, it made frequent statements in daily newspapers, and produced some short-lived, semi-regular publications, such as *Ketāb-e Jom'eh* (*Friday's Book*), edited by eminent poet Ahmad Shamlu, *Andisheh-ye Āzād* (*Free Thought*), and *Nāmeh-ye Kānun-e Nevisandegān* (*The Journal of the Iranian Writers' Association*, henceforth *NKN*.)[25] With a lifespan of just over two years and consisting of only six issues before it was banned, the semiannual *NKN* was the only one of these publications to survive past the summer of 1980 and into the first year of the war with Iraq. Each issue opened with a statement by the Association and featured articles engaging with contemporary international and domestic politics, followed by poetry, short stories, play scripts, illustrations, or photos, largely informed by a Marxist perspective. Many of the writers and poets who participated in the journal were already well-known at the time and went on to become even more famous. Many also found themselves in exile shortly after the government banned the Association. The first issue (spring 1979) is particularly noteworthy, with contributions by the well-known writers and poets M. Azad, Mahmoud Dowlatabadi, Amir Hasan Cheheltan, Shams Langerudi, Mohammad Ali Sepanlu, and Ahmad Shamlu, among others. Later issues featured the likes of Reza Baraheni, Bahram Beyzaie, Simin Behbahani, Nasim Khaksar, and Qazi Rabihavi.

NKN's fourth issue appeared in the winter of 1980 and was devoted to the war. Its two opening statements lay bare the nationalist and leftist political orientation of the Association. They name the war as one that the Iraqi government "imposed on the people of Iran and Iraq" and call upon peace-seeking, working-class people (*khalq-e solhju va zahmatkeshān*) of both countries, and the progressive, freedom-seeking intellectuals (*rowshanfekrān-e āzādikhā va motaraqqi*) of the world to resist the Iraqi occupation and end the war.[26] They go on to praise the bravery of the "people's resistance" (*moqāvemat-e khalq*), defend "the oppressed people of Iran and Iraq" (*mardom-e setamdideh-ye Irān va 'Irāq*), and connect the war to the recent revolution in Iran, by tying it to a greater fight "against imperialism."[27]

The issue features some of the first published poems and fiction about the war. The poems are largely defiant, with most of them expressing nationalist sentiments of resistance against the Iraqi invasion and occupation of the country. One such example is M. Azarm's "To That Shore of the Arvand River" which references well-known stories of Ferdowsi's *Shahnameh*, rooted in the country's pre-Islamic past, to express outrage specifically at a "second Arab invasion of Iran."[28] Qazi Rabihavi, who would go on to write much more about the war, published both a report from his hometown of Abadan, as well as a short, documentary-like story about the confused and desperate departure of a family from Abadan fleeing the invasion.[29] The issue's fiction, poetry, and nonfiction have a tone of urgency. Based on the time of publication, only months after the invasion, they were written quickly in the face of catastrophic and constantly changing conditions on the ground.

At the time, the Association's position regarding the war was nearly the same as that of the government. In fact, the Iraqi invasion had succeeded in bringing together Iranians in a way that nothing else over the prior two years could. Leftists, Islamists, nationalists, and supporters of the ousted Shah were overwhelmingly against the invasion.[30] What differed was the Association's framing of the conflict. A reader unfamiliar with events at the time could read *NKN* and come away thinking that Iran's war with Iraq was another front in the Cold War, with the Iranians representing the oppressed workers of the world, supported by the Soviet Union. Of course, this was not the case. Although the new Islamic state in Iran found itself caught by surprise by the Iraqi invasion and was initially unprepared for the fight both on the military and cultural fronts, its leaders knew that this was not how it would represent this "Imposed War." It was increasingly apparent that the ideological positions held by the Association's members did not align with those of the new government. In April 1981, in the midst of the ongoing Cultural Revolution (1980–1983) and just after the publication of *NKN*'s sixth issue, the Association's offices were raided by *komitehs,* revolutionary groups that "popped up in every neighborhood, in government departments, airports, factories, and business offices [and] carried out the self-appointed task of 'defending' the revolution."[31] This raid effectively signaled the end of the Association's life in Iran. Within the following year, the government banned it, and most of its members were either arrested or purged from their jobs; many soon found themselves in exile.[32]

Sureh

The closure of *NKN* and banning of the Iranian Writers' Association did not signal government opposition to literature or the arts. While the new state was "purifying" the cultural and educational spheres, it was also creating and sponsoring several institutions that espoused its ideological outlook. Among these were the Ministry of Culture and Islamic Guidance (*Vezārat-e Farhang va Ershād-e Eslāmi*, henceforth MCIG), the Organization for Islamic Propaganda (*Sāzmān-e Tablighāt-e Eslāmi*), and the Center for Islamic Art and Thought (*Howzeh-ye Honari va Andisheh-ye Eslāmi,* hereafter the Howzeh), which began publishing the journal *Sureh* in 1980.

Initially, the Howzeh was largely independent of the government, but financial and political pressures soon brought it under the wing of the MCIG. This move caused a split among some of its founding members, who advocated for political and financial independence of the state. Over the following decade and a half, most of its founding members, some of whom have been described as followers of Ali Shariati and part of the "Islamic left," departed.[33] Bringing *Sureh* into the MCIG allowed the organization's leaders to align the journal's ideas and artistic visions with the state's official outlook, perhaps best evidenced through its dedication to the cause of the war. Throughout the war, *Sureh* put the state's discourse on "Sacred Defense," and especially on the importance of resistance (*moqāvemat*), self-sacrifice (*isār*), and martyrdom (*shahādat*), into literary form. *Sureh* became the leading voice in Sacred Defense culture during the war and established the aesthetic standards of Sacred Defense literature.

Although *Sureh*'s writers were largely unknown when it began publication, the combination of their ambitiousness, the state's financial backing, and the censorship of other literary outlets gave the journal an outsized presence in the wartime Iranian literary scene. The journal's format was similar to that of *NKN*, consisting primarily of poetry, fiction, and literary and cultural criticism. The issues closed with an interview, illustrations, or the occasional script of a play or film, but without the political statements of the editorial board that opened each issue of *NKN*. *Sureh*'s criticism sections played a similar role by advocating the journal's political and cultural positions, often promoting the "Islamic arts" and portraying the war as a Sacred Defense. Many writers who published in *Sureh* are still remembered for their passionate positions on Sacred Defense culture. Some have remained active beyond the war years, even until today, among them: Hasan Hoseini (1956–2004), Qasem'ali Farasat, Mehdi Shoja'i, and Mohammad-Reza Sarshar (aka Reza Rahgozar). Others, who would become more famous, such as poet Qaysar Aminpour (1959–2007), and writer and filmmaker Mohsen Makhmalbaf, later distanced themselves from the Sacred Defense cultural scene and their hardline support for the state.

The case of Mohsen Makhmalbaf calls for closer attention, considering the international fame he would later gain as an arthouse filmmaker. In the early years of the war and the first years of the journal, he was one of the most prolific writers and advocates for Sacred Defense culture. In the second issue of *Sureh*, he has two articles of literary criticism and a short story. In both articles, he provides a blueprint for the type of prescriptive literary criticism that would later dominate state publications, advocating for a kind of "Gorky-inspired," uncomplicated fiction committed to telling the truth—a type of literature he calls "*maktabi* fiction." The term Makhmalbaf chose, *maktab* (adjectival form: *maktabi*), can be translated as "school," "path," or "school of thought." After the Revolution, supporters of the new government started using the term to "express their ideological militancy and populism, and to dissociate themselves both from the secularists (and secular intellectuals in general) and [. . .] 'liberal'—Muslims."[34] According to Makhmalbaf, *maktabi* fiction should be ideological and feature characters with "Islamic worldviews" in contrast to the vulgar, "humanist values" espoused in Western literature and "sex-obsessed" modern Persian fiction.[35] The four short stories in the same issue of *Sureh*, one of which is by Makhmalbaf and another by Qasem'ali Farasat, whose novel *Headless Palms* is treated later in this chapter, follow *maktabi* principles. Such work remained the norm for Makhmalbaf until he began critiquing the government's treatment of war veterans, first with the 1985 publication of his novel *Bāgh-e Bolur* (*The Crystal Garden*) and, more critically, with the widely viewed 1988 film *'Arusi-ye Khubān* (*Marriage of the Blessed*).[36]

As the war dragged on, the state encouraged the publication of the kind of war literature featured in *Sureh* and contributed to its mass production. Just with fiction alone, between 1981 and 1991, nearly 1,600 short stories and 46 novels about the war were published, most adhering to the Sacred Defense framework.[37] Additionally, with governmental support, more journals promoting the "Islamic arts" and Sacred Defense culture appeared, most prominently *Faslnāmeh-ye Honar* (*Arts Quarterly*).[38]

Ahmad Mahmud's Elegy for Destruction

In 1982, shortly after the closure of *NKN* and the appearance of the first issues of *Sureh*, eminent novelist and native of Ahvaz, Ahmad Mahmud, quickly published his novel *Zamin-e Sukhteh* (*Scorched Earth*). It was one of the first Iranian war novels and remains one of the most enduring Iranian novels of the war. *Scorched Earth* is based on the author's war front experiences, including his brother's death in the early days of the conflict. It features characters developed in two of Mahmud's prior novels, forming the final part of a loose trilogy that began with his landmark social-realist novel, *Hamsāyeh-hā* (*The Neighbors*, 1974), and continued in *Dāstān-e yek Shahr* (*The Story of a City*, 1978).[39] Taken together, the three novels narrate the story of a politicized, working-class family from Ahvaz during the second half of the twentieth century, from the early 1950s to 1980. *Scorched Earth* is set in Ahvaz during the war's first three months, a time of intense Iraqi shelling, urban fighting, and heavy losses for Iranian fighters and civilians. Mahmud was the most high-profile fiction writer to directly take on the conflict so early, and the novel sold well and was widely read, with two printings by 1984 and reprinted again after the war. It is currently in its twentieth printing.[40]

The novel begins with Ahvaz as a tense city on the brink of attack. As the capital of Khuzestan, with a sizable Arab minority and located only

64 kilometers from the Iraqi border, Ahvaz was in the Iraqi army's sights, literally, from the first days of the invasion. Although it was never occupied, it sustained heavy damage from Iraqi artillery fire, especially during the first year of the war. Typical of Mahmud's work, *Scorched Earth* is written tersely and narrated simply, with the unnamed narrator's thoughts and descriptions of Ahvaz. It relies on colloquial language often interspersed with news reports, radio broadcasts, and the multitude of slogans that quickly appeared painted on walls throughout the city. *Scorched Earth* presents an image of a tense and frightened population confused about the course of the Revolution, the Iraqi invasion, and the country's lack of military defenses. Raw emotions drive people's reactions to the circumstances and the novel depicts the first months of war as an utter disaster, characterized by the occupation and destruction of cities and communities along the Iraqi border, heavy Iranian casualties, and the complete breakdown of order. At the same time, the novel gives the early days of the war an epic quality through the heroism of the residents who stay behind to resist. Of these characters, perhaps the most memorable is Naneh Baran, whose son, Baran, is killed by Iraqis at the front lines. At his funeral she is "stone-faced, staring straight ahead, eyes raining fire. She stood rigidly like a tree trunk with the butt of a gun squeezed in the palm of her hand. The bandolier slung across her chest glistening."[41] The novel follows her trajectory from the mother of a resistance fighter to a militant who is eventually martyred defending the city. After Baran's death, she begins patrolling her neighborhood, telling the narrator that the war is a "matter of history! A matter of the revolution! History has given our generation this responsibility. If we don't fight, then we are traitors against ourselves! Traitors against our generation! Traitors against the Revolution!"[42]

The novel's narration adopts a militant, nationalist position on the war that portrays the defense of the homeland as an absolute necessity. However, its representation of the war is distinct from the fiction that appeared in *NKN* written by authors such as Qazi Rabihavi and, later, Asghar 'Abdollahi, whose early short stories sympathetically focused on the hardships of civilians under bombardment or displaced from cities and villages near the front. In contrast, *Scorched Earth* is unflinching in its defense of violence as a necessary means to resist the Iraqi invasion. Yet, its depiction of the war differs from that of government-affiliated cultural producers, who justified every act of resistance in defense of the homeland as both religious and nationalist. The new state's inconsistent ability to censor books, combined with Mahmud's position as a well-known writer who had been highly critical of the Pahlavi regime likely explains why the novel was published. For these reasons, it also attracted criticism from both independent and government-affiliated literary critics. Mahmud, who was unaffiliated with the Writers' Union and remained a member of the communist Tudeh Party (which supported the government's position on the war), was at once accused of being a nationalist warmonger who celebrated the war's violence, and of not being Islamic enough in his depiction of the resistance, and thus writing a book without literary value.[43] After the war, when questioned on the topic, he answered directly: "If this is what a warmonger [*jang-talab*] is, then I'm still one. So long as I know that the enemy is on our land, I believe that we should fight. Until they are driven out, I am a warmonger. I see no reason for giving up our territory and remaining silent. No, before anything else I'm first a nationalist and then an internationalist."[44]

THE INFRASTRUCTURE OF WAR LITERATURE IN IRAQ
Iraqi Journals Transformed

The pre-war and wartime governmental continuity of power and its dual strategy of co-optation and suppression, which had been at work for several years by the time the war broke out, was the most significant factor in distinguishing the early war cultures and literatures of Iran and Iraq. Iraqi literary and cultural magazines were more quickly and efficiently able to adapt to the ideological environment of the conflict and transform into mouthpieces for the war effort. Iraqi war literature appeared almost simultaneously with the start of the war, and several novelists and short story writers proved themselves capable of quickly creating works of fiction committed to the government's war narrative. These stories, along with similarly themed works of poetry and literary criticism, were usually published first in newspapers, magazines, and journals. In September 1980, as the Iraqi military launched their invasion, several cultural and literary journals abruptly began publishing content that supported Saddam's Qadisiyya. Among some of the most well-known were *Āfāq 'Arabiyya* (*Arab Horizons*), *Alif Bā'* (*A-B*), *al-Talī'a al-Adabiyya* (*The Literary Vanguard*), and *al-Aqlām* (*Pens*).[45]

The issues of *Āfāq ʿArabiyya*, the popular monthly arts and culture magazine published by the Iraqi Ministry of Cultural Affairs, printed immediately after the outbreak of the war, provide striking examples of how the visual and textual content of a monthly publication was immediately and comprehensively integrated into the state's cultural war machine. With the start of the war, *Āfāq ʿArabiyya* took a hard pro-war and explicitly anti-Iranian stance that had not been part of the magazine's previous content. For example, the October 1980 issue opens with an article entitled "In Memory of October" that commemorates the reclamation of Arab land from the Israelis during the 1973 war, and directly connects that conflict with Saddam's Qadisiyya, naming Iraq as the true defender of the Arab world. Saddam Hussein is quoted as saying Iraq will "teach the Persians a new chapter in the lessons of Qadisiyya."[46] The cover of the next issue depicts a menacing profile of Ayatollah Khomeini sternly staring at the reader. A black and white map of the Iranian province of Khuzestan, home to a sizeable Arabic-speaking population, is partly peeled away to expose a new Iraqi *ʿArabistān*, in green and red with Arabized names of Iranian cities. With the Iraqi invasion well underway, the issue features pictures of victorious soldiers at the front, drawings of the Islamic-Arab armies charging the Persians in the battle of Qadisiyya, and multiple photos of Saddam Hussein.

The same issue features several poems devoted to the war and Saddam Hussein, including one by ʿAbd al-Razzaq ʿAbd al-Wahid, a prominent poet who became the chief panegyrist for Saddam Hussein and one of the war's most vocal proponents. Then chief editor of the magazine, Shafiq al-Kamali, also wrote an article titled "Culture and the Battle," where he claims that Saddam's Qadisiyya will be a part of a larger cultural renaissance not just for Iraq but for the Arab Nation as well. "[T]he battle," he states, "puts three critical tests to our culture and intellectuals." The first of these is to draw inspiration from the historical role that Iraq has played in protecting the rights of Arabs and the expression of truth. The second is the necessity of culture to transform itself into a cry against corruption, decadence, and falsehood. The third is the obligation for all Iraqis to take a stand against "silent culture," an apparent reference to fifth columnists and any artists who were not actively supporting the war.[47]

The messages promoted in *Āfāq ʿArabiyya* were aimed at a broad audience of readers interested in contemporary cultural issues. Another monthly publication, *al-Aqlām*, demonstrates how a prestigious literary journal was mobilized for the war. *Al-Aqlām* had been in circulation for over fifteen years at the outbreak of the war and was among the leading literary journals in the Arab world, printing literature and criticism from authors writing in Arabic, as well as translations of works from various languages into Arabic. The inside cover of the August 1980 issue already presages the war with bellicose comments by the magazine's editorial board, then headed by Tarrad al-Kubaysi and Basim ʿAbd al-Hamid Hammudi, two critics who published several books and articles throughout the 1980s praising the war's literature and Saddam Hussein.[48] Their short editorial, entitled *"Mawqifunā"* ("Our Position"), claims the Iranians were already "occupying" Iraqi-Arab territory in and around the Shatt al-Arab waterway, territory they had "raped" and which could only "be taken back with force." The board writes:

> The Arabs should know that the liberation of Sayf Saʿd, Zayn al-Qaws and the Shatt al-ʿArab is a revolutionary uprising on the path to liberate Gaza, Golan and Palestine... [all] Occupations are one, whether it is in Palestine or Golan [...] or Arab Islands in the Shatt al-ʿArab [...] There is no difference between one occupier and another, American, Zionist or Persian. It [the liberation of Iranian-occupied lands] is a step on the path of liberation and uprising in all occupied Arab lands and a lesson for Khomeini's racist, corrupt gang...and a lesson to all Arabs, especially those who are still in occupied countries. Perhaps they, too, will rise up for themselves, for their dignity, and for the dignity of the Arab Nation.[49]

Subsequent issues of *al-Aqlām* devote more attention to the war, with the November and December 1980 issues each containing a special supplement preceding the table of contents entitled "Literature and the Battlefield" (*al-Adab wa-l-Maʿrika*). While this extra section was dropped by the early issues of 1981, during most of the first two years of the war, issues of *al-Aqlām* began with sections devoted to praising Saddam and the war with Iran, followed by stories, poetry, literary criticism, and discussions of the quickly developing genre of war literature (*adab al-ḥarb*), which soon became synonymous in Iraq with the literature of Saddam's Qadisiyya, at least until Saddam invaded

Kuwait in August 1990. Later issues were less forceful about the war and Saddam Hussein's cult of personality but nearly always contained some content devoted to the conflict. Within a year, a separate supplement was no longer included, but the war was still prominently featured in the journal's pages, in some cases plainly integrated into its contents, and at other times merged with the more extensive discussions of war and resistance in world literature, striving to draw a direct link between the literature of this war and the literature of Palestinian resistance.[50]

Stories from the Blaze

The fictional literature of Saddam's Qadisiyya that initially appeared primarily in journals would soon be anthologized through the multivolume series *Qādisiyyat Ṣaddām: Qiṣaṣ Taḥt Lahīb al-Nār* (*Saddam's Qadisiyya: Stories from the Fire's Blaze*), published by the Iraqi Ministry of Culture. These ten voluminous short story collections—the first of which appeared less than a year after the war began—were compiled by panels of famous writers and literary critics throughout the war years. Each volume numbered around five hundred pages, and they were occasionally introduced by a member of the editorial panel. They were meant to showcase contemporary war fiction, with each volume containing dozens of both prize-winning and other stories that were considered among the best by panels of judges, who, at times, included the likes of major writers and critics such as Jabra Ibrahim Jabra, Muhsin al-Musawi, and Fu'ad al-Takarli. Many of the short story authors appeared in multiple volumes; 'Abd al-Sattar Nasir, Warid Badr al-Salim, Ahmad Khalaf, and Jasim al-Rasif were some of the more well-known writers in the Iraqi literary scene before the war. Alongside those veteran authors were new writers, practically unheard of before (and sometimes after) the war, who were incentivized to publish war literature.

The tenor and content of these stories have been thoroughly reviewed and debated in Arabic and English. The first critical assessments appeared during wartime, simultaneous with the earliest pieces of literature. Alongside critical articles in literary magazines, entire books of literary history and criticism also appeared during the war, such as 'Umar Talib's *al-Ḥarb fī al-Qiṣṣa al-'Irāqiyya* (*War in the Iraqi Short Story*), published in 1982. Hawraa al-Hassan's observations of this book are instructive and applicable to other works of Iraqi state-sponsored literary criticism published during the war and in its immediate aftermath. Talib's book, she writes, was "part of a large corpus of state literary criticism designed to guide and direct propaganda writings in line with state imperatives. Literary criticism of this kind was also designed to lend weight to literary propaganda works as worthy 'objects of study.'"[51] More critical reviews of the official literatures began appearing in the immediate aftermath of the war, and their numbers have grown since that time.[52] Some critics have written wholesale dismissals of both the literature and the writers of the period, with several writers and literary critics originally from Iraq—among them Salam 'Abbud, Sinan Antoon, 'Abbas Khidr, Kadhim Jihad Kadhim, and Fatima Mohsen—writing the harshest critiques of the writers and intellectuals who participated in Iraq's 1980s cultural scene.[53] Others have been more forgiving of those who helped create the official literature of the war, highlighting the conditions in which writers and critics found themselves. Achim Rohde, for instance, writes that exile was often the only way to "stay 'clean'" for Iraqi writers not willing to publish about the war in the 1980s.[54] Others have noted how the literary trends changed over the course of the war, corresponding with Iraqi military victories and losses on the battlefield.[55] These changes made room for works that didn't entirely glorify the bloodshed or the cult of Saddam Hussein. Some stories published after 1982 (written after Iraq found itself on the defensive) even contained mild criticisms of war and its loss and pain. Khoury claims that the Ba'thist government "tolerated the implicitly critical stance of this literature in large part because it was not widely read beyond literary circles. It never explicitly challenged the conduct of war, and it was not picked up in mass media outlets, which continued to glorify the war experience in film, photography, and print."[56] Others have noted that some Iraqi writers, prominent among them Lutfiyya al-Dulaymi and Muhammad Khudayyir, managed to publish literature about the war that presented the conflict outside the state's narrative.[57] This is not to say that this literature was "anti-war," but rather that it was not outright "pro-war."

Despite these post-mortem debates over the details and qualities of Iraqi state-sponsored war fiction, there is consensus that it simply lacked the features of long-lasting literature. Above all, its derivative nature clearly meant to meet the state's propagandistic aims coupled with the state's decision to stop funding and promoting it once the war with Kuwait was underway in 1990, ensured that it would not endure. Yet, its massive quantity and the resources poured into its production makes it a historical marker of 1980s wartime Iraq, and lays bare the ideological and material conditions for cultural production in the country. Today, literary critics and historians cannot help but recognize it. Including the *Saddam's Qadisiyya* collections, eighty-seven writers contributed to creating ninety-five short story collections and seventy-five novels in the 1980s.[58] The best that can be said of this fiction is that with time, stories occasionally appeared that portrayed Iraqis as victims and the war as painful. The content of later stories was sometimes written with a degree of ambivalence toward the conflict and without explicit hatred toward the enemy. It is likely that the length of the war and the Iraqi population's fatigue led to greater tolerance on the part of the censors. However, this did not mean that the state tolerated criticism, or debate about the fundamental reasons behind the war, or its representation as anything but a necessary cause. This is why ʿAbbud claims that wartime literature "was an authoritarian literature [*adab sulṭawī*], whether written by Baʿthist or non-Baʿthist."[59] It was all part of the same war machine. Literature that was explicitly critical of the government or the war did not appear in Iraq until after the war ended.

DYING FOR THE CAUSE

Iranian and Iraqi official wartime literatures were produced quickly and copiously, mainly with the aim of flooding the literary sphere with pro-government messages. While Arabic and Persian wartime literatures were primarily set on the war front, writers also addressed, in lesser quantities, stories of veterans, women, and children on the home front. Literary critics were just as active as writers of fiction. Typically, they lauded the stories being produced as revolutionary landmarks in the history of Arabic or Persian literature, or tempered their critiques by first recognizing the importance of the war and its literary byproducts, then noting that its literature still needed development.

In both countries, the content and form of most wartime literary fiction adhered to the prescriptive writing of literary critics, who were often the judges for prizes for the best works of war literature. Equally important were the censors in each country that gave final permission for any work to be printed. The combination of these factors ensured a level of consistency in most wartime fiction. There was a tendency in each official literature to draw from the didactic nature of socialist realism by teaching the aims of wartime governments, glorifying war front heroism and righteous victimhood, emphasizing the binary nature (good/evil, friend/enemy) of the war, keeping depictions of enemy combatants largely anonymous and distant, and stressing the importance of the collective at the expense of the individual. However, more than anything else, the veneration of martyrdom emerged as an essential element of both Iraqi and Iranian war cultures and featured prominently in the official literatures of both countries.

The war's proponents extolled martyrdom both to maintain support for the war effort among combatants and civilians, and to instantly commemorate those who fell in battle, exalting the martyr's social status. In both Iran and Iraq, on the most basic level, this included giving financial support and an elevated category of citizenship to the families of martyrs. Scholarly and journalistic writing on the Iran-Iraq War has tended to emphasize the importance of the concept of martyrdom in Iran, while largely ignoring its immense importance in Iraq, when in fact both states promoted cultures of martyrdom, albeit with different points of reference. Although the active promotion of the culture of martyrdom specifically related to "Saddam's Qadisiyya" in Iraq essentially came to an end in 1988, the culture of martyrdom connected to the Sacred Defense has continued in the postwar era in Iran, with the massive expansion of the Martyrs' Foundation (*Bonyād-e Shahid*).[60]

Because of the 1990–1991 Gulf War, the 2003 U.S.-led invasion of the country, and consequent collapse of the Ba'thist regime, the definition of "martyr" has never been as stable in Iraq as it has been in Iran. The wartime Iraqi state's most drastic attempt to claim victims of the Iran-Iraq War as martyrs exemplifies this. Because martyrdom was exclusively defined by the Ba'th party until 2003, during the war with Iran, Saddam Hussein's government posthumously inducted all non-Ba'thist war dead into the party, claiming them as Iraqi Ba'thist martyrs. However, if their families took part in the rebellion against the states in the aftermath of the 1990–1991 Gulf War, the state revoked their status as martyrs.[61] More recently, martyr status has been redefined with the establishment of the Iraqi Martyrs' Foundation in

2006, and debates over who is considered a martyr throughout the history of modern Iraq continue today, although with far fewer ramifications for literary production.⁶²

In the Iranian context, martyrdom during the war had a clear religious signification and was one of the pillars of the state's official discourse. During the early years of the war, there was a zealous public discourse of martyrdom that reached an apex when *shahādat-talabi*, or "yearning for martyrdom," became an increasingly common theme in public speeches and popular media. Citing from the widely circulated newspaper *Etteläʿāt* (*Information*), Saskia Gieling writes, "[s]tories were circulated about people from all strata of the population who sought martyrdom. A very revealing connection between the death of Iranian soldiers and Husayn's death at Karbala was made through accounts of those whose heads had been cut off or even stories about potential martyrs who wished that their heads would be cut off from their bodies as had happened with Husayn at Karbala."⁶³ References to martyrdom remained constant throughout the conflict. Khomeini and others repeatedly praised martyrdom in public speeches, it was dramatically visualized in large-scale murals, and names of streets and alleys were changed to honor both well- and lesser-known martyrs.⁶⁴

The Iraqi regime's employment of martyrdom as a trope during the war was also a crucial component of the country's war culture. In one respect, the "Baʿth Party undertook a systematic effort to sanctify the deaths of soldiers by developing rituals that gave meaning to their deaths within the narrow confines of a secularized reading of martyrdom in Islam and a Baʿthist interpretation of Iraqi Arab nationalism."⁶⁵ In this way, it limited the way families could mourn fallen soldiers, prohibited the formation of associations meant to commemorate the dead, and worked to instill the idea that all soldiers died for Iraq, despite their religious background, ethnicity, or political affiliation.⁶⁶ Nonetheless, while the Baʿth Party attempted to present Iraq as the face of secular Arab resistance to the exportation of Iran's Islamic Revolution, it also opportunistically drew from its pre-Islamic past as well as its important place in Islamic history to mold Iraqi war culture to its needs. This resulted in a pastiche of images and statements that framed the Iraqi goals of the war in terms of Arab unity, the Battle of Qadisiyya, and even the principles of the first Shiʿi Imam and fourth Muslim Caliph, ʿAli ibn Abi

Talib. Within this context, the regime stressed the importance of martyrdom while carefully avoiding the points of reference utilized by the Iranian government, which early on framed the war entirely through the martyrdom story of the third Shi'i Imam, Hussein, arguably the most dramatic and famous story of martyrdom in Islamic history. Rather than attempt to counter-co-opt that story for its own purposes, the Iraqi government nodded toward Shi'i martyrology as an explicitly non-Persian, Arab phenomenon, stressing the fundamental Iraqiness of Babylonian history as a symbol of national unity, and making use of a wholly different martyrology rooted in the Battle of Qadisiyya and the Arab-Islamic defeat of the Persian Sassanian empire.[67] For example, the Ba'thist regime named one of its ballistic missiles *al-Hussein*, and Saddam Hussein was often compared to Nebuchadnezzar, with variations of the slogan "Yesterday's Nebuchadnezzar is Today's Saddam Hussein" (*Nabūkhadh-naṣr al-ams Ṣaddām Ḥusayn al-yawm*) frequently heard in public ceremonies.[68] Details in the story of the Battle of Qadisiyya helped the regime create its own "cult of martyrdom" where "the mother of all martyrs was Khansa' who lost four sons [. . .] in the battle of al-Qadisiyya against the Persian Empire." Khoury goes on to note that the "figure of Khansa' as the historical mother of the modern martyrs of Qadisiyat Saddam was frequently invoked by Saddam Hussain in his well-publicized visits to the families of martyrs."[69] As in Iran, the Iraqi state also undertook far-reaching projects publicly commemorating the war's martyrs, such as the Martyr's Monument and the dedication in 1982 of December 1 as Martyr's Day (*Yawm al-Shahīd*).

The wartime regimes' discourses on martyrdom quickly appeared in each country's literature. In both countries, the war years saw the publication of hundreds of poems, memoirs, works of fiction and literary criticism that lionized the war's martyrs. Thus, Mir- 'Abedini calls martyrdom "the most important theme in [Iranian] war stories" and identifies martyrdom in Iran's earliest war literature as the "highpoint of the life of the protagonist." He goes on to explain that in most war fiction from the 1980s, the narrator of the story is "transformed" by witnessing the martyrdom of others and is then heroically set on "a path towards becoming a martyr" himself.[70] On the Iraqi side, Mohsen points out that the function of the massive body of wartime literature written about the conflict "was to glorify martyrdom, making life inferior to death."⁷¹ Muhsin al-Musawi has also stated that the Ba'thist regime launched an "enormous propaganda effort to make martyrdom acceptable" during the war with Iran, alongside Saddam Hussein's efforts to secularize any specifically Shi'i conception of martyrdom.⁷²

For their partisans, martyrs are not controversial or divisive figures. Throughout the war years and, in both countries to differing extents in the postwar years, the martyr's dominant role in literature has been that of a unifying figure, a blameless and untouchable character, immune to criticisms that might have been leveled against either government during or after the war. Furthermore, aside from notions of redemption and sacred vindication, which we often tie to the idea of martyrdom, both the Arabic and Persian words for martyr and martyrdom, "shahīd" and "shahāda/shahādat," carry essential meanings of seeing, testifying, and witnessing. As such, it is implied that the martyr has seen the war and can truthfully attest to what they saw. Both governments drew from the martyr's inherent reliability and infallibility to produce numerous representations of meaningful death in the war's literature.

Heroic Martyrdom at the Front in Saddam's Qadisiyya

In 1986, *Afāq 'Arabiyya*, in cooperation with the Iraqi Ministry of Culture, published a collection of articles titled *Qādisiyyat Ṣaddām wa-l-Khiyār al-Qawmī* (*Saddam's Qadisiyya and the National Choice*). The book's chapters on various aspects of the war's culture and interviews with experts in strategic affairs, celebrate the war while analyzing and criticizing the Iranian enemy. It was part of the Ministry's special book series titled *"Fī al-Thaqāfa wa-l-Ḥarb"* (On Culture and War), which featured hundreds of books of literary and cultural criticism, fiction, and poetry. This volume featured an article titled "Ḥawla Mafhūm al-Istishhād" ("On the Concept of Martyrdom") by 'Abd al-Jabbar Mahmud al-Samarra'i, a Ba'thist intellectual, prolific writer, and advocate for Saddam's Qadisiyya in the 1980s. The author traces a consistent history of martyrdom in Iraq that goes back to the pre-Islamic period and leads directly to this contemporary moment and the war against Iran. According to al-Sammar'i, martyrdom is rooted in Iraqi culture's love for the homeland, dignity, and honor. The martyr "is not just an example, but a school from which our glorious students learn the meaning of sacrifice in defense of truth and honor." Samarra'i claims that Iraqi history already contains the "original Islamic Revolution," which occurred during the first Islamic conquests, thus invalidating the claims of the recent Islamic revolution in Iran. He connects that first so-called revolution to the ongoing revolution of the Ba'thist Socialist Movement emanating from Iraq, which he calls "the only revolutionary movement that has presented caravans of martyrs on the path toward the Arab nation's revival." According to him, the Ba'thist Revolution was "the second great Arab Revolution," one that also carried with it "an emphasis on sacrifice." As such, Ba'thist ideology has a "direct connection to the concept of martyrdom in Islam."[73]

This profound weight given to martyrdom appeared repeatedly in Iraqi fiction throughout the war. The 1981 short story collection, *al-Shahīd 1777 (Martyr 1777)*, by 'Abd al-Sattar Nasir, is an early work that dramatizes martyrdom while also displaying the other traits that were typical of the many stories in the growing canon of Saddam's Qadisiyya literature.[74] The title story from this collection is particularly telling. "Martyr 1777" refers to the story's protagonist, Tawfiq Zahir, the 1,777th martyr for the Iraqi cause against the Persian enemy. He is a Moroccan who travels to Iraq to fight for the defense of the eastern Arab flank. Exhibiting a superlative personality and exceptional bravery, Zahir, arriving at the front, innocent, chaste, and pure, "wanted only freedom for the entire Arab Nation, from the ocean to the sea and from the clouds that travel westward to the ones that settle in the east."[75]

The short story, which reads partly like a eulogy to a fallen pan-Arab fighter and partly as a first-person account of combat, serves two didactic principles essential to the state's war narrative. Firstly, the battle against the Persians was for the freedom of the entire Arab World. Secondly, Zahir's martyrdom forever makes him a hero. Zahir's battlefield coordination with his fellow Arab fighters is nothing short of perfection, matched only by his admiration for his new Iraqi comrades-in-arms. It reads: "Tawfiq Zahir said to one of the soldiers... 'It has been two long years, and I have fought everywhere. But the truth is that I have not lived among soldiers who laugh in the face of death like you [Iraqi soldiers] do. This is something to add to the many great lessons I have learned in the past.'" Smiling, Zahir is martyred on the December 7, 1980, and his last words spoken to an Iraqi soldier were "I have learned from you how to laugh in the face of death. And this is the most beautiful of lessons."[76] The story ends there, lamenting only that the martyr will never know how the other soldiers spoke of his bravery and sweet smile, and that he will never be able to read his own story. The story places undeniable importance on Zahir's sacrifice for the Arab cause. As a martyr, he is not to be mourned because he has been redeemed. The description of the hero as fearless, zealous for combat, and happy to die, follows patterns identified by scholars of the period.[77] The pan-Arabist, didactic story recalls the heyday of Arabic committed literature in the 1950s.

Throughout the war, novice writers were sent to the front to be embedded with soldiers, record their experiences, and produce this type of literature.[78] Older, more experienced writers who were already known in the Iraqi literary scene were incentivized and sometimes coerced into writing about the war. 'Abbud cites the example of Ahmad Khalaf, a fiction writer who came of age with the generation of well-known Iraqi novelists in the 1960s. With the outbreak of the war, he was brought into the Ba'thist cultural establishment and began churning out dozens of crass war stories. According to 'Abbud, the Iraqi soldiers in his stories "borrowed from Rambo movies" and "derived pleasure from death."[79] For example, in his story *"Nuqṭat Tamās"* ("Point of Contact"), his main character "laugh[s] at his own pain" while mowing down "Magi" soldiers with rounds of bullets.[80] Stories such as these made up the literature of Saddam's Qadisiyya, a literature in which "weapons dance and bullets sing."[81] As the war dragged on, there was support for literature that was less celebratory of the war's violence, and occasionally grieving the loss of life that the seemingly never-ending conflict was causing. Al-Hassan demonstrates how another Iraqi writer, Jasim al-Rasif, wrote prolifically throughout the war and won three prizes for Saddam's Qadisiyya literature, and suddenly published two novels in the war's final years that put the limelight on civilian suffering in the cities and the pain of losing loved ones. As previously indicated, though, even in these cases, explicit criticism of the war or the government remained impossible.[82]

Stories such as these were part of a plethora of ideologically-charged literature that created a literary bank of images associated with the war: fearless heroes, the war as an Arab-Muslim cause, selfless Iraqi soldiers, cruel, anonymous enemies, and death in combat always coded as martyrdom. The volumes of the *Ṣaddām's Qadisiyya* series were chock full of these motifs. Martyrdom was the most important part of this symbolic cache. More than any of the other elements, it attempted to render the war, and dying in it, as both religiously and nationalistically meaningful.

Sacrifice and the Sacredness of Defense

With few exceptions, much of Iran's wartime literature was written by writers the Iranian readership was initially unfamiliar with when the war began, but who gained name recognition by publishing prolifically during and after the war. Censorship ensured that wartime literature remained largely homogeneous by embodying the viewpoint of the state's official narrative of the conflict. While anthologies of fiction in the scale and scope of the *Saddam's Qadisiyya* collections in Iraq did not exist in Iran, writers who wrote Sacred Defense literature were published by presses that received funding and support from the state. Writers and critics such as Mohammad Reza Sarshar, Seyed Mehdi Shoja'i, Qasem'ali Farasat, and Ebrahim Hasan Baygi, were among the first writers to gain prominence as Sacred Defense writers, many publishing their first stories and articles in *Sureh*. These writers consistently produced war stories featuring characters who saw the war as a way to extend the Islamic Revolution's principles.

As both a critic and fiction writer, Sarshar, who has remained active in writing literary criticism and fiction about the Iran-Iraq War until the present day, epitomizes the figure of the staunchly committed Sacred Defense writer and intellectual. His short stories written during the war and later compiled in the collections *Khodāhāfez, Barādar* (*Goodbye, Brother*, 1990), and *Posht-e Divār-e Shab* (*Behind the Night's Wall*, 2008) typify Iranian wartime fiction. Originally published in 1986, "Māndāb" ("The Marsh") is one such story. It is told in the form of a long letter written by a professional writer, Jalil, to his dear friend, Naser, who is fighting at the front. The letter is prompted by Naser's four-year-old daughter asking Jalil when her father will return, and why Jalil himself does not go to the front when her father does repeatedly. Jalil is guilt-stricken and writes to Naser to express his shame for not participating in the war. In the letter, he recounts his interaction with another soldier named Parviz, who has just returned from the front. Parviz, for his part, bemoans and criticizes non-committed, professional writers who do not visit the war front and who, six years into the conflict, remain unable to understand the extraordinary significance of the war front soldiers' sacrifices. "The front, brother!" Parviz tells Jalil, "Every subject is there: martyrdom, sacrifice, divine intervention, Islam, moments of spirituality, purity, mysticism, love, God, the *Mehdi*, stories, history, everything!"[83] Parviz continues:

> We're going into our sixth year of war and every moment of it has been an epic. But until now, only a few novels and short stories have been written that do justice to the issue [...] Maybe it's because our patient and noble fighters haven't told you anything. But how are you going to answer to history? [...] If, in 20–30 years a young person asks you 'Mister, you're a writer, during all those war years, where were you, what were you doing?' How are you going to answer? [...] Brother, our soldiers have seen so much during this war and our artists do nothing! They [the soldiers] are now forced to shoulder the burden of writing, too. [...] But their writing is just full of feelings and emotions. There's nothing artistic in it.[84]

The letter contains multiple such moments that allow the writer to teach readers about the principles of the Sacred Defense. In this case, Sarshar metafictionally addresses what he and other Iranian critics saw as a crisis of representation vis-à-vis the war with Iraq. It is a position that calls to mind how contemporary Iraqi critics viewed mobilizational war literature as being of the utmost importance while still wishing to see it improve artistically. Sarshar's story functions as didactic literary criticism camouflaged as fiction and identifies the qualities that war literature must contain from the perspective of the Sacred Defense ideologue: the selfless heroism of the war front soldiers, the need for literature to capture the "truth" of the front, and the importance of their martyrdom. Ironically, his characters agree with Mir-'Abedini's critique of wartime fiction that the war front soldier-writers were "afraid of forgetting the value of war," "wrote in a rush," and were unable to create "a natural, fictional world with living characters."[85] By the end of the 1980s, both the Sacred Defense literary critic and his independent counterpart could agree that war literature was stylistically weak, but they saw the remedy for that situation differently. The pro-regime critic doubled down on the necessity of Sacred Defense ideology, while the independent critic saw a need for war literature to be liberated from state ideology.

It is safe to assume that one of the "few novels" referred to in Sarshar's story was Qasem'ali Farasat's *Nakhl-hā-ye bī Sar* (*Headless Palms*), which was published in 1983 and was one of the first war novels to receive attention by Iranian literary critics. It continues to be referenced in articles and academic studies about the war's literature and especially by critics affiliated with Sacred Defense culture, who hail it as one of the first literary works celebrating sacrifice and resistance, two hallmarks of this literature.[86] Set in the cities and villages scattered along Iran's border with Iraq, *Headless Palms* takes place during the first two years of the war. It centers on the Iraqi invasion and occupation of the city of Khorramshahr in September 1980 and its subsequent liberation by Iranian forces in May 1982.

Headless Palms revolves around Naser, a young man from Khorramshahr who joins the initial resistance to the invading Iraqi forces.[87] The novel tells the story of a young man learning bravery through faith in God and experience in combat. Its simple narration is told through Naser and a third-person narrator. The dialogue and narration are full of laudatory references to the Islamic Revolution, Imam Khomeini, and the martyrdom of Imam Hussein. As a work of early war fiction produced by a Sacred Defense writer, *Headless Palms* offers an interesting comparison to the simultaneously produced works of Saddam's Qadisiyya. The soldiers are portrayed as brave fighters, several scenes reinforce the government's vision of the conflict, and the enemy is anonymized or, at best, stereotyped. In a telling example, after a battle with Iraqi troops Naser is assigned to lead a group of Iraqi POWs away from the front. He is reminded by a superior that "everything with our revolution must be Islamic, even taking prisoners," a command that he honors by treating the prisoners lawfully. Soon after, a local religious leader, Sheikh Sharif, congratulates him on the operation and asks about his platoon's name. The scene informs readers how this war should be understood:

> Sheikh Sharif: "What is the name of your division?"
> Naser: "Scorpion, ['*aqrab*] sir!"
> Sharif: "'*Scorpion!*' Why '*Scorpion?!*' Call it '*Towhid*' [God's oneness], call it '*Ashura,*' call it '*Shahid*'[martyr]!"[88]

Similar moments recur throughout the novel as Naser is transformed into a battle-hardened warrior. Early on, before Khorramshahr is entirely occupied, he fights under the command of the now-famous general, Mohammad Jahan-Ara (1954–1981), who rallies his troops by telling them, "We can't forget the Imam's words. We must remember what promises we've made to the martyrs. If we think that this is Khorramshahr and that is Iraq, that we're facing all those weapons, we'll be defeated. We should imagine that this is not Khorramshahr. This is Karbala!"[89] Other battle scenes contain elements that are on par with what was being produced by contemporary Ba'thist writers. For instance, during another battle, the commander of a partly destroyed Iraqi tank tries to escape. To the shock and horror of the Iranian soldiers, the commander turns out to be a woman. Falling out of the hatch, she is ridiculously described as a "naked and drunk woman...bloated and staggering." In response, Saleh, one of Naser's fellow soldiers, turns away and spits out of disgust.[90]

Martyrdom emerges as the most prominent theme in the 212-page novel. Several of Naser's platoon members are martyred in battle; his brother Hosein is killed by Iraqi bombs; his sister Shahnaz is later killed by Iraqi shells while volunteering at the local mosque that doubles as a hospital. The novel concludes with the liberation of Khorramshahr in May 1982 in Operation *Beyt ol-Moqaddas* (Operation Jerusalem) in which Naser, badly injured and recently hospitalized, participates. Following his departure from the hospital to fight at the front, Naser's mother waits by the phone for days until it finally rings. Saleh, one of the platoon's survivors, tells her that Khorramshahr has been liberated. She is overjoyed and tells him, "If Naser has been martyred, then I won't be sad." He responds in kind: "Well...Naser has been martyred!" and the novel abruptly ends.[91] In the contemporary emulation of Imam Hussein, Naser sacrifices himself for the defense of his country. The story ends with total conviction and commitment to the Islamic Revolution and war. Naser's mother, who has already been displaced and lost two other children to the war, should not mourn the loss of her third but rather should be thankful for it. She exemplifies the mothers of martyrs the Islamic Republic championed during and after the war as the heroic backbone of the nation while their sons were fighting at the front.[92]

LEGACIES OF OFFICIAL LITERATURE

When the war officially ended on August 20, 1988, the Iranian and Iraqi wartime governments were firmly in place, and two new canons of officially sanctioned war literature had come into existence. This literary legacy of the Iran-Iraq War accompanied the war's other legacy of mass death and destruction. The focus here is fiction, but the literature of Saddam's Qadisiyya and the Sacred Defense each also consisted of thousands of poems, memoirs, and works of cultural criticism dealing with the Iran-Iraq War from the perspective of the official narratives. In both countries, most wartime literature was state propaganda, written partly by an older generation of coopted writers and partly by younger authors who "established themselves by writing about the war experience."[93]

Despite its ubiquity, the stated purpose of mass mobilization, and the supposedly prize-worthy status of many works, wartime literature was not widely read by anyone outside the circles of critics and writers who produced and commented on it. At the same time, the very writers and critics who were involved in creating and promoting this literature were sometimes the ones who bemoaned its weaknesses and still yearned (at least in writing) to see the war adequately memorialized. The incessant production of repetitive, cliched official war writing created a thick film of familiarity over the war's cultural representation. By the end of the war, images of heroic soldiers who didactically ventriloquized the official discourse, predictable scenes of martyrdom, and constant claims to exclusive truth and victimhood had become stale and dull, offering nothing new or nuanced to readers. By 1988, with a ceasefire signed and hostilities over, politicians and establishment critics remained anxious over how the war might be remembered and continued to wait for the appearance of their own great novel of Saddam's Qadisiyya or the Sacred Defense.

Of course, there were Iranian and Iraqi writers and intellectuals who opposed the war and remained unaffiliated with the state, but they were marginalized. The war allowed each government to consolidate power and crush internal political dissent, including criticism of the war. While there was pressure on writers and intellectuals in both countries, the circumstances in which they found themselves differed: some were coopted to write for the government; others were pressured and intimidated into silence; others chose or were forced into exile; some were even killed. The pressure on more established Iraqi writers and artists was arguably more substantial than on their Iranian counterparts in the 1980s. This is likely why, among the limited number of nonconforming works of fiction from each country, two Iranian war novels—Ahmad Mahmud's *Scorched Earth* and Esmail Fassih's *Zemestān-e 62* (*The Winter of '83*, 1987), continue to be read much more than any contemporaneously published work of Iraqi fiction.[94] Critics writing about Iraqi fiction and poetry from the period completely dismiss wartime fiction more frequently than their Iranian counterparts. While searching for salvageable wartime literary texts, some point to the few works of fiction that mourn death and avoid celebrating violence, occasionally finding that "poems and stories were published which teemed with ambiguity and Sufism, while others contained sparks of rejection and rebellion."[95] These include some of Muhammad Khudayyir's short stories (covered in the next chapter) that were published during the final year of the war but which appeared more prominently after the war, collected in the books *Basrāyāthā* (1993), and *Ru'yā Kharīf* (*Autumn Visions*, 1995).

This chapter's review of 1980s war fiction in Iraq and Iran demonstrates how the material and intellectual conditions for cultural production in the two countries creates a basis for comparison between the two literatures and their relationship to the war. Today, the twin corpora of Saddam's Qadisiyya and Sacred Defense literatures may be quite justifiably seen as "bad literature" by all but the few remaining ardent ideological defenders of wartime Iran and Iraq. However, from the perspective of the wartime regimes, these literatures were successful in fixing the boundaries of two discursive environments within and against which subsequent writers would craft new and different narratives of the war. In that sense, these literatures served their purpose by setting the limits of the war's representation and defining the horizon of expectation for the literature of the Iran-Iraq War. The following chapter will turn to the early postwar period, defined roughly by the first decade after the war's end, during which the state's grip over the war story loosened slightly, and readers of Arabic and Persian fiction began to read war stories that challenged the limits of Saddam's Qadisiyya and Sacred Defense literature.

Two
REPRESENTATIONS OF SURVIVAL AND LOSS

THE BLOODSHED THAT CONSUMED THE GREATER PART OF THE 1980S in Iran and Iraq ended in August 1988 with borders unchanged, both governments firmly in place, and hundreds of thousands dead. After the war, the priorities of both states changed, and the official war cultures no longer had the same importance. In Iraq, the narrative of Saddam's Qadisiyya rapidly receded following the disastrous invasion of Kuwait, which set the stage for the 1990–91 Gulf War, the 1991 Iraqi Intifada (uprising), the crippling sanctions leveled against the country until 2003, and the relative self-autonomy obtained by Iraqi Kurdistan. The state's international isolation and dire financial situation throughout the 1990s would mean that the prizes and support that it had previously given to writers of fiction and poetry would disappear. The Iraqi state, as Dina Khoury has described, began to promote a "new narrative of memorialization" that defined Iraq and Iraqis primarily by their victimization and steadfastness (ṣumūd) in the shadow of the army's crushing defeat following its invasion of Kuwait, and a U.S.-led campaign of sporadic bombing and punishing sanctions.[1]

The Iranian state faced no such comparable pressures. The immediate postwar years in Iran witnessed a wave of economic liberalization unprecedented since the 1979 Revolution, part of what Ali-Akbar Hashemi-Rafsanjani, the first president of the Islamic Republic after the death of Ayatollah

Khomeini, would call an "Era of Reconstruction." This would be the precursor to the 1997 election of Mohammad Khatami, who presided over two terms of relative sociopolitical openness lasting until 2005. During this time, the fairly uniform nature of the state-led narrative of the war would crack, giving birth to a more diverse discursive environment with various subcategories of government-subsidized producers of Sacred Defense Culture, as well as more independently-minded cultural producers—literary or otherwise—creating work both domestically and abroad.[2]

Although the state war cultures in Iran and Iraq were never totalizing, at the tail end of the war and during the first decade after its conclusion, the aesthetics of storytelling began to change and genuinely new narratives of the Iran-Iraq War emerged. This was the environment in which Iraqi and Iranian writers overcame the legacies of an overdetermined, ideologically-saturated war literature and began to rewrite the content and form of the war story. Publishing fiction centered on survival, doubt, and loss during the first decade following the end of the conflict, authors gave voice to war narratives that had previously been silenced. Treating the war largely from the perspective of the home front, their stories feature civilians on the receiving end of bombardments, survivors who deal with the death and disappearance of loved ones, and those who have lost faith in both the "official truths" and the good-evil binary that animated the states' narratives.

In addition to changing the content of the war story, writers like Muhammad Khudayyir (b. 1942) and Lu'ay Hamza 'Abbas (b. 1965) in Iraq, and Shahriar Mandanipour (b. 1957) and Amir Hasan Cheheltan (b. 1956) in Iran, also broke away from the literary aesthetic inspired by socialist realism that typified state wartime literatures. While the wartime prose fiction of Saddam's Qadisiyya and the Sacred Defense had grown stale and predictable, stressing the heroism of soldiers, the righteousness of each state's cause, and cliched actions and speech of non-combatants, these writers opted for different approaches, drawing from relatively recent literary trends of literary modernism and experimentation in Iran and Iraq. In doing so, they shunned the dominant and official representations of the war and their associated ideologies. The directions taken by these writers highlight the failure of state-sponsored wartime fiction and emphasize its role as state propaganda. In addition to the many flaws of these literatures that Chapter 1 highlighted, the failure to produce a "poetic evocation of the unbearable atmosphere" of war remains one of the greatest failures of state-sponsored wartime fiction.[3] The works of fiction in this chapter are imbued with poetic elements that separate them from the rigid, predictable stories of the war years. Indeed, much of what separates the texts examined here from the overdetermined heroism of the official wartime literatures is precisely their formal elements: fragmentation, impressionism, repetition, and silence. These elements push the texts toward a poetics and politics that were both new and different from state literature and ideology. In so doing, these writers activate the creative and political potential of postwar survival and loss to shine a light upon silenced narratives of the war.

In writing a war without enemies, Mandanipour and Khudayyir, the first two authors examined in this chapter, effectively defang the most militant element of the official narratives of the war. Writing later, 'Abbas and Cheheltan, discussed in the chapter's second half, build off the aesthetic choices of Mandanipour and Khudayyir to focus on the loss of life and call attention to what remains in war's aftermath.

A WAR WITHOUT ENEMIES
Muhammad Khudayyir's Poetics of Survival
By the time the war had started with Iran, Basran writer and literary critic Muhammad Khudayyir had gained acclaim as a short story writer with a fresh and distinct voice.[4] However, during Iraq's eight years of cultural militarization, he wrote relatively little, and his name never appeared in the *Saddam's Qadisiyya* collections. He published a handful of short stories in literary magazines and newspapers but had no book-length publications from 1978 to 1993.[5] Some of his stories from the war years would be later included in two books that he published in the early postwar years: *Baṣrāyāthā: Ṣūrat Madīna* (English translation: *Basrayatha: Portrait of a City*, hereafter *Basrayatha*, 1993) and *Ru'yā Kharīf* (*Autumn Visions*, 1995).[6] Here, I focus on Khudayyir's *Basrayatha*, and specifically its final chapter, "Ṣabāḥiyyāt wa-Ṣabāḥiyyāt: Yawmiyyāt al-Ḥarb" ("Morning Airs and Nocturnes: A War Diary," henceforth "War Diary"), because the book remains Khudayyir's best-known work, not least because "Basrayatha," as a place and idea, recurs throughout Khudayyir's other writings. He makes references to it in several short stories

written since the book's publication, most notably in *Autumn Visions*,[7] and it is also the name of an eponymously titled literary magazine and publishing house in Basra that was founded in 2004 and still exists.[8] As of this writing, it is the only book-length publication by Khudayyir that has been translated into English.

Basrayatha is a memoiresque, fictional tribute to a real city, Basra, as well as to Basrayatha, a fictional, heterotopic double of Basra. Published in 1993, it takes readers on cultural, historical, and, at times, magical journeys through Basrayatha and Basra, the city where Khudayyir continues to live today. As the book's narrator, Khudayyir grants readers intimate company with other contemporary Basran writers with whom he was close, among them the poet Jawad al-Hattab and short-story writer Mahmud 'Abd al-Wahhab, figures who appear on multiple occasions throughout the work. By the time *Basrayatha* was published in book form, Khudayyir had already published half of its ten chapters in Iraqi newspapers and journals between 1987 and 1990 as standalone texts. The "War Diary" first appeared across two issues of the Iraqi newspaper *al-Thawra* in February 1987 and June 1988. *Basrayatha* was not Khudayyir's first engagement with the Iran-Iraq War or war at large. His first short story collection *al-Mamlaka al-Sawdā'* (*The Black Kingdom*), published in 1972, contained stories that referenced the 1967 war and the First Iraqi-Kurdish War (1961–70). Even at that early point in his career, his texts invited readers to think "about war in general, but always through very specific depictions of the impact of war on people without power: the traumatized soldier; the soldier on leave and his lover; the women often depicted as waiting for their husbands or lovers to come back from the front, sometimes in vain."[9] Those perspectives informed Khudayyir's writing on the Iran-Iraq War in *Basrayatha*.

The "War Diary" provides an account of life in Basra over the course of a day during the Iran-Iraq War. As a major city located around twelve kilometers from the Iranian border, Basra was the target of several major Iranian campaigns that sought to capture it and cut off Iraq's access to the Persian Gulf. Consequently, by 1988, large parts of the city and its surroundings were depopulated by the Iraqi government and decimated by shelling and the major battles that took place nearby. Khudayyir's "War Diary" consists of eight entries, each one a vignette that tells of a different aspect of daily life during wartime Basra. They describe nights filled with terrifying bombing campaigns, civilians who insist on working despite shells falling around them, and the surprise that the narrator feels when first seeing the bombed-out city and its environs in the daylight. The chapter departs from both the battlefield drama and victimizing tone of Saddam's Qadisiyya and shifts the setting from the war front to the home front, focusing largely on civilians' fear and their attempts at survival. Gone are narratives of heroism, praise of martyrdom, and devotion to the Qadisiyya narrative, and in their places are human, animal, and material survivors of nearly a decade of brutal, obligatory warfare in the closest major Iraqi city to the ferocity of the frontlines. Moreover, the "War Diary" also does away with the decisive narrative arcs offered by most works of Saddam's Qadisiyya fiction. As very short, inconclusive, and often abstract vignettes, each entry in the chapter offers a formal alternative to the overdetermined novels and short stories published with the blessings of the Ba'thist government. In this way, Khudayyir offers essay fragments as formal and genre-based alternatives to short stories and novels that usually concluded with unequivocal support for the war.

The first survivors Khudayyir focuses on are mothers, who are valorized in a way that the official literature usually reserved for soldiers and the parents of martyrs. In the opening paragraph of the chapter's first vignette titled "al-Layla al-'Āshira" ("The Tenth Night"), mothers confront "thousands of artillery rounds" during the darkness of the night, whose "fangs clacked together" while it "raged, terrifyingly black." The narration continues:

> Mothers let their cloaks hang down to cover the great heart of the city, holding their hands to enclose and protect it. A million sleepless hearts, thumps that continued in rapid succession, [...] a roar and a fading away, a sobbing and a declamation, fear and prayer. Then these were organized and harmonized into a single rhythm: a beat in a gracious evening that cloaked the terrifying lament for a tattered night with disheveled hair so that it quieted down, became calm, and softly hummed a familiar tune that traveled from house to house until it reached the soldiers in the trenches beyond the river.[10]

Khudayyir prioritizes the home front mother and her role as both a survivor of the war and a protector from violence that comes, significantly, from an unnamed enemy. While the literature of Saddam's Qadisiyya also featured mothers, they were the proud parents of war front heroes and martyrs, not maternal pillars of serenity that calmed the nation. Mothers in the official literature often expressed their rancor toward "Khomeinists" or "Magi." In Khudayyir's work, however, a motherly collective provides security during the night, and he and others make reassuring phone calls in the morning to check on one another and celebrate the individual, personal victory that is survival—a distinct focus from the militant tropes of revenge, heroism, and martyrdom that dominated Iraqi war culture in the 1980s. At the end of the first vignette, Khudayyir hears a nocturne by Chopin, a "sweet reverberation" that "caresses sleepless eyes with dawn's delicate fingers." He exclaims, "The world is alive. The nation is alive. We are alive."[11] In positing one of Chopin's nocturnes as a soundtrack of survival, Khudayyir identifies a slow, meditative, solo piece of music that is everything that the songs of Saddam's Qadisiyya are not. Their difference from the songs composed for mass consumption and war mobilization is clear and emblematic of how the "War Diary" views the war with the Iranians: a struggle for survival in the face of bombardment, without concern for state-endorsed war narratives.

By stressing life and survival over martyrdom and the glorification of the war front, the "War Diary" works against what has been called the governmental routinization of warfare in Iraq during the war with Iran.[12] One aspect of the nation's total wartime mobilization was maintaining the normalcy of daily life on the home front, despite the number of corpses and returning wounded soldiers, and despite the aerial bombardments that clearly transformed the fabric of life in the cities. The changes and disruptions to home front life that Khudayyir depicts are changes that the official narrative conveniently overlooked and the wartime literature largely ignored. In this way, Khudayyir's "War Diary" gives voice to a narrative of the war that was otherwise silent throughout most of the 1980s. One of the ways in which he does this is by writing about the war without ever referring directly to it. The "War Diary" never mentions the Iraqi state's directives, nor does it openly refer to the Iranian forces that threaten the city. The words "Qadisiyya," "Saddam," or any of his epithets never appear in the piece. Khudayyir manages to do this even when he does write about the actual war front, in three separate entries, and those who have returned from it.

In the first such entry, "al-Ikhtiyār al-Waḥīd" ("The Only Choice"), the narrator sees a wounded war veteran who stands out among a crowd of civilians going about their daily business. The sight of him reminds Khudayyir of his own imagined war front, a place that civilians, such as he, have not "been granted the opportunity" to experience, leaving them healthy and able-bodied. For a moment, his eyes meet those of the veteran, and his fleeting glance reminds Khudayyir of "the only choice" referred to in a poem by Soviet poet and war veteran Mikhail Lukonin (1918–76): "In that stormy reverberation / The choices were limited / and returning with an empty sleeve / Was preferable to returning / With an empty spirit."[13]

Like the previous sections, "The Only Choice" is written in a spirit of survival that emphasizes the need to carry on and live during an unnamed war with an unnamed enemy. Khudayyir's contemporary readers would know which war he refers to. They would also know what singular "choice" he writes about, and that it was not a choice in any real sense. Soldiers were conscripted and hunted down when they tried to escape; if they were caught, the consequences were punishable by death. Civilians were left with little choice but to bear the brunt of bombs from an enemy who appeared fanatical and whose government wanted nothing less than to topple the Iraqi regime. The only choice, then, was to carry on, to fight when necessary, and to choose the "empty sleeve" over the spiritless, empty corpse, to choose life. At the same time, by initially referring to the war front as a privileged opportunity, Khudayyir appealed to the Iraqi censors.

"Al-Thaʿābīn al-Alīfa" ("Familiar Serpents") is the fifth entry in the "War Diary."[14] It offers a short meditation on "the encounter between wild animals and men with weapons." The entry begins with Khudayyir paging through his small personal archive of twentieth-century Arab wars, a folder with newspaper and magazine clippings of stories from the wars of 1967, 1973, and the contemporaneous Lebanese Civil War, linking the current war with Iran to a series of contemporary wars plaguing Arab nations. In this private archive, an image of a hyena-like animal growling and facing off against a tank in the Sinai desert catches his attention. Its caption reads: "a strange encounter in the desert." Khudayyir, however, disagrees, writing in the next line that such encounters are, in fact, common in every war:

There is nothing strange about an encounter like this, where the roar of tanks mingles with that of wild beasts. In their stubborn confrontation, a common bond unites them in a single ditch with a single goal: to shred the enemy with fangs, claws, and shrapnel. The man, however, is amazed by another, opposite state: the wild beast's respect for the corpse tossed on a no man's land [fī al-arḍ al-ḥarām]. It approaches the body, sniffs, and toys with it, but shuns its blood and flesh. What's more, for this beast, the corpse's unknown nature makes it equivalent in status to other corpses by which it will squat and bear its snow-white teeth."[15]

Readers steeped in the narrative of Saddam's Qadisiyya might have expected a description of the enemy soldiers as savage animals ready to tear apart the enemy, but Khudayyir's wild beasts are far more ambiguous. They share the violent attributes of combat weapons yet shun the flesh of a corpse killed in war. In fact, they "respect the corpse" even if it is like the corpses of other animals that it might feed on. Two readings are possible here: on the one hand, the animals might teach Iraqi soldiers to respect the enemy through their treatment of the corpses. They are humans who have fallen in battle and deserve respect. On the other, they are corpses—nothing more, nothing less. They are neither Iraqi nor Iranian. They are not to be mutilated, but they are not to be venerated either, as martyrs or otherwise.

The actual serpents, after which the entry is titled, also have an ambiguous presence on the war front. They live side-by-side with the Iraqi soldiers in the trenches, falling from a nook when shaken by an exploding shell and, in the soldiers' minds, eavesdropping on the stories they tell each other during long evenings. They neither frighten the soldiers, nor do they feel threatened by them. Rather, they "decrease the desolation" of war-front soldiers, "granting them memory of a friendship with a familiar creature, even if it is a snake."[16] In presenting wild beasts as man's familiars and friends, Khudayyir inserts a third being into a setting where the typical Other is the dehumanized enemy: the Iranian soldier. The animals become a foil to the binary of good and evil, suggesting that "perhaps more effectively than anything else in the world, the 'question of the animal' prompts us to think about 'the wholly other'."[17] The presence of animals here prompts the thoughtful reader to think outside of the dyadic world of Saddam's Qadisiyya.

A third entry, titled "Amḥū wa-Arsim" ("I Should Erase and Draw"), connects the two fronts.[18] Here, Khudayyir sets off with two companions to assess the damage caused by a recent bombing of the ʿAshār neighborhood, a part of the city through which the eponymously named narrow river runs. He compares the car and the speed with which they whiz past the bombed-out businesses to an eraser "rubbing out the scenery around it." He thus commands himself "to erase and draw." He first erases the establishments and businesses that he knows and replaces them with "burned-out structure[s]" resembling the damaged buildings they pass. As they approach the corniche and the river, the quotidian scenes of what Khudayyir erases and draws are suddenly militarized: "I erase a boy swimming and draw a soldier. I erase a fishing pole and draw a rifle. I erase a skiff and draw a military bridge. I erase embarrassment and hesitation and draw manliness and daring."[19] As their excursion comes to an end, all three passengers think about what they have erased and drawn. Their thoughts go towards a hopeful future where they would put the remnants of warfare in the past by "sweeping up the shattered glass and building a new façade," by "erasing a river and drawing one with a lighthouse that will glow with a green light that does not slumber," by "erasing a city and building a paradise."[20] As a formulation, "erase and draw" conveys the author's spirit of survival during the war while also echoing his previous utterance, "the only choice." He has no choice but to see the militarization of life along the river, to see boys turn into soldiers and their fishing poles into rifles. Erasing and drawing is a means of surviving the conditions of Saddam's Qadisiyya at home; building a paradise over an erased city gives hope that one day the war will end and the city will be built anew.

Against the discursive backdrop of the state's bellicose rhetoric, the absence of a clear pro-war sentiment is striking. There is a sense of national pride in the wounded veteran in "The Only Choice" and a sympathetic recognition of the hardship and loneliness of the war-front soldier in "Familiar Serpents," but the only clear commitment in both is to survival. Even in "Erase and Draw" as the narration momentarily shifts—militarizes, in fact—when Khudayyir sees the front, the transformations that create soldiers, manliness, and courage are nothing more than a blink of an eye, quickly overshadowed by his proclamation "How quickly everything will rise again!"[21] Taken together, the diary entries highlighted here defamiliarize the scenes of warfare that had become commonplace by the time of their publication. Moreover, there is an implicit criticism of the war in "Familiar Serpents." By using animals in place of humans, Khudayyir puts the behavior of humans in war in a new light, showing their actions to be something strange, below even that of wild beasts. Similarly, a critique of the war project appears in his commandment to "erase and draw." He honors the request for an instant, without the slightest notion of fidelity to the cause of Saddam's Qadisiyya. He and his travel companions salute the idea just long enough to pass by, or, put differently, just long enough for the authorities to notice, before skipping to their real desire: to move beyond this moment, forget the conflict, and have life return to a time before the war.

Some critics have framed Khudayyir's writing as purposefully abstract, written in a way to beat the censors.[22] Others have criticized him "for appearing to endorse *distance* and *anachronism* [via Agamben]" as he veers from "a realistic depiction of the events surrounding him."[23] Yet, those views fail to consider Khudayyir's oeuvre and the style he has been cultivating since the late 1960s, a style that continues to characterize his fiction today. Caiani and Cobham rightly note that Khudayyir never published stories with the same adherence to the mimetic realism of so many Iraqi writers of his generation, and that he has been critical of more recent (post-2003) writers who cannot "imagine a Baghdad without corpses." In his own writing, Khudayyir has defended "his right to be inspired not only by the real world of his surroundings but also by the exhilaratingly mysterious coincidences that happen in the borderland between reality and imagination, dream and literature: the land where visions are realized."[24] That borderland and its relation to the aftermath of the Iran-Iraq War is also explored in a short story by Iranian writer Shahriar Mandanipour.

Breaking Binaries: Shahriar Mandanipour's "The Color of Fire at Midday"
In the 1990s, with his distinct voice and symbolically loaded style, Shahriar Mandanipour began to earn a reputation as a well-known writer of Persian fiction. From 1990 onward, he published several popular short story collections that made an impact on the Iranian literary scene, with some of his work eventually making it into translation in English and other languages. Most notable were his short story collections, *Sharq-e Banafsheh (East of Violet,*

1990) and *Māh-e Nimruz* (*Midday Moon*, 1997). In 1998, he published a 900-page, two-part novel, *Del-e Deldādegi* (*The Courage of Love*). Mandanipour enlisted in the military in 1981 and fought at the front for eighteen months; his experiences there undoubtedly inform some of his stories that deal with the Iran-Iraq War, perhaps most significantly in *The Courage of Love*, *Moon Brow* (2018), and several short stories, some which have been translated into English in two edited short story collections, *Sohrab's Wars* (2008) and *Seasons of Purgatory* (2022). Since 2006, he has been living in the United States, and since 2009, two of his novels and one short story collection have appeared in English translation, both novels prior to their publication in Persian.[25]

Here, I offer a reading of Mandanipour's short story "Rang-e Ātash-e Nimruzi" ("The Color of Fire at Midday"). The story was completed in 1994 and published in *Midday Moon*. Like Khudayyir's texts, this story keeps the violence of the war largely at a distance. Similarly, it dwells more on the consequences of war than on the experience of combat, which is never experienced by the story's narrator. As a piece written and published shortly after the war concluded, it demonstrates how some writers in Iran, like their Iraqi counterparts, also resorted to a self-questioning style to write about the war, a characteristic of both Iraqi and Iranian modernist fiction. As demonstrated below, this style challenges one of the most fundamental components of the war's official narrative: the duality of friend and enemy, here expressed as self and other.

"The Color of Fire at Midday" contains a frame story that takes place shortly after the war has ended. The story's unnamed narrator has recently returned from an unspecified "exile" to live on what was presumably once a much larger piece of land, a likely reference to his status as a pre-Revolutionary elite who returned to Iran in the late 1980s to reclaim what had not been confiscated in the Revolution.[26] More important is the story within the frame story: the narrator's recounting of the events surrounding the death of the young daughter of his longtime friend, an airborne brigade captain whom he calls "Captain Mina," to a small audience sitting around a nighttime fire on his land. Its fifteen pages in the original Persian are written entirely in a single paragraph with occasional ellipses breaking the narrator's thoughts. In a conversational mode of narration that borders on stream of consciousness, the narrator flows seamlessly between his recollection of Mina's visit and his past and present observations of himself and his family. In the process he makes casual remarks to his guests, mostly to share a pipe, point out the fire's beauty, or contemplate the meaning of darkness.

The narrator's story happened shortly after the Iran-Iraq War. Long before, he had befriended Mina, who at the time was only an "obscure lieutenant" stationed at a military base in his region. Through a mutual love of hunting, often illegally on one of the Shah's hunting grounds, they came to know one another.[27] "It was with me that he first tasted the still-pulsating liver of a deer [...] I taught him to sink his teeth into it while it still had blood," the narrator tells us.[28] When the war breaks out, Mina goes to the front, in time rising through the ranks. The narrator, meanwhile, flees the country, probably soon after the Revolution, and lives in exile abroad. Mina's experiences in the airborne brigade leaves him battle-hardened and injured, both psychologically and physically. Following doctor's orders to take a mandatory sick leave, he comes to spend a few days with his old friend the narrator, in the countryside, bringing along his wife and young daughter, Neda. This is when the narrator's campfire story begins. A few days into the trip, while the group is resting by a mountain stream, Neda wanders off, "chasing after dragonflies."[29] A moment later, they hear a scream, and the girl is missing. A bloody trail, ripped clothes, and, later, bones, reveal that she was killed by a leopard, setting off a crisis and a complicated story of revenge.

In recounting the events around Neda's disappearance, the realization that she has been killed by a leopard, and the ensuing hunt for the animal, the narrator also offers various philosophical reflections that serve as commentary on his own behavior within his story, as well as his current existential struggle in life. He opens the story by addressing his audience around the fire with the following:

> Darkness, ah, darkness . . . it's mysterious, darkness. A man wonders what to do. But it's clear that man is one species and leopard is another, if they're around one another, like it or not, they'll confront one another. Then, they'll have to fight until only one of them returns and the other stays on the ground—the earth's share—or for the vultures or hyenas, which at times like this are certainly around. It's because of thoughts like

those that I run away from the city. When I returned from exile abroad, I came directly here. No matter how much the Khan's land is taken away by revolution or land reform, enough remains to provide his grandson with fresh milk in the morning, kebab in the evening, and cartridges for his five-round hunting rifle. And that's enough for me to finish off this life full of tribal enmities. At least that was the plan, but we never know what tomorrow might bring. How was I supposed to know that this peace would fall apart, and I'd find myself caught between a man and leopard? And I hate in-between solutions...Look at this fire that I asked them to light especially for you! It's the color of blood. Because in this fire, too, is a temptation to fight. As I was saying...[30]

From the start, the narrator presents his outlook: man and animal are meant to be enemies and a problem between them should be solved with a fight to death. For him, solutions should present themselves clearly and simply. One side should win, the other should lose. One side is right, the other is wrong. That is why he does not like the darkness and why he hates "in-between solutions." This mindset pervades the story that he tells his guests. It haunts him until the present moment.

References to the Iran-Iraq War appear through Captain Mina relating his war experiences to the narrator. When the two are alone, away from the wife and child, he recounts stories from his time at the front and the narrator embeds these war stories into his own narrative and descriptions of the Captain. Simultaneously, the time Captain Mina spends with his family, away from the front and visiting his friend, is clearly precious for him. The narrator tells us that when Neda spoke, Mina was enamored by the child's speech and sweet mannerisms. He is at once a hunting partner, a loving father, and a hardened war veteran with the lingering effects of combat and killing persistently interrupting him. The narrator says "I told him, c'mon, let's go hunting. He paid no attention. He was engrossed in being with the child. He had been hit by shrapnel a few times and [even] after two or three surgeries there were still pieces of shrapnel near his vertebrae. He sat up straight and stared ahead."[31]

Heroism, masculinity, and the ferocity of combat saturate Mina's war memories. In the narrator's telling, they merge with his own memories of the two hunting together. At one point, as the two sit on the rooftop of the narrator's house, they recall a hunting trip and the time they each felt "helpless looking at the eyes of a wounded deer" they had shot at twilight. When they reach the animal, they find it half paralyzed, and "in its eyes was neither fear nor an appeal for mercy." The two hunting companions freeze. They felt "helpless because of the way the wounded deer was looking at them."[32] The narrator tries to elaborate on their state and struggles to define the situation: "I can't say that the deer's gaze scared us, but we were in a state of fear, but not only fear. Remorse, but not only remorse."[33] Mina's solution, however, quite literally cuts through any indeterminacy that the two have: he slices the deer's artery with a serrated knife. The scene ends. Cutting open the deer's artery gives way to Mina's war stories, which are disturbing enough to prevent the narrator from sleeping and continue to give Mina nightmares.[34] The narrator explains how Mina's resolve in killing the deer carried over into the battlefield. His recollections of the war are comprised of controlled, ruthless decisions to destroy the enemy. According to the narrator, Mina would go behind enemy lines at night on reconnaissance missions looking for Iraqi dugouts, "Every pair of commandos for a trench [. . .]. Like leopards, they would crawl behind the sleeping enemy and throw a wire—a garrote—around his neck and with a swift pull, the head of the soldier would fall to his chest."[35]

Although the narrator admits that these war stories terrify him, both men, in fact, are guided by a determination that refuses any self-doubt or second thought; they both prefer certainty, firm decision-making that eschews the "in-between solutions" that the narrator derides at the beginning of the story. It is the backbone of their friendship. Thus, when area villagers confirm that Neda has been killed by a leopard by locating her "stripped and masticated bones" in the surrounding mountains, the narrator tells Mina he *must* kill the animal because it is his right. He is not the only one with that position. Mina's wife, who otherwise says nothing in the story, also becomes a barefaced proponent of vengeance:

> His wife raised her outstretched hands like claws. She could hardly utter a word. She was saying things like 'Kill it . . . kill it, tear it to shreds'. . . She raised her hands into the air as if she wanted to pluck out the eyes of the leopard . . . The woman clawed at his face and screamed: 'Kill it! Kill it!'[36]

After recovering the bones, Mina and his wife leave the village. He returns alone a week later to kill the leopard. Initially, he insists on going into the mountain and hunting it alone but ends up nearly killed by the animal, which slashes his face and shoulder and badly wounds him. He returns to the village and after a few days' rest, he and the narrator set out together with a baby goat in tow as bait. Mina, seemingly convinced by everyone around him, insists that only he should kill the animal and forces the narrator to leave his gun behind. Arriving at the point where he and the leopard fought just a few days prior, the pair tie the baby goat to a rock and take a position on higher ground to wait for their prey. The following morning the leopard appears. It immediately kills the goat and begins devouring it. At that point, according to the plan, Mina should shoot the animal to avenge the death of his daughter. What follows in the story's final pages, however, upends that logic. While the leopard feasts on the goat, Mina stares at the it through his rifle's scope and the narrator, beside him, through binoculars. The leopard raises his head and notices the two men. In a move that mimics the dying deer earlier in the story, it stares coldly at the pair, with the liver of the freshly killed goat in its mouth. Increasingly agitated, the narrator pleads with Mina to fire: "Shoot, go on, shoot! . . . Shoot dammit . . . Shoot [. . .] for your kid . . . Shoot so that the animal's teeth fly everywhere . . . for your kid, goddammit . . . shoot for her!"[37] Mina begins to fire. Totally unmoved, the leopard continues to stare. The narrator hears more shots from Mina's rifle as he stares at the leopard, who is now yawning, teeth shining in the sun.

Dumbfounded, the narrator throws his binoculars to the ground and sees Mina emptying his rifle's cartridge into the air. The leopard turns away, climbing higher up the mountain. Mina turns in the opposite direction and begins descending, leaving the narrator stunned. When he comes to, he is furious. He chases after the Captain and catches him:

> I wanted to punch him. He didn't answer. I shouted at him again, "You're worthless! Why didn't you kill the leopard? You wasted your kid's blood!" His knee buckled, and he grabbed a boulder. "It's impossible," he cried. I didn't give up. I dug my fingers into his shoulder. "God damn you, why didn't you shoot?" "I couldn't. . .I can't! My child's flesh is in its body . . . it's impossible . . . my child's blood is in its veins" . . .and he cried silently all the way down the mountain . . .[38]

"The Color of Fire at Midday" ends there. Its content, with the war distant yet palpable through Mina's vivid memories that are interspersed by encounters between man and animal, invite a two-layered allegorical reading of the text. Specifically, the story uses animals to create a world of mirrors wherein the characters see reflections of themselves in their enemy. Thus, Mina's wartime actions resemble the leopard's actions, first in killing the girl and later by harassing the villagers. For his part, Mina recounts ambushing sleeping Iraqi soldiers "like a leopard," and the trap that he and the narrator later set to capture the animals conjures up the trap Mina and other commandoes once set for Iraqi soldiers, blowing up their vehicle, and then sniping them off one by one. The leopard, for its part, stealthily kills Neda in a manner reminiscent of Mina's actions as a wartime sniper. In the final scene, the leopard stares at the two hunters while devouring the liver of their freshly killed goat, evoking how the two men once ate the liver of a freshly killed deer. Taken further, the story leads readers to wonder if perhaps the leopard also stared into Neda's helpless eyes, just as Mina and the narrator once stared into the eyes of a helpless, dying deer, with confused feelings, before Mina swiftly delivered the death blow. Of course, the most suggestive case of allegorical mirroring appears in the story's final scene, where Mina finds himself unable to kill the leopard, because his daughter's blood now flows in its veins.

That moment, when Mina refuses to shoot the leopard—by now an obvious metaphor to Iraqi soldiers—is when "polarized dual systems no longer function."[39] It marks the breakdown of the Sacred Defense narrative's duality of friend and enemy or, in the view of the narrator, self and other. By creating a world in which these categories are disrupted, the story exposes the impossibility of the narrator's worldview, which conveniently exists alongside—and is in fact validated by—the Iranian's government's official narrative of the war as a sacred defense. The narrator's fragmented, stream of conscious narrative that strives so hard to comprehend what has taken place perfectly reflects the failure of his worldview, just as the lack of paragraphs and punctuation in the original Persian-language text effectively conveys the confusion accompanying the breakdown of a weltanschauung that maintained the "truth" of good and evil during wartime. The narrator repeatedly states his dilemma to his audience when he breaks out of the story to address them directly. Darkness is what bothers him. Darkness obscures and troubles his understanding of a dichotomized world. As the story concludes, he feels compelled to confess that "maybe darkness is not the right word. I don't know. Things that are not clear and straightforward to me, I call darkness. I don't like them. Mundane affairs should be obvious. Everyone ought to know the answers to different things. Inhale, exhale; thirst, satiation; friendship, friendship; enmity, enmity."[40]

Darkness blurs the lines between friend and foe, self and other. In the sober aftermath of war, those previously clean categories lose their definitiveness and give way to a new, hazy reality. This state of uncertainty characterizes much of Mandanipour's fiction and especially his short stories, which are populated by characters who are full of ambivalence and doubt, and whose very identities are often fluid, constantly pulled by opposing beliefs.[41] The narrator's view of darkness, which opens and closes the story, functions like the title: the color of fire against the backdrop of the midday sun obfuscates the view and blurs the boundaries of anything around it, including the definitions of man and animal.

Aside from darkness, the presence of animals in "The Color of Fire at Midday" also plays a role in breaking down the dyadic wartime system of self and other. The leopard offers an allegorical representation of the Iraqi enemy, yet as an animal, it inserts itself into the story in another way as well. Commenting on the presence of animals in modernist fiction globally, Efthymia Rentzou notes that such texts, in her view, "rediscover animals as a common universal denominator that upsets certainties: everyone knows animals, but no one really does. Entrenched in the textual intricacies of modernist grappling with the real, the animal emerges as a global encoding of experimental positionings."[42] The leopard's non-human presence in the story inserts itself as a third pole in an otherwise bifurcated world of friends and enemies. This is reinforced by Mina's refusal to kill it because his daughter's blood now flows in its veins. The animal may have been an enemy, but it is also a neighbor; the war is over and neighbors must learn to live with one another.

As short works of modernist fiction written late in the war or early after its conclusion, the presence of animals in both Mandanipour's "The Color of Fire at Midday" and Khudayyir's "War Diary" is striking. For both writers, animals go beyond simple allegories of the enemy. Rather, they "gaze [...] and exist as open possibilities for a different signification of the world as they are for a different human."⁴³ Their presence upsets the very definition of what it is to be human for the stories' characters during a time of war, by disrupting a world easily categorized into known and unknown. In this way, and without creating entirely contradictory and combative counternarratives of the conflict, both texts are attempts to overcome the strict dualities of the war's official discourses to present alternative narratives.

WHAT REMAINS
Silence and the Search for the Dead in the Short Stories of Lu'ay Hamza 'Abbas

In 1997, a younger Basran writer, Lu'ay Hamza 'Abbas, published his first collection of short stories, *'Alā Darrāja fī al-Layl* (*On a Bicycle at Night*), with Amman-based publishing house Dār al-Azmina. 'Abbas, then thirty-two years old, had already published short stories in Iraqi literary journals, among them *al-Aqlām*, and won two awards for "Ẓahīra Wāṭi'a" ("A Low Midday Sun," 1992) and "Khuṭaṭ Masā'iya li-Ḥarb ghayr Muntahiyya" ("Evening Plans for a Never-Ending War," 1993). Like Khudayyir, 'Abbas has chosen to remain in Basra until today, making it the setting of many of his stories and novels, and drawing inspiration from its space, sites, and the events that have taken place there. Since 1997, he has published six short story collections, four novels, and four collections of literary criticism and history.

'Abbas's writings show the influence of Khudayyir through a genealogical relationship that can be seen in his subtle narratives and attention to the minutiae of everyday life. His themes, however, are decidedly darker, a consequence of the generational difference between the two authors. 'Abbas is nearly twenty-three years younger than Khudayyir and came to age in the shadow of the Iran-Iraq War, while Operation Desert Storm, the sanctions years, and the U.S.-led invasion dominated much of his twenties and thirties and the beginning of his publishing career. His stories often revolve around death, loss, and the consequences of war, spanning the Iran-Iraq War to the present. Critics have pointed out that 'Abbas is part of a generation that matured in the shadow of intense political oppression under Saddam Hussein's dictatorship, violent wars, poverty and malnourishment, and the explosive entrance of religious and sectarian politics in Iraq and the region after 2003. This background is also one of the most important factors differentiating his generation of writers from those of prior Iraqi literary generations, namely the prose-fiction pioneers of the 1950s and 1960s, of which Khudayyir is a part, even if exceptionally so.⁴⁴

Here, I offer readings of two stories from 'Abbas's first short story collection, *On a Bicycle at Night*, that typify the aforementioned themes and styles. The collection's stories generally articulate the experience of war through grief and mourning, often doing so by harnessing the poetic potential of silence and the unspoken, elements that had an exaggerated power in the wake of a war dominated by the overdetermined, propagandistic, and decidedly loud discourse of Saddam's Qadisiyya. The first story I examine, "*'Add al-Mawtā*" ("Counting the Dead"), is a work of flash fiction. Like 'Abbas's other writings, it narrows in on the minute details of a place—in this case, Basra's Ma'qal train station in the early morning. The narrator observes a man, a woman, and a worker at the station's restaurant. Its description—"the wall clock, the air heavy with the smell of burning oil"—is what one might find in any other restaurant, the narrator writes, and the station itself is dreary but sanitary: "The gray sky cast down on the station, dissolving everything: people and wet iron dissipated in the cloudiness of the glass. The station remained dreary, its tracks indiscernible but clean, a cleanliness not found anywhere but in hospital lounges or train platforms."⁴⁵

The comparison between the train station and a hospital sets the micro-story's mood and anticipates a connection soon made between the station's general colorlessness and death. The man asks the station worker if the train due to arrive that day will bring the hearse-car. That, the worker tells them, depends entirely on the number of bodies that need to be transported.⁴⁶ The narrator then approaches the couple and asks them the same question. The man responds, "Three bodies are enough for the train to bring the car." There is a pause. The woman stares silently into the distance. The narrator hears the following:

> We've been waiting for two days. He is in the forensic office, while we count the dead. Whenever another one arrives, I mean every time the family of another deceased arrives [...] they find themselves waiting forever for the 1:00 a.m. train. Some don't even believe it, that whether or not the train will bring the car, depends entirely on the number of dead.

We're the only ones who've remained here, waiting for them to reach the quota that will make it possible for the train to bring the hearse-car.[47]

The story quickly ends after that interaction, with the narrator reflecting that he cannot remember who actually spoke, and he can only recall a quiet sob coming from one of the two, though who or what caused the tragedy goes unnamed. However, the story's setting tells readers all they need to know. During the Iran-Iraq War, the train transported young men to the front, particularly during some of the fiercest battles, which took place in the Faw Peninsula and the Jasim Canal; for some, the train was also the primary method for bringing back their corpses.[48] It bears mentioning that the train between Baghdad and Basra in modern Iraqi literary culture is not an empty signifier, its presence in Iraqi literature dates to the 1950s and 1960s, when foundational figures of modern Iraqi fiction such as Fu'ad al-Tarkarli and Mahmud 'Abd al-Wahab wrote about the train in the context of urban migration to Baghdad from the Iraqi south. Khudayyir, in *Basrayatha*, also writes about this train in his chapter "Madīna Mutannaqala" ("Mobile City"), citing 'Abd al-Wahhab's 1954 short story, "al-Qiṭār al-Ṣā'id ilā Baghdād," ("The Train Going Up to Baghdad"), originally published in the Beirut-based journal *al-Ādāb* (*Literature*), as an example of a sophisticated realist fiction that gives us "an understanding of an exemplary, mobile slice of life in a vast, stationary reality."[49] The story brings together various social classes, ethnicities, and urban and rural people in what was a relatively new experience of traveling to Baghdad by rail early in the history of the modern nation-state. By the time 'Abbas wrote about this train, it had been dragged into Saddam Hussein's war machine and become another marker of the Ba'thification of society.

The melancholic, hazy grayness of "Counting the Dead" finds parallels in other stories in the collection where war, whether it is the war with Iran or the 1990–91 Gulf War, lurks in the background and only appears briefly in the forefront. Moreover, when it does, rather than identifying the cause of melancholy, 'Abbas's stories remain silent, dwelling on grief rather than placing the blame on one side or another. In the collection's opening story, "al-Saḥālī" ("The Lizards"), for example, we see a man arriving at a house, wearing khakis, and riding a motorcycle with a green emblem (a clear reference to the military), delivering a death notice. It interrupts what would otherwise be a warm recollection of childhood but appears without commentary. In another, "al-Bāzdār" ("The Falconer"), a grandmother's relationship to a man who passes by her house daily, and with whom she would chat, suddenly ends. She feigns belief in his return, but knows, the narrator tells us in the story's final line, that without a doubt, "wars will not bring back what they take away."[50]

Nowhere else in the collection is death as ubiquitous (or absurd) as in the title story "'Alā Darrāja fī al-Layl" ("On a Bicycle at Night"). The story's narrator, like most others found in the collection, is an unnamed man. He is searching for his friend among the "the dead of 1988," a phrase that he and others repeat throughout the story. While it appears that the meaning of the expression is clear to the narrator and others in the story (and it is more than simply all the people who died in 1988), for readers no definition is ever ascribed to it. Like the other stories in the collection, "On a Bicycle at Night" has a poetic, dreamlike quality to it. It consists of eleven impressionistic vignettes—scenes abruptly separated by hollow square boxes that break the text—spanning less than a day in the narrator's life as he searches for the names of those who died in 1988 to see if his friend's might be among them.

The story opens in a mortician's office, where the narrator learns that there are no lists of the dead from the year 1988 and that the only place where such a list might be found is in the "new cemetery." The dialogue between the narrator and an employee at the mortician's office establishes the story's terse, minimalist mode of conversation:

"There are no lists for the dead of 1988."
    I remained silent, and he repeated in a dry voice before turning around:
    "There are no..."

The narrator does not respond and exits the office to go and find the cemetery. In the next scene, he is the last passenger to exit a bus whose route ends at the "new cemetery:"

The cemetery spread out far and wide, under the sweltering midday sun. It was silent, save for the rumbling of engines, and it was lined by locked houses that stood in cryptic expectation. Piles of bricks were spread about on both sides of the dusty road.

I asked the driver: "The new cemetery?"

He gave me a sharp, sidelong glance, lowered the speed and, in a commanding voice said: "Get out."

And I got out.[51]

From the outset, the narrator's conversations during his search for the dead of 1988 continually draw attention to silences and the unspoken. He either remains silent in the face of questions from his interlocuters, or they refuse to answer his questions about "the dead of 1988." In the new cemetery, he encounters a masked man who gives him a ride on the back of his bicycle further into the sprawling burial grounds, telling him he will drop him off soon, at which point he will have to continue the journey on his own. The emphasis on silence allows the slightest sound to trigger the narrator's memories, such as when the squeaking of the bicycle's wheels prompts him to think of a story his missing friend once told him about his grandfather. Thinking back to that moment, the narrator recalls:

> The old man would polish his bicycle every morning, and then ride it to the nearby girls' school at the same time every day, bringing along an old newspaper which he would never read. I don't know why I imagined at that moment the grandfather's bicycle leaning on the cement bench across from the school and the newspaper, with its yellowing pages and torn edges, placed between the two shiny bars of the bike frame. On the paper's folded-over page I can nearly make out a picture of him—the grandfather—as a young man, smartly dressed in an ironed black suit, with small gray faded buttons, a wandering look in his eyes, his hands covered in oil.[52]

After they stop for a second time, the biker rings his bell and disembarks. The narrator suddenly steals the bike and rides it deeper into the cemetery, presumably in search of the dead of 1988. As evening approaches, he leaves the bike in the muddy road and walks ahead with the grandfather's image in his head. The story then takes an abrupt turn toward the fantastic, with the grandfather materializing, separating himself from the newspaper and approaching the narrator on a bicycle. The narrator, although terrified to see a bicycle whizzing by him at night, is comforted by the man's voice, which resembles that of his lost friend, the old man's grandson. Without any words exchanged between the two, the grandfather knows that the narrator is searching for those who died in 1988 and, as he had done with others before him, the old man tells him that he will not be able to help, even if he had wanted to. "I can't guide you to anything," he says, "the new cemetery is immense, and I don't think I know anyone in it."[53]

The grandfather starts to leave but then turns around to ask whom the narrator is looking for. At first, the narrator does not respond, preferring to remain silent rather than bring up the painful issue of his lost friend. The grandfather then admits that "every evening I find someone looking for the dead of 1988 or another year, [. . .] Did you say you were looking for one of them?" The narrator replies, "Since the morning, I've been looking for the dead of 1988. I'm simply looking for the dead so that I can ask them about my friend . . . who went missing that year."[54] As in "Counting the Dead," the story ends abruptly and inconclusively, denying readers any sense of closure. The narrator does not find his friend, no one knows where those who died in 1988 can be found, and no one seems to know who could guide the narrator to someone who might know. Thus, the narrator's search for his missing friend, who may or may not be dead, continues among the unidentifiable, numerous "dead of 1988," alongside a combination of fantastic and absurd elements that create an environment of uncertainty about what took place that year. This uncertainty challenges the feigned certitude that dominated both the Iraqi state's narrative of the war with Iran, as well as its domestic politics under the rule of Saddam Hussein. During the war, the dead, outside of those categorized as insurgents, political dissidents, and deserters, were declared martyrs by the state and buried as such. The state kept diligent records of such deaths, even if the laws concerning who was or was not a martyr were malleable and constantly being renegotiated.[55] The lack of any record of the narrator's missing friend or the "dead of 1988" raises the question of what happened that year that caused such an aberration to take place.

In 1988, the war's final year, both sides witnessed enormous death tolls from operations that took place in the Iraqi south between Faw and Basra as each side attacked and counterattacked, attempting to control access to the

Shatt al-Arab waterway and either regain or hold the Faw Peninsula.[56] In describing these battles, Khoury quotes the Southern Bureau's director of the Baʿth Regional Command Council, who wrote:

> The battles resulted in a large number of deserters from the army, and they increased crime in the city [Basra] by stealing. We worked actively at limiting the crimes of the people. Our party organizations were given the authority to execute [deserters] and we were very successful in apprehending a great number of them. We also worked at persuading their families to surrender deserters.[57]

Like other fronts in the war, the southern front turned into a stalemate, and new campaigns with large battles opened in the Iran-Iraq border zone in Kurdistan in northern Iraq. It was here that the Iraqi army massacred thousands of Kurds, whose Peshmerga militias sided with Iran during the war, during the brutal Anfal Campaign that peaked from February to September 1988. Although technically separate from Anfal, the gassing of the Kurdish border town of Halabja on March 16, 1988 was the single most destructive and now well-known event from this especially dark period, with up to five thousand civilians killed and thousands more suffering from life-long injuries from the use of chemical weapons.[58] Human Rights Watch estimates that as part of the Anfal Campaign "50,000 and possibly as many as 100,000 persons, many of them women and children, were killed between February and September 1988."[59] This story's repeated references to "the dead of 1988" call forth, without directly naming a place or campaign, those who died in that last year of combat including those who were killed fighting the Iranian military, the civilians who lost their lives to Iranian shelling, and Iraqi Kurds, Arabs, and others who were killed by their own government in the final year of the long war.

For a reader familiar with the history of Iran at the same time, "the dead of 1988" immediately conjures its own horrific imagery. That year, between July and September at minimum 5,000 political dissidents, largely but not exclusively from the Mojahedin-e Khalq (PMOI), were executed in Iranian prisons and their bodies dumped into mass graves.[60] This followed the PMOI's incursion into Iran and attempted capture of the city of Kermanshah in one of the last major operations of the Iran-Iraq War, codenamed

"*Forugh-e Javidān*" ("Eternal Light") by the PMOI and "*Mersād*" ("Ambush") by the Iranian military and government.[61] The phrase "the dead of 1988" has an unfortunate relevance to both sides of the war.

"On a Bicycle at Night" creates a nightmarish world of torture and repetition for those who are looking for missing persons from the war, where the only ones who might know where they lie are the dead themselves. The living are left to reckon with the shadow of war, with its painful—both physically and figuratively—references appearing throughout the story: the narrator's wanting to spare his missing friend's grandfather the heartbreaking knowledge about his grandson, the mortician's gesture in which he "extends his arm . . . sluggishly, as if an invisible pain had begun creeping into it," the narrator's feeling, after he disembarks from the bus and is walking in the sweltering heat of the midday sun, that he likens to "the twist of a dagger."[62] But even more than such direct references, it is the stark silences in the story's dialogues that recall a ubiquitous and unspoken pain, a symbol of the inconsolability of those who remain and survive the dead, and an allegory for the silence of a state (or states) around the lack of accountability for a war that it fueled for nearly a decade.

Refusing Martyrdom in Amir Hasan Cheheltan's "Munes, Mother of Esfandiar"
By the time the war ended, Amir Hasan Cheheltan had already begun making a name for himself within the world of Persian fiction. In the late 1970s, he started publishing short stories in high profile literary journals and by the end of the 1990s he had published four short story collections and two novels. At the time of this writing, he has published 12 novels and eight collections of short stories. Like Shahriar Mandanipour, most of his novels and short stories written in the past two decades have not received permission for publication in Iran. His story "Munes, Mādar-e Esfandiār" ("Munes, Mother of Esfandiar"), first appeared in 1996 in a collection of stories about the war published by the MCIG and was republished two years later in his own collection of short stories, *Chizi beh Fardā Namāndeh Ast* (*Not Much Time Until Tomorrow*).[63] The story revolves around an elderly woman, Munes, whose son, Esfandiar, has been missing in action for years. It takes place in a small, unnamed Iranian village shortly

after the war ends, at a time when the names of POWs are being announced in newspapers and on the radio.

The initial release of the Iranian POWs in 1988 was reason for celebration. In 1988, the International Committee of the Red Cross registered approximately 70,000 prisoners of war, consisting of approximately 50,000 Iraqi POWs in Iran and 20,000 Iranians in Iraq.[64] The first of several exchanges took place in November 1988 and quickly ended due to a diplomatic fallout over the exact number of prisoners. In the story, the entire village is glued to the news in the hopes of hearing the names of family, loved ones, and neighbors who had been captured by Iraqi forces. In the village, everyone has read the same list of returnees in the same newspaper and listened to the same radio broadcasts that announced their names. Munes' son, Esfandiar, is not among them. Yet, as soon as the first POW names are announced, Munes declares to her neighbors that her son is finally home. An elderly man in the village named 'Abd ol-Baqi reminds her that it is not possible for Esfandiar to have returned yet. "They're held for a day or two in quarantine," he tells her. "It can take some time to get here from the border, you understand?" She retorts: "No. I don't. I don't understand anything anymore. He [Esfandiar] took away my ability to do that when he went to war, and only he can bring it back."[65] Her reaction goes further still, as the third-person omniscient narrator tells us that after the announcement, it seemed as if Munes had become young again—she stopped limping, lost the wrinkles in her face, and her hair seemed to have regained its color.[66]

Munes' behavior creates confusion among the neighbors and fodder for their gossip. The story opens with them trying to make sense of the situation. The woman, who lives directly next door, claims to have heard Munes talking to someone in her apartment. Meanwhile, Munes tells everyone that Esfandiar is recuperating at home and shoos away visitors when they arrive at her door so they do not wake him. She has the village tailor sew a suit for his upcoming engagement, asks neighbors about suitable brides, and claims that once Esfandiar is rested and better, they can come to see him at the engagement party. She begins taking his clothes to be cleaned and pressed regularly, until one day the cleaner asks her if Esfandiar has been wearing them at all, since they appear unworn.

As time passes, most of the neighborhood begins to think that Munes has gone crazy, but they cannot bring themselves to tell an old woman that her child, seemingly her only relative, has been killed in the war and will not be coming home. Instead, some neighbors go along with her, quietly accepting everything she says. Others seem to want to prod her into admitting the truth by maliciously telling her that she is holding her son captive just like the Iraqis once did, or by offering to help find work for her son. She snaps after one neighbor suggests he can get Esfandiar a job as a security guard: "'My son studied for nine years so that he could become a doorman [*darbān*]?' Khojasteh's husband replied, 'No, not a doorman, Ms. Munes, a security guard [*negahbān*]! Security guards have total control over who comes and goes. If they don't give permission, the president of the bank can't even enter.'" Soon afterward, another neighbor enquires sarcastically, "So how is Mr. Prime Minister doing today, Ms. Munes?"[67] The constant questioning and sarcasm break her. From that point forward, she begins avoiding others in the street and rarely leaves her house.

There is one exception in the village: a young woman named Tahmineh, the last person to have seen Esfandiar alive before he went off to war and who not only believes Munes, but also claims to have caught glimpses of Esfandiar after his supposed return. Moreover, based on Munes' descriptions of her recuperating son, Tahmineh falls in love with him. By the end of the story, Tahmineh, along with Munes, are the only two who seem to believe that Esfandiar has returned. Before the story ends, Munes goes absent. After a few days, the neighbors who start to notice a foul smell from her house, break in to find her body in a bedroom:

> They saw Munes sitting on the ground at the foot of the bed with clean, untouched sheets. Her forehead was resting on the corner of the mattress. On the bed were an ironed shirt, pajamas, and a clean undershirt carefully placed next to each other. They lifted Munes's head from the mattress and saw bloodstains the size of her palm on the white sheets.[68]

The story ends with the neighbors calling for a hearse to take Munes' body to Behesht-e Zahra cemetery.[69] The men gather near her house smoking cigarettes and chatting, and the women distribute food in the neighborhood to mark her death. The only person who seems affected by Munes's passing is Tahmineh who "stood by the window, alone, tears dropping from her eyes."[70]

Cheheltan's story, which first appeared in a state-sponsored publication, was part of a wave of Persian fiction that appeared in the decade after the war that signaled an opening around representations of grief and loss related to the conflict. On a more subversive level, however, it also questions the sanctity of the war. One way this happens is through the use of the names "Tahmineh" and "Esfandiar," which immediately conjure prominent characters from Ferdowsi's *Shahnameh*, the nationalist epic of pre-Islamic Persia. They feature prominently in the cycle of stories involving Rostam, *The Shahnameh's* most famous hero. Although different, their roles are echoed in Cheheltan's story. In *The Shahnameh,* Tahmineh was a princess from Samangan, located in today's north-central Afghanistan, whose one-night stand with Rostam results in the birth of Sohrab. Sohrab is raised by Tahmineh and quickly grows to be a warrior nearly equivalent to his father. He grows anxious to meet him and eventually rides out with an army to face Rostam in combat, but no one reveals to Rostam that Sohrab is his son. The two fight and Sohrab nearly defeats Rostam before being sneakily killed by the old champion, at which point he reveals who he is. The story of Sohrab's death in combat at the hands of this father is the epic's most famous tragedy. It sends Tahmineh into a terrible state of mourning that eventually kills her a year later. Separately, Esfandiar is another hero in *The Shahnameh*. A divine warrior blessed by the Prophet Zoroaster, Esfandiar is also tragically killed by an aging Rostam in a battle. Esfandiar is nearly invincible, but Rostam learns that he can be killed with an arrow shot through his eyes. He is also foretold that anyone who kills Esfandiar will face a terrible fate. Later, Rostam does indeed die in an especially gruesome manner: his jealous half-brother pushes him into a pit of spears.

In "Munes, Mother of Esfandiar," the combination of Tahmineh's lonely tears, the near certainty of Esfandiar's death in combat, and Munes dying in anguish over her son call forth the tragic stories of *The Shahnameh*. The very evocation of the epic in the context of the Iran-Iraq War can be read as an alternative to the myth of mourning and sacrifice used in the Sacred Defense narrative's framing of the war: the story of Hussein's martyrdom at Karbala.[71] The disappearance of Esfandiar's body denies Munes closure and complicates the role of the martyr in official war discourse as well. Upon entering Munes' house, the neighbors see "bloodstains the size of her palm on the white sheets." The scene reinforces the idea of her own death for another cause—that of Esfandiar—not for a sacred defense of the homeland. Had his corpse been returned from the front, it would have been wrapped in a white sheet, bloodied perhaps, and Esfandiar would have been considered a martyr of the state. The image of the bloody palm had become a well-known part of the visual iconography of the 1979 Revolution, calling forth the martyrdom of Imam Hussein and symbolizing the blood of fellow protesters killed in the revolution.[72] Through Munes's denial of her son's death, the story quietly rejects the state's martyrdom discourse and undercuts the unique status of the martyr in the larger official culture of war by placing more importance on the anguish of families of the martyr than the martyr himself and his supposed sacrifice for the Sacred Defense.

LOSS AND THE LIMITS OF PERMISSIBLE DISCOURSE

In the short-term aftermath of the Iran-Iraq War, Iranian and Iraqi fiction emerged as two separate sites of struggle between differing narratives of the war, as writers sought to give voice to otherwise silenced stories of grief, loss, and anger. Like many European modernist writers after the First World War, these writers rejected "the sentimentality and lies of wartime propaganda [. . .] the patriotic certainties [. . .] euphemisms about battle, 'glory' and the 'hallowed dead.'"[73] Instead, they wrote about the damaged remains and the painful absences the war left behind.

It is important to note that three of the four writers whose works this chapter focuses on wrote and published in their countries of origin. Only ʿAbbas published his first short story collection abroad in Jordan, and even then, it contained stories already published in the Iraq-based literary journal *al-Aqlām*. Their overlapping aesthetic practices not only demonstrate how some Iranian and Iraqi writers found themselves drawn toward similar approaches to writing about the war in the first decade after its conclusion, but also how abstract narratives of loss emerge as a permissible way through which to write about the war in both countries. As David Eng and David Kazanjian write, "[A]ttention to remains generates a politics of mourning that might be active rather than reactive, prescient rather than nostalgic, abundant rather than lacking, social rather than solipsistic, militant rather than reactionary."[74]

Throughout the four stories presented in this chapter, more than any other character, the figure of the mourning survivor, often the mother, is the character who most embodies Eng's and Kazanjian's claim. The survivors of the war, those who remain after the death of children and other loved ones, turn their mourning into politically potent messages that contrast the state war narratives. In the short stories by ʿAbbas and Cheheltan, the focus on the postwar absence of those who died and the pain of those who remain amounts to subtle but piercing critiques. Read within the larger context of literature related to the Iran-Iraq War, they opened the door for more direct counternarratives of the conflict to develop later in Persian and Arabic fiction, both through an interrogation of the martyr figure and the non-combatant survivors. Approaching the war's legacy with a starting point of loss, employing silences, a focus on the individual, and a move away from the desire to produce mimetic realism—some of the hallmarks of modernist fiction from both of these countries—allowed these writers to engage with the war but from a distance, while still operating and often publishing in the countries they lived in, rather than the relative distance and safety of exile. Thus, I consider these types of writing to constitute the first stage of a discursive confrontation between the two regimes and their detractors. Over time, these confrontations would take even more direct forms.

Three
WAR FRONT APOCRYPHA

IN THE POSTWAR PERIOD, MANY WRITERS, ESPECIALLY THOSE WHO had experienced combat firsthand, continued to set their stories on the war front. However, the passage of time and changing sociopolitical circumstances opened spaces to depict events at the front in ways that diverged from the Sacred Defense and Saddam's Qadisiyya narratives. Some writers used these new circumstances to critique the foundations of the state narratives and challenge their monopoly on the "true" representation of the battlefront. The two state-sponsored wartime literatures often sanitized representations of the war for its readers. Essential components of these "truths" included the sacralization of violence, the enchantment of martyrdom, the prioritization of narratives of heroism, and the maintenance of anonymous, dehumanized representations of the enemy. The states' narratives were not interested in critiquing military decisions or showing soldiers who questioned their duties.

Truth for these two warring governments should be understood in its Foucauldian sense as "a system of ordered procedures for the production, regulation, distribution, circulation and operation of statements. 'Truth' is linked in a circular relation with systems of power which produce and sustain it, and to effects of power which it induces and which extend it." All of this constitutes what Foucault calls "a 'regime' of truth."[1]

Through censorship and rewards, the cultural arms of the Iranian and Iraqi states determined how their truths about the war would appear, resulting in the literatures of Saddam's Qadisiyya and the Sacred Defense. Because the state narratives of the war hinged upon the supposed righteousness of each belligerent's wartime cause, and because they were each so invested in the creation of cultural production that promoted these narratives, the "truth" became a manufactured, mass-produced, and widely distributed "reality."

This chapter draws from novels and short stories written by Iraqi writers Janan Jasim Hillawi (b. 1957) and Muhsin al-Ramli (b. 1967), and Iranian writers Ahmad Dehqan (b. 1957) and Hossein Mortezaeian Abkenar (b. 1967), to demonstrate how Iraqi and Iranian writers have defamiliarized the banal and ubiquitous wartime representations of battlefront violence to undermine and redefine aspects of the official "truths" of the war front. My readings of these authors' texts expose how they have challenged the official representation of martyrdom, depicted soldiers' confessions that taint official accounts of combat, and presented the war front experience as dystopic. By vocalizing unheard and visualizing unseen aspects of the war, the contents of these literary works constitute what I call, drawing from the work of Brian McHale, "war front apocrypha" in the eyes of the Iranian and Iraqi wartime states.[2]

These works of fiction demonstrate attempts to create counternarratives of the war front experience through techniques that are related to, but ultimately distinct from, the short stories highlighted in the previous chapter. Those texts doubt the certainty of each state's war story and mourned its losses, without directly attacking state ideology or putting forth a clear counternarrative of the war. They present alternative discourses of the conflict that offer criticism of the war or the state's narrative of martyrdom, but do not overtly attack the martyr's sacrifice. In this sense, the previous chapter's war narratives rely on a presumed consensus of unity around the martyr, a figure whom the state characterizes as voluntarily sacrificing himself for the war and immune to criticism. By extension, the promise of redemption and sacred vindication intrinsic to the very concept of martyrdom is preserved.

The approaches of the writers featured in this chapter range from disenchanting the war's martyrdom tropes, to exposing the "darker corners of history" through confessions about the war front, to breaking down the binary logic of wartime ideology by giving voice to characters such as the uncommitted soldier and the army deserter. Notably, the critiques made by these authors target aspects of the "truth" of the official narrative and therefore take aim at the heart of wartime ideology. These well-known works of Iraqi and Iranian fiction have a bone to pick with the state ideologies of the war. They aggressively challenge the literary depictions of the war that appeared in both countries during the 1980s and that have continued to appear in Iran in the postwar period.

DISENCHANTING WAR FRONT DEATH

One of the most critical ways state war narratives were deconstructed through literary fiction was through transforming the representation of the martyr, the figure most used to play up the nationalist and religious aspects of the war and to glorify death in battle. By the mid-1990s, an important shift was underway: some writers of fiction began turning the tropes of war front heroism and martyrdom from static representations of serving and dying for the state into polyvalent signifiers. The wartime discourse of each state had mostly enchanted the experience of fighting and dying on the battlefield. The postwar period witnessed critical rewritings that disenchanted these discursive foundations, signaling a crack in the representation of these previously untouchable concepts.

Another representation of the martyr emerged after the war that moved further away from the official discourse. In it, the figure of the martyr becomes a flashpoint, and its trope becomes a space wherein to challenge the routinized state discourse of martyrdom. Here, martyrdom is desacralized and stripped down to its most visceral and physical meaning: corporeal death. This representation is a starting point for a counternarrative to those of the Sacred Defense and Saddam's Qadisiyya. It challenges the idea that martyrdom is inherently redemptive and rejects the assumption of meaningful death in combat. More than simply a challenge to the war itself, this depiction of death and martyrdom can also be seen as a site of resistance to the ideologies of the Iranian and Iraqi wartime states.

In this discursive transformation of the martyr into an unsanctified corpse, we see what Sarah Cole, in her study of representations of violence and war in English and Irish literatures, calls "disenchantment." In Cole's formulation, enchantment in war literature "is the tendency to see in violence some sort of transformative power." It is "to imbue the violent experience with symbolic and cultural potency."³ Disenchantment undoes what she calls a "symbolic valorization." She writes:

> The general principle is this: that violence—especially the rampaging violence of war—demands a style or technology of representation that pinpoints its experience and consequences without justifying or celebrating it. To oppose the mystification and mythologization of violence, texts with such a goal often focus on a moment of bodily injury (and the consequences that ensue from that violation), drawing the reader or viewer back to the moment of destruction, rejecting the thematics of metamorphosis and the idea of a purifying or cathartic violence.⁴

Drawing on Cole's notion of disenchanting wartime violence, in the first half of this chapter I analyze novels and short stories written by two war veterans-turned-writers that are set on the war front, exiled Iraqi writer Janan Jasim Hillawi and Iranian writer Ahmad Dehqan. To differing degrees, in texts by each of these writers, martyrdom and the war front emerge as sites of symbolic struggle, with the writers using them to challenge the official representation and ideologies of the war, as well as the notion of redemptive death on the battlefield.

Grisly Details and the Physicality of Death in Ahmad Dehqan's Fiction
Ahmad Dehqan established a name for himself within the literary and intellectual circles of government-sponsored writers during the 1990s when his first novel, *Safar beh Garā-ye Devist va Haftād Darajeh* (*Journey to Heading 270 Degrees*), was published in 1996 with Sarir, the publishing house connected to the Foundation for the Preservation and Publication of Sacred Defense Works and Values (*Bonyād-e Hefz-e Āsār va Nashr-e Arzesh-hā-ye Defā'-e Moqaddas*). The following year, it received multiple awards from government sponsored cultural foundations, including the fourth annual prize for Best Sacred Defense Novel. It went through several reprintings and was later republished in 2005 by the much larger publisher, Sureh-ye Mehr, which is connected to the Howzeh. After an initial printing of five thousand copies, it has subsequently gone through eighteen printings, and

in 2006 was translated into English by Paul Sprachman. Although Dehqan is a writer who is part of the government-sponsored literary establishment, his nonconformist depictions of the war front in his novels and short stories have provoked the ire of his peers and earned him praise from writers and readers working outside the Sacred Defense literary scene.

The title of *Journey to Heading 270 Degrees* refers to the due west direction of the Iraq border and war front. It begins with the novel's eighteen-year-old protagonist, Naser, and his arrival home after years at the front and his quick return to participate in the Karbala Five campaign—an attempt by the Iranian army in early January 1987 to capture the Iraqi port city of Basra. The battle was connected to two other operations codenamed "Karbala" in the same area that lasted from late December 1986 until April 1987. Taken together, these military campaigns were the biggest of the entire war and resulted in a staggering number of Iranian casualties: nearly 40,000 Iranian combatants were killed, with twice as many wounded, while 10,000 Iraqi soldiers were killed. The battles were ferocious. They featured Iranian human-wave attacks, oftentimes undertaken by teenage boys, and prompted the Iraqis to launch another "war of the cities." The Iranian forces came within twelve kilometers of Basra before being pushed back, ultimately unable to claim any victory. For his part, Saddam Hussein "congratulated his generals for this 'superb victory' and named it 'the Great Harvest' [al-Ḥiṣād al-Akbar] for the impressive number of Iranians killed."[5]

In the novel, Naser is excited to leave his home in Tehran and return to the war, even though his parents oppose it. His desire to get back to the action has nothing to do with the war itself, though. What draws Naser back to the front is the desire to see his friends and regain the camaraderie lost since returning home. His reunion with the platoon is buoyant and comedic. Brought together again, the mostly teenage soldiers hardly act as if they are at war. In the days leading up to the battle, no one speaks of combat, the "Sacred Defense," or the sacrifices of martyrs. Instead, they play soccer, drink tea, reminisce, roughhouse, curse irreverently, and play slapstick jokes on each other. Their youthful energy is set in counterpoint to the Iranian state radio, which, like a stern father, reprimands the teenage soldiers for their rambunctious behavior when they should be serious, and broadcasts martial music and slogans supporting the war cause.

Not long after arriving at the front, Naser and his platoon are sent into battle. The tone changes abruptly as the embanked soldiers come under heavy fire. The incredibly ugly and violent reality of the battlefront is brought to readers unfiltered. With his platoon arriving at the first position, Naser is on the verge of vomiting from the stench and sight of enemy corpses being run over by Iranian bulldozers as they attempt to mold the geography to their advantage. Gripped by fear, he describes a dead body by saying, "Trucks have repeatedly run over it, picking up pieces of the corpse in their threads, leaving only a flattened piece of flesh."[6]

Most of the novel takes place on the battlefield. It is a fast-paced story that brings to the fore the details of multiple horrendous deaths. One by one, the platoon thins out as soldiers are badly injured or die. Here, the novel's narrative departs from the official narrative of martyrdom. As exemplified in the scene of the death of Naser's dear friend, 'Ali, *Journey*'s representation of the war front is defined by gory violence, stripped of any mention of the glory or heroism that distinguishes the official representation of the soldier. Naser reaches 'Ali just moments after he has been run over by a tank:

> I stand over what is left of his body. He stares up at me with a look of horror and disbelief. I sit. The thread has crushed his midsection. His main artery is still spurting blood and his left eye is moving. He has been cut in half, exactly in two pieces. I take his head and upper part of his body in my arms; the lower half is mashed into the tank tracks. His crushed limbs smell like blood, and steam rises from them like snakes into the air.[7]

Naser knows that 'Ali will die there. The novel does not hesitate to show the sense of futility that he feels witnessing the violent death of his best friend.

'Ali's death is the first of many, with nearly everyone in the platoon suffering a gruesome end. The Iranian soldiers instinctually fight and retreat, their own survival becoming their only cause. They are depicted as fragile and dispensable; bullets and shrapnel rip through their bodies, they are lit on fire, blown up, and torn apart. After being hit with shrapnel in the mouth, Naser describes the scene around him, "I find myself lying with my head on the ground and the smell of kabob in my nose.... I sniff the air ... but as I rise slowly, I am gripped by a terrible fear. Human flesh is roasting; someone who was once alive is now a headless piece of meat."[8]

Dehqan's attention to grisly detail and directness in describing the horrors of combat remain unique for Persian language war novels. His emphasis on the physicality of death is in sharp contrast to the valorization of martyrdom in Qasem'ali Farasat's *Headless Palms* (Chapter 1) and other works of wartime fiction. Martyrdom and its enchanted characterization in the Sacred Defense are not described here but corporeal death is. In the novel's real-time narration, the term "martyr" is defamiliarized, ripped out of its context of supposed meaningful death, and repurposed to refer to the details of battlefront combat and being horrifically killed. Relatedly, the novel's present tense narration has as much to do with disenchanting war front death as the gory content. *Journey* offers no time for reflection or retrospectively recasting death in combat as worthy, either for the cause of the war or for spiritual salvation. Its immediate account of combat works in tandem with the novel's details to reject what Cole calls "the idea of a purifying or cathartic violence."[9]

Stripped of the ideological tone that characterized most Iranian official war front literature, the publication of Dehqan's *Journey* marked a breakthrough. Furthermore, the novel's first publication with the relatively small publishing house, Sarir, and then later with Sureh-ye Mehr, the largest state-sponsored publisher in the country, signaled a fissure within official literary representations of the war. Now, even some writers whose books were printed and distributed by state-sponsored publishers were willing to go against the calcified modes of official representation of the war. Dehqan's *Journey* presaged other forms of cultural production that were put out by state-sponsored publishers, film production companies, or news media, that broke, or claimed to break, with the official representation of the war. The most prominent example is Masoud Dehnamaki's 2007 comedic war film, *Ekhrāji-hā* (*The Outcasts*), about a group of neighborhood troublemaker friends who go to the war front for the sole sake of impressing their girlfriends. In the process, they are transformed into loyal fighters for the Sacred Defense by some of the devoted volunteers.[10] Dehqan's books can be seen as contributing to the debates around the war's memorialization and representation among war veterans-turned-cultural producers who consciously distinguish between "the official" (*rasmi*) and "the real" (*vāqʿei*) versions of the war.¹¹

A related element to Dehqan's emphasis on the carnal aspects of war front violence is his tendency to spotlight events that are not acknowledged by the Sacred Defense narrative, and in this sense, his fiction has more in common with non-Sacred Defense fiction writers. The stories contained in his 2004 short story collection, *Man Qātel-e Pesar-e-tān Hastam* (*I Killed Your Son*) emphasize the second element. The book contains ten short stories about the Iran-Iraq War and its aftermath. Dehqan published the slim collection with Tehran-based publishing house Ofoq, an independent publisher, just before Sureh-ye Mehr reprinted *Journey*. The following year, likely aided by the fanfare that *Journey* had already garnered, *I Killed Your Son* was nominated for several literary prizes from foundations without connections to the state, including the prestigious Mehregān Prize for best short story collection, and the prize for best short story by the once highly respected, but now non-operational, Hushang Golshiri Foundation.¹² To date, the collection has gone through eight printings. If *Journey* sought to muddy the Sacred Defense battlefront story by reorienting the narrative of martyrdom toward physical violence and senseless loss, this collection's title story can be read as an attempt to shine light on the darker corners of the war and its aftermath.

"I Killed Your Son" is a confession written in the form of a letter by military veteran, Faramarz Bonakdar, to a man named Reza Jabbarzadeh, the father of a soldier killed in combat, whose name was Mohsen. Bonakdar writes the letter shortly after the mourning ceremony commemorating the fortieth day since Mohsen's death. He tells Jabbarzadeh that he was at the ceremony and saw him but could not bring himself to speak with him. "[W]ithout you knowing me, I was ashamed to see you. I did not know what impact it would have had on you to know that I killed your son. Yes, Mohsen was killed by my hands, not those of the enemy soldiers."¹³

The story continues with Bonakdar revealing to Jabbarzadeh the true nature of his son's death. His son, Mohsen, was not shot and killed on the battlefield, as Jabbarzadeh had been told. Rather, he was first shot by enemy fire and then drowned by Bonakdar after his unconscious grunting and flailing threatened to reveal their position to Iraqi soldiers. Bonakdar writes,

"I decided to tell you how things went after your son's friend, who was also my friend and fellow combatant, took the megaphone [at the funeral] to speak about Mohsen. Everything he said was true, but he was not entirely honest about Mohsen's martyrdom. This letter is to make up for what was missing."[14]

What ensues is an explanation of events during an operation gone awry, as a group of Iranian divers, to which Bonakdar and Jabbarzadeh belonged, attempted to cross into Iraqi territory via the Arvand Rud/Shatt al-Arab waterway. Jabbarzadeh was hit in the neck by a bullet and presumed dead, and Bonakdar was commanded to bring his body ashore. While doing so, he realized that Jabbarzadeh was still alive, and he initially hoped to save his life. However, once on enemy territory and reunited with the other divers, Jabbarzadeh, unconscious and unable to control himself, began to grunt and wheeze loudly as he tried to breathe. Bonakdar writes that he was commanded to "shut him up" and he could not:

> The commander again told me to stop him from making noise. How? I asked. He said, put his head under the water. [. . .]
>
> Mohsen [. . .] was still snorting. A wave hit him and water poured into the hole in his neck, sprouting up like a fountain. I took him by the hand and pulled him under the water. Even though he was unconscious while above the water, as soon as his head went under his body jerked up and he pulled his arms away from me to come above the surface. The commander [. . .] said in a firm voice to pull him under because if we were discovered the lives of all the fighters would be in danger. I went behind Mohsen, took hold of his arms, and pulled him underwater.[15]

With the help of his commander, Bonakdar drowned Mohsen's flailing body and attached him to one of barbed wires set up along the shore so that the tide would not drag it into the river. The last time Bonakdar saw him, "his arms were spread out in either direction and his head tilted downward between the barbed wire, like Christ on the cross."[16] Bonakdar tells the father of the friendship that the two men shared and how it flashed before his eyes as he took his friend's life to save the rest of the platoon. He ends by saying, "I killed your son and must bear the punishment for that. I submit myself to whatever fate you decide for me."[17]

As a letter, the confessional aspect of "I Killed Your Son" targets the assumed heroism of the war front soldiers. The short story is a continuation of the critique of martyrdom that Dehqan launched only a few years prior in *Journey*. The aesthetics of the story harken back to that novel as well, with Dehqan continuing to emphasize the disenchanted, corporeal elements of violent death on the battlefield by invoking the sounds and physical aspects of the unconscious body attempting to remain in the realm of the living. Without providing any firm answers, the story asks what it means to have the received narrative of a son's martyrdom turn out to be a lie, and rather than dying at the hands of the enemy, being killed by one's own comrade and friend. When Jabbarzadeh's mother screams invectives at her son's killer at the ceremony marking forty days since his death, she is actually calling for the death of an Iranian soldier who killed her son for the sake of his fellow fighters, or so we are led to believe. It is easy to forget that within the story of Mohsen's death that Jabbarzadeh proffers in the letter, Mohsen is finished off by his fellow soldier because of the commander's sense that his flailing and snorting *might* give away their position. As much as Bonakdar wants to believe so and hopes that Jabbarzadeh's father also believes him, there is a noticeable lack of certainty in the story. In other words, no one knows what might have happened if Jabbarzadeh had not been drowned there and then. Bonakdar's comrade's death might have been entirely meaningless.

Much like the stories examined in Chapter 2, the unspoken plays a role in this story and begs readers to ask if Mohsen's death at the hands of a fellow soldier affects his status as a martyr. In telling Jabbarzadeh's father that he last witnessed his son in a position that resembles "Christ on the cross" (replete with a barbed wire crown that recalls Christ's crown of thorns), Bonakdar at once reinforces a specific narrative of martyrdom while simultaneously relating a story that undercuts the assumed qualities of meaningful death at the battlefield. Understood this way, readers cannot help but view Bonakdar as an unreliable narrator, nervously caught between a conviction of Jabbarzadeh as a martyr, and the fact that he was the one who killed his fellow soldier for the possibility of a battlefield advantage. In its format as a letter from a battlefield participant and witness, "I Killed Your Son" disobeys the official narrative's exclusive claim to truth and offers a revisionist narrative of the war front.

By the end of the war, readers of Iranian war fiction had come to expect predictable portrayals of the war front in writings by establishment writers, particularly those affiliated with the Howzeh. In *Journey*, Dehqan broke many taboos of writing about the war front and the ideological convictions of the soldiers. "I Killed Your Son" works similarly by showing another side of the battlefield, stripped of the sacralizing language of the governmental narrative around combat and martyrdom, and shedding light on a darker side of the war that the state-sponsored narrative ignored.

Escaping Martyrdom in Janan Jasim Hillawi's Night of the Lands

Janan Jasim Hillawi, who left Iraq for Sweden in 1992, had written many short stories and poems before writing his first novel, *Layl al-Bilād* (*Night of the Lands*), which was published in 2002 by Beirut-based publisher Dār al-Ādāb and translated into French in 2005. As a novel in which battlefield combat features prominently, and published roughly around the same time as Dehqan's *Journey*, it offers an interesting comparison from an Iraqi perspective on similar combat experiences. Spanning the decade between 1981 and 1991, the novel follows the story of its main protagonist, 'Abd Allah in a bildungsroman-like manner. The third-person omniscient narrator recounts 'Abd Allah's development through three stages: his treatment by Ba'th Party members as a political independent, his time in combat at the battlefront with Iran, and his participation with the Kurdish rebels before his eventual return to his destroyed hometown of Basra.

The novel begins with 'Abd Allah's return to his family in Basra following an extended absence from his university studies. Almost immediately, he is conscripted into the Iraqi army and sent to a training camp, where he is imprisoned for not being a Ba'th Party member. Living conditions in the military prison are appalling, and 'Abd Allah endures regular verbal and physical abuse. After witnessing the torture and the death of another prisoner, he and a fellow prisoner attempt to escape, but are caught and as a punishment transported to the front lines of war, which makes prison seem like a distant luxury. 'Abd Allah then participates in multiple battles with Iranian forces, which are described in horrifying detail. After suffering a wound on the battlefield and spending time in a military hospital, he is sent to the front in Kurdistan, where he and a fellow soldier are ambushed and taken prisoner by Kurdish revolutionaries aligned with Iraqi Communists battling the Iraqi military.[18] He eventually gains their trust and fights alongside them against the Iraqi forces, likely on the opposite side of the Anfal campaigns. Again, he is injured—this time badly burned. The novel concludes with his return to Basra, now decimated after years of heavy Iranian shelling and just following the Iraqi state's merciless punishment of the city following the 1991 uprising, when between late February and early April of that year, Iraqi Kurdish militias in the north, Shi'i militias in the south, and army detractors rose against the Ba'thist state but were brutally crushed.[19]

Hillawi's novel sets itself up in opposition to both the war and the ideology of the Ba'th Party. This is perhaps best illustrated by the scenes in the army base where 'Abd Allah is conscripted and trained, as well as in the prison where he is incarcerated for remaining a "political independent." In his first encounter with an army political guidance officer (*ḍābit al-tawjīh al-sīyāsī*) after conscription, the life of the uncomplacent conscript is laid bare. The officer interrogates him:

"You're not a member of the party?"
"No sir."
"Why?"
Terrified, his face quivered and he blushed; his earlobes were on fire. He responded as if his voice were coming out of another person's mouth: "I don't like to get involved in politics, sir."
The officer's eyes bore into him. His forehead was sweating, heart pounding. But he remained direct, composed and stood his ground.
"The party is not politics, the party is the nation."
"True, sir. But I will remain independent."
"'Independent.' That's a political word. A big word for a disorderly soldier, a prisoner, a weak-hearted coward. 'Independent' from the party, the government, the state, and the army. What are you? A maggot, filth, a rag, a laughingstock. 'Independent,' you son of a bitch. Who are you to become independent? An officer? A leader? The president? of the country? And what have you become independent from? How? You sick, filthy bastard." There was a storm exploding in the officer's mouth, who was now looking at 'Abd Allah, curling his lips as if to spit out of disgust.
"Who are you to become 'independent'?"

"I'm nothing, sir."

"Of course you're nothing... you shit... you woman!"

'Abd Allah turned his head away and swallowed. He was utterly confused. Had he committed a crime in the past? Where? When? With whom? His head swirled with questions and he shrank back, expecting another round of insults. He heard the officer ask him, scornfully, "Are you going to register or not?"

"No, sir."

"Get out of here, you son of a bitch."[20]

Throughout Hillawi's novel, the Baʿth Party is depicted as a wholly oppressive apparatus. From conscription to incarceration to warfare, the novel's protagonist is subjected to escalating levels of pain administered by party apparatchiks whose propensity to commit acts of violence against its internal or external enemies only increases with their level of authority. The prison scenes make it clear that Hillawi's ideological position is staunchly anti-Baʿth. As such, the descriptions of death on the battlefield devalorize the act of martyrdom entirely, stripping it down to its most visceral meaning and chipping away at its mythic status. Not once is the word "martyr" used to describe Iraqis who die in battle. Instead, there are repeated references to "severed limbs," "torn corpses," and the "smell of blood and gunpowder." In one of the most graphic sections of the novel, ʿAbd Allah lifts his head out of a trench in the morning to find a hellscape in front of him. He sees:

> corpses that he hadn't noticed during the night when he had waded into the blood in the heat of the battle, not feeling himself among the whizzing of shrapnel, bullets, and canon fire. He was deafened and unable to see, his eyes tearing from gunpowder and sand. The corpses were piled atop each other, limbless. The pressure from the rockets and shrapnel had ripped them apart and then melded them together. They now appeared as one body with multiple heads and arms pointing in every direction, bound together by blood, dirt and mud, torn camouflage, hole-ridden helmets and half buried broken guns. Iranian insignia adorned the heads of the dead, torn to shreds now stained with red blood, with "Oh Martyr of Karbala" written upon them.[21]

Later battle scenes describe the hysterical fear that soldiers felt while engaged in hand-to-hand combat. Gone is the clean kill of bullets; instead, the war front is akin to a medieval battlefield where soldiers wield "bayonets, knives, shovels, rocks and teeth" while the injured "groan, gasp and scream." Whatever logic the war and the battlefield supposedly had disappears. If the war front soldier of the official literatures was a coolheaded hero, the narrator of *Night* describes his shock in describing human wave attacks: "with an incomprehensible human charge, the Iranians were quickly dying, mixing into the darkness in front of the ferocious Iraqi soldiers who were terrified of being taken as prisoners."[22]

Like Dehqan's *Journey*, Hillawi's *Night* presents a gripping and action-packed storyline that focuses on graphic depictions of senseless death and destruction. Moreover, the novel also gives voice, albeit limited, to the Kurdish opposition, further demonstrating the multifaceted nature of this conflict. That said, the Iranian soldiers remain anonymous and silent, just as the Iraqis do in Dehqan's works. Astrid Ottosson al-Bitar rightly notes that there are scenes that feature Iranian soldiers, including one in which a soldier is found gurgling blood just before being shot, or a similar scene where the narrator describes the religious, bellicose chants heard coming from the charging Iranian soldiers.[23] However, this hardly represents an insight into a separate ideological position.[24] In a short story published two years before *Night*, Hillawi makes a similar move by writing about an Iraqi conscript's experience watching over an Iranian POW. The POW escapes, and they are both punished equally by the Iraqi commanding officer.[25] In contrast to the official literatures of both states, these scenes are interesting for their more humanizing portrayal of the enemy, even if they do not attempt to truly engage with the voice of the opposition.

Witnessing a Transformation: From Martyr to Corpse
With their graphic depictions of death on the battlefield, *Journey to Heading 270 Degrees*, "I Killed Your Son," and *Night of the Lands* engage with a war setting whose literary representation had been dominated by state-sanctioned, sanitized depictions of combat and death. Their portrayals abstain from the celebratory tone of most wartime literature. These novels instead

use those scenes to divest martyrdom of "all forms of symbolic valorization."[26] Martyrdom is questioned and stripped down to its physical meaning: corporeal death. Both authors wipe away the film of familiarity that had settled over the figure of the martyr in the official literatures of the war. In this sense, the novels are a further testament to the idea that time and distance from this war broadened the discursive field around it in different ways.

Beyond physical descriptions and ideological challenges, a close, comparative reading of these two writers' texts illustrates how they also invert the meaning of martyrdom by directly calling forth its other meaning: to witness. The word used in both Arabic and Persian contexts for "martyr," *shahīd*, and martyrdom, *shahāda* (Persian cognate: *shahādat*), like its English translation, carries the meaning of witnessing. Unlike English, the three-letter root (*sh-h-d*) of the Arabic word *shahid* reveals its connection to an array of verbs related to bearing witness (to testify, to certify, to confirm, to watch), in addition to the profession of the Islamic faith, and to die as a martyr, as well as several nouns (a witness, a testimony, a scene). The protagonists of Dehqan's and Hillawi's texts upend the deeper meaning of martyrdom. Rather than becoming martyred themselves and witnessing some sort of spiritual truth, they witness the gruesome deaths of others around them. In the case of Hillawi's protagonist, 'Abd Allah, he even makes note of the mutilated corpse of an enemy soldier whose head is ironically wrapped with a headband calling out to Shi'ism's "Prince of Martyrs" with the proclamation, "Oh Martyr of Karbala!" (*Yā Shahid-e Karbalā'*).

Examining how Dehqan's and Hillawi's texts challenge the state narratives of the Iran-Iraq War also illustrates how they do not function entirely on the same level. Hillawi is ultimately far more critical of the state's war apparatus than Dehqan. Essential to his ability to express that position is his place as a writer working and publishing from exile. He wrote the novel from Sweden and published it in Beirut at a time when writing this way about the Iran-Iraq War and the Ba'th Party would have been unthinkable in Iraq. The hero of *Night* is valorized precisely because of his stance against the Ba'th, which comes to full fruition at the end of the war as he fights side-by-side with the armed Kurdish opposition against the Iraqi state. His critique of the war, outside of a general critique of violence, also happens primarily through his critique of the state—something that is a hallmark of other Iraqi exilic writers covered in the next two chapters. While *Night* is interested in depicting the war's horrors, it replaces the Iranian fighters with the Ba'thist regime as the actual enemy of the victimized Iraqi people, who are championed through the figure of the army deserter ('Abd Allah), the armed Kurdish rebels, and the Iraqi citizens and soldiers who participated in the 1991 uprising. In this way, *Night of the Lands* presents a view of the Iran-Iraq War not unlike other postwar Iraqi novels by 'Ali Badr and Nasif Falak, for example.[27]

Although also a rebellious writer in his own right, Dehqan has an entirely different relationship with the Iranian state and this war. As a writer who not only still lives in Iran, but who works with the state-sponsored literary establishment, he refrains from the type of raw criticism of the Islamic Republic that Hillawi levels against the Ba'thist regime. Even if Dehqan is explicit in exposing the horrors of warfare on the battlefield, he does not question the necessity of war, nor does he portray the soldiers in a negative light like Hillawi does, or even like another Iranian veteran writer, Hossein Abkenar, whose work is treated in the following section. Because of his status as a veteran and biographer of war heroes, as well as his affiliation with the Howzeh, his writings are immediately associated with pro-regime cultural producers who maintain the nationalistic and religiously-informed view of the war found in the Sacred Defense narrative. Paradoxically, this positionality as an "insider" allows him to write the type of fiction that critiques the war front and represent it from an "outsider" perspective. It is unlikely that an independent author would have been able to publish the same type of fiction within Iran at the time (or any time since). Dehqan has also drawn the ire of the Islamic Republic's most zealous cultural critics supporting the war. One example is Ahmad Shakeri, who has accused Dehqan of being fundamentally antiwar and writing what he called a "materialistic" work that ignores the "benefits and virtues" (*husn va mahāsen*) of the war, instead choosing to only focus on the negative aspects (*ma'āyeb*) of the conflict.[28] His collection *I Killed Your Son* caused even more controversy for some of its depictions of war front combat and postwar traumas.[29] For his part, Dehqan has found himself on the defensive several times against accusations that he is uncommitted to maintaining the proper memory of the war, once stating that he has "no position on their [pro-regime critics'] definition of what is pro- or anti-war in our country's literature and this is not the basis on which I write.

The eight-year war is one of the honors of the nation. I am proud that I write about it."[30] He is not entirely alone, as other Iranian writers affiliated with the Howzeh, such as Davud Ghaffarzadegan, Mohammad Reza Bayrami, and Habib Ahmadzadeh, have also tried to challenge the inflexibility of the official narrative of the war, albeit with fewer graphic details.[31] Their works in the 1990s and early 2000s represent fissures in the official narrative, recalling in fiction what Shahla Talebi similarly identifies in the letters of veterans as "the contested meanings of martyrdom in Iran after the revolution."[32]

THE WAR FRONT AS DYSTOPIA

The critique of martyrdom is not the only way that Iranian and Iraqi writers have challenged the official representations of the war front. The second part of this chapter turns the spotlight on the ways in which Iraqi writer Muhsin al-Ramli and Iranian writer Hossein Mortezaeian Abkenar, two writers who have written several works of fiction that deal with the Iran-Iraq War, have portrayed the war front and the space between the war and home fronts as dystopian nightmares. Their short novels examined here, al-Ramli's *Fatīt al-Mubaʻthir* (*Scattered Crumbs*) and Abkenar's *'Aqrab ru-ye Pelleh-hā-ye Rāh-āhan-e Andimeshk, yā, Khun az in Qatar Michikeh, Qurbān!* (*The Scorpion on the Steps of the Andimeshk Railroad, or, Blood is Dripping from This Train, Sir!*) are harshly critical of the both the war and the Iranian and Iraqi wartime states. Published in 2000 and 2004 respectively, their novels, like Dehqan's and Hillawi's, use the martyr as a critical symbol against the wartime regimes, but they are less interested in using corporeal descriptions of death to critique the states' martyr myths. Instead, their novels focus on the entire space of the war and home fronts, portraying them as dystopic zones where none of the ideals of Saddam's Qadisiyya or the Sacred Defense exist.

Reorienting Martyrdom at Home: Muhsin al-Ramli's Scattered Crumbs

Published in 2000 in Cairo, Muhsin al-Ramli's *Scattered Crumbs* is one of the earliest examples of a novel that subversively moved the focus of the war story away from the soldiers on the front and reoriented it toward both the home front and exile abroad. The novel was al-Ramli's first, and clearly contains elements that parallel his own life, including the village setting and the place of narration, Madrid, where he has lived since 1995.[33] Prior to the novel's publication he had published short stories and poetry. Following *Scattered Crumbs*, he published several novels, poetry and short story collections, and critical essays in both Arabic and Spanish, as well as multiple translations of Arabic literary texts into Spanish. Notably, since 2008, three of his novels have appeared on the longlist of the International Prize for Arabic Fiction. *Scattered Crumbs* was his first work to be published and distributed widely in the Arab world.

The novel tells the story of Hajji 'Ijayel's family (Arabic: *'Ujayl* or *'Ajīl*),[34] which consists of his wife and seven children—all sons, save for one—and their downfall throughout the 1980s in an unnamed Iraqi village. Although the setting is clearly Iraq, the country is named only once throughout the entire novel. Other factors that play major roles in the text, especially the Iran-Iraq War and Saddam Hussein, also go unnamed or are referred to only euphemistically. The nameless narrator tells the story from his adopted country of Spain, where he arrived searching for Mahmud, Hajji 'Ijayel's utterly nondescript son, about whom no one seems to remember a thing. He will not find Mahmud, nor will the narrator tell the readers much about him. In fact, we learn nothing about Mahmud from start to finish. Nearly halfway through the text, the narrator tells us that he does not even know whom he is looking for, that Mahmud is "very ordinary, even more ordinary than an ordinary person."[35] However, his one-time existence and current non-presence become an excuse for telling the story of the rest of his family, particularly one of 'Ijayel's sons, Qasim, and his difficult relationship with his father.

The narrator focuses on Mahmud's siblings: Qasim and, to a lesser extent, Saadi, paying even less attention to the others, who are each essentially reduced to one major eccentricity: 'Abbud (mentally handicapped and often pretending to be a wolf-like animal); Ahmed (a brilliant child who leaves the village for the city to become a judge), 'Abd al-Wahid (the "good son" who is killed in the war with Iran); Warda (the beautiful daughter, who marries numerous times, begets multiple children, and swears revenge on "the Leader" at the end of the novel). For his part, Qasim is a peace-loving artist, electrician, and the creator of his very own style of calligraphy, which he calls "Qasimicalligraphy" (*al-khaṭ al-Qāsimī*), and Saadi (*Saʿdī*) is characterized by his sexual perversions. These latter two have deserted the war front, immediately putting them at odds with their highly nationalistic father and family patriarch, 'Ijayel. For his part, 'Ijayel is a supporter of Saddam Hussein (referred to only as "the Leader" in the novel), and considers his proclamations to be nothing less than the absolute truth. He proudly ascribes to the notion that his eldest son, 'Abd al-Wahid, died as a martyr in the Iran-Iraq War and did so for the sake of what he calls *"nashinan,"* a mispronunciation (described as "Bedouin barbarism") of the English word "national," a word to which he ascribes to all things he deems positive and good for the nation. As described in the novel:

> Ijayel did not buy a product on which "nationon" [*nashinan*] was not written or suggested. If he wished to describe a man or a thing that he liked, he would call it nationan. Among these things were my aunt's beans. He used to say, "Her beans are nationan." [. . .] And among his children he singled out Ahmed, who became a judge, as a nationan son. This was also how he described Abdul-Wahid after his death in the war. As for Qasim and Saadi, "They are not nationan at all because they deserted the army just when the war heated up!"[36]

The conflict between 'Ijayel and his artistically inclined son, Qasim, takes center stage after the latter's refusal to paint a picture of the Leader for his father and his army desertion. Somewhat predictably, this pits the two characters against each other: one who represents the independent artist, on the one hand, and the representative of state power, on the other. With Qasim's refusal, the narrative takes a sharp turn in a sustained critique of the Iraqi Ba'thist regime that lasts for the remainder of the novel, laying bare the repression of political prisoners, war deserters, and anyone who dares dissent. After this moment, the narrative explicitly treats the Iran-Iraq War (referred to only as "the war") and the madness that it creates in the village, depicting Iraqi society under the Ba'th as a nightmare. "The war" becomes the source of the family's complete unraveling, through which the novel offers a counternarrative of the conflict that culminates in the death of 'Ijayel as well as three of his sons.

The second half of the novel is essentially the government narrative of the war recast in a dystopian light. If Saddam's Qadisiyya was a battle cry that pushed the nation forward to the front, the war narrative offered by *Scattered Crumbs* is the story of those who hesitated and who refused to join the war chorus. The novel's alternative to Saddam's Qadisiyya is the home front dystopia where, as the narrator recounts, the "summer grew hotter and the war more voracious. It brought convoys of flags, medals of honor and village youths in coffins back to us."[37] Qasim and Saadi, already imprisoned for deserting the military, are released into this environment. The narrator tells us:

> The war intensified, so the Leader pardoned all military prisoners and returned them to their units. He also released all political prisoners from life and returned them to the belly of their mother earth after they had impregnated the refrigerators for a period long enough for their parents to pay the cost of nooses, the importation of which would have cost the government hard cash.[38]

Scattered Crumbs relies on this ironically subversive mode of narration to describe the system the Ba'thist state foisted on the Iraqi people during the 1980s and tells the story of the family during the Iran-Iraq War. The novel uses a similarly ironic tone to mock Ba'thist wartime ideology through the blindly nationalist character of 'Ijayel, whose speech is a caricature of the party apparatchik. In this way, his speech "over-identifies" with Ba'thist ideology and adds to the general critique of the state and the war offered by the novel. Inke Arns and Sylvia Sasse define "over-identification" as a strategy of resistance writing. This is part of what they recognize as the broader tactics of "subversive affirmation," defined as an "artistic/political tactic that allows artists/activists to take part in certain social, political, or economic discourses and affirm, appropriate, or consume them while simultaneously undermining them."[39] It accurately describes the mode of narration featured in *Scattered Crumbs* as well as in other novels (see Chapter 4) about the same authoritarian period.

As the war intensifies, bringing with it the deaths of 'Ijayel's son, 'Abd al-Wahid, and his son-in-law, Fawzi, so does this mode of writing. The local party head and police chief arrive to give 'Ijayel a medal of honor and congratulate him on the martyrdom of his son-in-law, telling him that Fawzi "was a valiant hero who watered the soil of the precious homeland with his noble blood."[40] The party representative's speech slaps 'Ijayel with the same over-identified, ideological discourse of the state, which he had previously espoused without question. Later, it will be this very ideology that will kill the other son, Qasim, the war deserter, and lead to 'Ijayel's own death. Estranged from his father and refusing to live like a fugitive, Qasim is eventually apprehended by the authorities, who swiftly execute him in public. His final moments, before he is shot and his body left in the open for three days, are dramatically depicted. On the one hand, his death reorients martyrdom toward a different Iraqi nation and away from Saddam's Qadisiyya. On the other, Qasim is sublimated from a man into an idea that encompasses a grieving Iraq:

> A white sun glaring, women weeping, old men trembling, children shrieking, date palms wilting, sparrows flying and Qasim's head and disheveled hair drooping. They shackled his feet, and his hands behind his back. His clothes were stained the colors of red, green, white. And memories of him hovered in the heads that surrounded him.[41]

Qasim's death sets off the final collapse of Hajji 'Ijayel's family. Before his own death as a grief-stricken mute, 'Ijayel witnesses the imprisonment or death of all his children except Warda and Mahmud. The heartbreaking story that was previously punctured by moments of comic relief, now gives way to a purely tragic narrative of anger and loss. In the aftermath of the war, Warda marries Isma'il, a local musician, and together they dream of concocting a plan to kill the Leader, who has turned them all into "scattered crumbs."[42] The postscript, like the preface, returns to the narrator in Spain, giving the book a deliberate and self-conscious feeling of an exilic novel, where the narrator, whose life seems to mirror al-Ramli's own life, writes:

> Here in the streets of Granada, we weep with the Palestinians. We cry like women over homelands that we did not know how to preserve like men. How often have we spat at our mustaches before the mirrors of the West and then ended up shaving them off? We are no good except for blackening the pages of sorrowful cries. I wonder if paper-recycling companies can supply enough sheets for the flood of stories about my homeland.[43]

"Scattered crumbs," then, is a metaphor for the fate of so many Iraqi families that were broken apart under the Ba'th during the war, and whose members were killed, disappeared, and dispersed across the globe. Al-Ramli, like

Hillawi, is one of those scattered crumbs spread across the world because of wars, political repression, and violence in Iraq. The novel narrates the Iraqi experience of the Iran-Iraq War from a perspective that connects the war front to both the home front and the life of a political exile through the character of the war deserter, creating the sense of two wars in the country: the war on the foreign enemy and the war on the domestic political dissident. In so doing, *Scattered Crumbs* is not as concerned with the violence of the war front, but of connecting that violence with the political violence enacted upon civilians and those who tried to escape. By employing a darkly comic and ironic narrative, the novel creates an individualistic counternarrative of the years of the Iran-Iraq War, by focusing on one family and one individual in particular, Qasim, and his story during and preceding the war. The use of humor to balance the otherwise exclusively tragic narrative of the life of one family under dictatorship and war, gives way to complete dystopia following the death of Qasim and 'Ijayel's realization that his total devotion to the state has brought about the reality in which he is forced to live out his remaining days. *Scattered Crumbs* creates an alternative literary narrative of the war to the reality promoted in the literature of Saddam's Qadisiyya. Although the novel is less concerned than Hillawi's with the experience of soldiering on the war front, they both express their opposition to the war foremost through opposition to Ba'thist ideology, first by mocking it, and then vilifying it.

Desacralizing the Sacred Defense in Hossein Mortezaeian Abkenar's Scorpion

The transgressive elements found in the texts analyzed above come together in a surreal mix in Hossein Mortezaeian Abkenar's 2006 novel, *The Scorpion on the Steps of the Andimeshk Railroad, or, Blood is Dripping from this Train, Sir!* (henceforth *The Scorpion*). In chapter 8 of the award-winning Iranian novel, 'Ali, a fellow conscript and friend of the novel's main protagonist, Morteza, rants to him about having to stay at the front while Morteza and another conscript from the unit, Siavash, will soon depart:

> What do you mean you two get to leave and I have to stay here all alone in this middle-of-nowhere desert for another three months? No, I can't, I can't . . . I'm not like those idiots you see who get off from kissing ass

and ratting on others [. . .] They're saying I'll have to stay another four months, but we all know that in four months if the war's not over they won't let us go. We'll end up like those guys over there who do their military service for five years. Poor things. You've seen 'em. Most have white hair, they're old, they have wives and kids, they're hopeless [. . .] I can't deal with this . . . son of a bitch, where can I go to get outta here . . . give me a lighter . . . to hell with this ass of commander [. . .] Here, look, take a souvenir from us, make sure that the MP doesn't catch you . . . do you have a match? No? Forget about it, I have one. Look at its tail, there's a reason they call it a crooked tailed scorpion [*kazhdom*] . . . you know what it does when it's surrounded by fire and can't escape? . . . You don't know? . . . Well, look at this![44]

'Ali then presents Morteza with a scorpion that he encircles with fire. Surrounded by a flame, the scorpion goes into spasms from the heat. Its writhing, bony body thrashes about within the circle, giving the impression that, in a fit of uncontrolled paranoia, the scorpion commits suicide by stabbing itself with its venomous stingers.[45] The crazed, burning scorpion is a metaphor for the Iranian conscript throughout Abkenar's novel. Following its publication with Nay Publishing House, an independent, Tehran-based publisher, *The Scorpion* won several Iranian literary prizes, including the once-prestigious prize for best first novel given by the Hushang Golshiri Foundation. It received a great deal of press and went through three printings in Iran before it was suddenly banned.[46] Paris-based Persian-language publisher Naakojaa reissued the novel in 2012.[47]

The Scorpion presents the most dystopic view of the war front that has been published in contemporary Persian literature. Moreover, beyond pushing the limits of content, Abkenar's novel is also one of the most formally complex fictional representations of the Iran–Iraq War. Set in the final days of the conflict, the novel focuses on Morteza Hedayati, a conscripted soldier from Tehran, discharged and attempting to make his way back home from the war front, via the small town of Andimeshk, which was ravaged during the war.[48] What ensues is a series of nightmarish vignettes framed in a wandering, non-linear narrative that blurs dreams and reality. Before its publication, neither the experience of the battlefront nor the return home had been described in such a hellish and surrealistic manner. Aside from its breaks with what had become conventional modes of writing about the war front experience, the novel incorporates elements of the uncanny and fantastical. Its portrayals of Iranian soldiers are anything but patriotic, with depictions of senior officers and military police as corrupt and cruel, and soldiers as frightened drug users who hate the front and the filth of the trenches. In *The Scorpion* the defense of the homeland is anything but sacred.

Despite all of this, the first page of the novel opens with the following sentence, which a number of Iranian literary critics have latched onto in their critiques of the novel: "All the scenes of this novel are real" (*Tamām-e sahneh-hā-ye in romān vāqeʿi ast*).[49] Not only is this an inversion of the more typical opening statement that absolves the author of all responsibility for any similarities between the events and characters of a fictional work and those of real life, but it makes a claim to a representation of reality that is more typically found in memoirs or biographies, a claim that is even more striking given the plethora of Iranian war memoirs largely published by state-sponsored presses. For a fictional work that relies so heavily on the fantastical, it is no wonder that critics have found it difficult to reconcile that sentence with novel's content. In an interview shortly after the book's publication, Abkenar stated, "Yes, all the novel's scenes are, in fact, true. [But] they have been recreated after passing through my own mental filter."[50] This approach was lauded by some critics for "opening horizons and breaking all the clichés of Iranian war literature,"[51] while doing little to assuage Sacred Defense critics, who condemned the book as "worthless" and "overly pessimistic."[52] These comments demonstrate the bifurcated world of literary criticism as it relates to the Persian literature of the Iran-Iraq War. After assessing whether a literary work is pro- or antiwar, critics, often with known political affiliations, proceed to judge texts along those lines, either faulting them for not sufficiently recognizing the epic, historic nature of the event and the religious and nationalistic sacrifices of soldiers who fought for the survival of the Islamic Republic during the war, or criticizing the writer for being part of the state propaganda machine and glorifying a war that lasted far too long.

The Scorpion's opening scene sets the mood of the novel with a third-person narrator describing the nightmarish world in which Morteza lives:

> Private Morteza Hedayati, dispatched March 1986, from Tehran, sat on the steps of the Andimeshk railroad station, waiting to be taken away. Squatting with his legs up against his chest, he rested his chin on his knees and stared ahead at the asphalt, the trees and green grass covered in blackness. From near and far he could hear bursts of gunfire and the single shots of snipers.
>
> The eyes of soldiers hidden in the brush flashed in the darkness. Military police officers with white boots and tassels hanging from their shoulders were pushing aside leaves and branches as they searched for deserting soldiers. They did not have firearms but carried large flashlights in their hands and batons. A truck trailed nearby, and for any soldier they found two men would take his hands and feet and hurl him into it atop the other soldiers.
>
> [...]
>
> One of the MPs held a large pitchfork. He would stab it into any pile of dirt or a dense bush that he saw and then pull it out, stabbing down and pulling out, stabbing down, and pulling out. Sometimes a soldier would cry out in pain and the MP would forcefully pull up the pitchfork and throw the soldier into the truck, arms and legs flailing in the air. The moaning of soldiers could be heard from inside the truck, as well as the crushing sound of their broken bones.
>
> The weather was hellish. The smell of gunpowder and fish filled the hot air.
>
> [...]
>
> It was around 11:00 pm. Around the year 1988.[53]

In its final chapters, the novel returns to this scene. Its depictions of the military police and other senior officers and platoon leaders are decidedly negative, casting them as the villains of the story. The chapters that connect the opening scene to the end of the story are flashbacks to time spent at the front or the brutal journey to Andimeshk, made first with a crazed, bloodied driver of a dump truck used primarily for the transport of supplies and men, as well as on foot. As an entirely dystopian experience, the war front in *The Scorpion* is represented as a place from which any conscripted soldier wants only to escape, and the journey back is arduous, if not impossible, even if the soldier has properly received his leave, since all soldiers away from the front are assumed to be deserters and are pursued as such.

The novel's description of the war front oscillates between the real and the fantastical. The journey to the Andimeshk Railway Station and the experiences in the war front trenches are its most surrealistic scenes. Yet, scenes such as the opening passage cited above contain a plethora of "realistic" details, largely in the form of olfactory and auditory descriptions. Despite Abkenar's statement that all the novel's scenes are true, its narrative is purposely repetitive and written in a way that defies the possibility of a singular truth from a reliable narrator. The dream-like narration constantly shifts, moving from the first-person narrative of the novel's primary characters, Morteza and Siavash, to a third-person narrator, and occasionally to the monologues of others, such as that of 'Ali above. The other characters whom the narrative treats in passing are given little description and generally say very little. Thus, readers are left with nightmarish impressions, such as that of the large, silent MPs who, like grim reapers, silently beat and kill conscripts, or the bloodied driver of the dump truck peppered with bullet holes who speaks sparsely, eyes glued to the road.

Other scenes explicitly depict nightmares or states of being plainly induced by opium, sleeplessness, or a combination of both, such as when Morteza finds himself offering a cigarette to what appears to be a ghost or zombie.[54] Or, when following what appears to be the death of Siavash for the first of multiple times, he disappears into a flooded foxhole for five days only to reappear in a nightmare in a later chapter.[55] In one scene narrated in the first-person, we read how the water in the foxhole, first clear, becomes muddy, melding into various colors, now disappearing, now reappearing. The punctuation-free paragraph leading up to this scene suddenly shifts: "then there was a sound it was loud like an explosion it was silent the sound reverberated the pool caught on fire yellow orange they screamed a scream echoed a ring of fire surrounded the pool fire and orange yellow fire the sound of screaming was everywhere everyone up in this and that direction they flew past me they fell into the water out of fear of the fire[.]"[56]

This recurring, experimental mode of narration gives *The Scorpion* its sense of instability and unreliability, calling into question everything that might (or might not) have happened at the war front. It is also this mode of narration that largely characterizes Morteza's return to Tehran from the front as well. However, once he boards the train and eventually returns home, the narrative switches to a second-person narrator who talks to Morteza reassuringly, in a way that confirms that the nightmare of the front is over. He boards the train and we read the following:

> The train conductor comes. He asks if you are a deserter. You say no. Show your release papers! They are in your pack. They are torn. That MP 'Abdol Khan tore them up. The conductor is kind. He leaves ... He comes again and says that before you reach Tehran, you must get off the train. The railway station is full of officers. They will think you are a deserter.
>
> [...]
>
> When you reach Tehran you run, faster and faster from the main street, to the alley, to the door of your house. Run! You're panting. When your mother hears the door open, her heart drops.
>
> She opens the door: Oh! Oh! She puts her head on your chest and weeps. You kiss her veil. Your father stands behind her, his pride not allowing him to cry.
>
> [...]
>
> The next day your father rushes home. He puts a box of fruit on the floor and turns on the radio. He says that cars are honking their horns. Their lights are on. People are passing out sweets in the streets. It is peacetime. Your mother cries in her chador. She says "Thank God! Thank God!"
>
> That night your father leans back against the wall and holds the radio up to his ear. Your mother spreads the mattress and sheets on the floor, and you sleep.[57]

The difference between the lines in this chapter and those in the remainder of the novel is clear. The stability of home is associated with a mode of writing that is stable and well-defined, confidently voiced by a seemingly omniscient second-person narrator. There is no doubt as to what happens in this scene, and it is clearly written outside the circular and winding narrative of the rest of the novel. The nightmare of the war front is over.

The representation of the war front in *The Scorpion* goes beyond what other literary works that challenge the official narrative offer, which is usually on the level of content. This is not to say that the novel does not put forth content-oriented challenges to the official representations of the war; it clearly does—as in its portrayal of the war front and the senior military officers that completely defies the Sacred Defense's cultural representations of the war. The novel depicts a war that is at once macabre and monotonous, a war whose only givens are uncertainty and self-doubt. It relies on a narrative that constantly calls into question its own record of events while simultaneously claiming that it is a truthful record.

In this way, I propose a reading of *The Scorpion* guided by Brian McHale's definition of a post-modernist historical novel, which he calls "revisionist" in two ways. Firstly, he states that this type of writing "revises the content of the historical record, reinterpreting [. . . and], often demystifying or debunking the orthodox version of the past. Secondly, it revises, [. . . and] transforms the conventions and norms of historical fiction itself."[58] According to McHale,

> The two meanings of revisionism converge especially in the postmodernist strategy of apocryphal or alternative history. Apocryphal history contradicts the official version in one of two ways: either it supplements the historical record, claiming to restore what has been lost or suppressed; or it displaces official history altogether. In the first of these cases, apocryphal history operates in the "dark areas" of history, apparently in conformity to the norms of "classic" historical fiction but in fact parodying them. In the second case, apocryphal history spectacularly violates the "dark areas" constraint. In both cases, the effect is to juxtapose the officially-accepted version of what happened and the way things were, with another, often radically dissimilar version of the world. The tension between these two versions induces a form of ontological flicker between the two worlds: one moment, the official version seems to be eclipsed by the apocryphal version; the next moment, it is the apocryphal version that seems mirage-like, the official version appearing solid, irrefutable.[59]

This describes *The Scorpion* well.[60] The novel approaches the war not only in a radically different manner from works of Sacred Defense fiction but also in a way that is distinct from other works of subversive fiction dealing with the Iran–Iraq War, such as the novels and short stories of Ahmad Dehqan, or similarly-minded writers like Habib Ahmadzadeh, Hasan Bani-Ameri, or Davud Ghaffarzadegan. These authors, whose works are often hailed as straying from the state narrative of the conflict despite sometimes having published their books with the primary state publishing house, Sureh-ye Mehr (Ahmadzadeh, Dehqan, and Ghaffarzadegan), write war stories that operate solely in the "dark areas" of the official narrative. In so doing, their texts, such as Dehqan's *Journey*, or the stories contained in *I Killed Your Son* or Ahmadzadeh's *Chess with the Doomsday Machine* (*Shatranj bā Māshin-e Qiāmat*), do not seek to displace the sanctioned, "official-accepted" historical record. Rather, they work within it, in the manner of an exposé or with the intention of deromanticizing or challenging aspects of that narrative.[61] Herein lies the significance of Abkenar's novel. On the level of content, it attacks the assumed heroism of the Iranian military and is totally devoid of the ideological language of the Sacred Defense narrative. At one point, when Morteza finds himself in the coffeehouse with the truck driver, it even takes a clear stab at the highest levels of governmental war leadership by mocking the television broadcast of a bumbling "beardless sheikh," who struggles to explain Iran's massive losses near the end of the conflict—a barely concealed epithet for the late Akbar Hashemi Rafsanjani, one of Iran's leading politicians and de facto commander in chief during the war.[62] However, beyond the cruel MPs and misery of the trenches, the novel's dystopic vision of the front attacks the war itself,—not simply for its negative consequences, like Dehqan, but for its very existence. On a formal level, *The Scorpion*'s fragmented and repetitive narrative and constant questioning of events cast doubt on the self-assured narrative of victory promoted in Sacred Defense literature, and the forms that Sacred Defense fiction usually take, epitomized by the war memoir of soldiers loyal to the state's framing of the war or war novels that follow such characters. In contrast, *The Scorpion* iconoclastically refuses to engage in the portrayal of Iranian soldiers as heroes, disenchants their sacrifices, and grinds away at the narrative of Sacred Defense's monopolistic claim to truth about the war.

THE BATTLEFIELD OF REPRESENTATION

In some works of postwar Iranian and Iraqi fiction, the war front—the site of most state-sponsored wartime literature—has emerged as a site of struggle over the representation of the Iran-Iraq War. The strategies of the highlighted writers contesting the official narratives' monopoly on truth range from attempting to redefine the meaning of war front death, to shedding light on the elements that the official narrative has silenced, like doubtful and deserting soldiers. In both cases, they upend the utopian image of the war propagated most by early official literatures and elevate the dystopian nature of war front soldiering and combat. The texts examined in this chapter deliberately sully an otherwise sanitized history of heroism presented by state-sponsored narratives and are, therefore, apocryphal in the eyes of officialdom.

While the exact themes and approaches to the war highlighted here vary, there are clear sites of thematic and formal overlap between the writers of these two countries. Perhaps the most important of these is the focus on the individual and hence, the rise of subjective narratives of difference vis-à-vis the sonic boom of state-sponsored war choruses. Regardless of thematic focus, each text in this chapter uses the individual as a vehicle of dissent to create narratives that deviate from the ideological limits of war writing in Ba'thist Iraq and the Islamic Republic of Iran. Moreover, these novels also challenge the official literatures on a formal level. On the one hand, they transform the war novels promoted by the wartime states by emptying them of their heroic content and filling them with graphic horror and fear. On the other, they offer fragmented narratives that upend the chronology and easy understandings of what really happened at the war front, defying the official literatures' supposed "truthful" representation of the war.

That said, this chapter's texts also highlight some of the salient differences in postwar Iraqi and Iranian literary responses to the war. Iraqi literary condemnation of the war inevitably brings with it the denunciation of Saddam Hussein and the Ba'th Party. The cult of personality, authoritarian state, and the war with Iran, are conflated and attacked in a way that is unparalleled in Iranian literature and is a defining characteristic of critical Iraqi literary responses to the war. Additionally, Iraqi writers who took increasingly condemnatory positions on the war and its consequences—Hillawi and al-Ramli among them—did so from exile and published outside Iraq. This harkens back to the tension between "internal" and "external" literatures (*adab al-dākhil* and *adab al-khārij*) in the Iraqi literary scene that began in the 1970s and continued until at least 2003.[63] The relevance of exilic writers since the mid-1970s to Iraqi literature may very well surpass that of Iran and this is particularly true regarding writers who have written about this conflict. Exilic Iranian fiction has largely been muted on the war front experience of the Iran-Iraq War, with writers far more often choosing instead to focus on the 1979 Revolutionary moment, the status of women in the country, or political prisoners, for example. When it does appear in exilic Iranian literature dealing with the 1980s, the war with Iraq is usually treated as background noise or a passing incident rather than the main event.[64] By contrast, many exilic Iraqi writers have chosen the path with which al-Ramli and Hillawi are associated: the writer who uses fiction to recover Iraq's recent past from Ba'thist historiography and critique the regime that silenced all forms of dissent. These writers often write the war with Iran as the first episode of multiple wars into a larger narrative of conflict and loss that has afflicted the Iraqi people since 1980.[65] The ideological positions of these oppositional writers vary, but they are unified in their resistance to the war and the state. Their approach is not to write around or reorient the terms of the conflict but to attack fundamental elements of the state, the war with Iran, and Saddam Hussein.

In Iran, sustained state support for literature and other forms of cultural production related to the war, alongside the absence of any other major international conflict comparable in size to the Iran-Iraq War, has meant that since 1988, Iranian writers have written more works of fiction dealing exclusively with this war than their Iraqi counterparts. This makes a writer such as Dehqan not only relevant, but also extremely important within Iran. He can be a rebellious writer precisely because of his status as a privileged "insider" to the official cultural establishment. As a writer supported by the state and who writes largely in defense of it (despite his works analyzed here), he does not find a contemporary parallel among Iraqi writers in the years of Ba'thist rule following the Iran-Iraq War, despite the existence of "formal antonyms" described in Chapter 2.[66] This difference in the sociopolitical conditions of literary production is a factor that must be considered when comparing how writers from both countries have approached the conflict in the postwar period.

The following chapter continues the survey of Iran-Iraq War counter-narratives by returning to the home front, as examined in Chapter 2, but looking at texts published primarily in the early aughts and centering the very role of the artist and their ability to resist the power of the wartime state. In doing so, it demonstrates how exilic Iraqi writers told a home front war story that was far more critical of the war and the Ba'th Party in the first years of the twenty-first century just before or after Saddam Hussein's overthrow. Their Iranian counterparts employed similar techniques but with a different temporality, demonstrating the changing importance the state has given the war in that country. In all cases, stepping back from the war front to the home front gives rise to a different perspective of the conflict and allows writers to reorient the narratives of war around language and civilian experiences of home.

Four
WRITERS' HOME FRONT WARS

THE HOME FRONT, THE CIVILIAN CENTERS THAT WERE NOT SITES OF direct clashes between the Iranian and Iraqi militaries, was part of the story of the Iran-Iraq War from the very beginning. Cities and villages across Iran and Iraq supplied the war front with thousands of men for combat and they received these veterans afterward, physically well, wounded, or dead, and in all the equivalent mental states. With their strategies of total war, the two wartime governments called upon civilians to play a part in the effort by boosting the morale of the troops. As such, men, women, and children, willingly or unwillingly, showed their support for the troops through rallies, parades, and donating money and time to support the war effort.

The "wars of the cities," as they were called, brought the war front violence directly to the home front through extensive bombing campaigns by each country's air force and the use of long-range missiles, primarily between 1984 and 1988. Although each side strategically bombed the other's civilians in an attempt to beat those populations into submission, in the war's early stages they had the opposite effect. The severe disruptions to daily life in both countries and the number of casualties angered civilians and caused them to rally around the governments' causes.[1] In the last four years of bombings, nearly 1,500 Iranian and 300 Iraqi civilians were killed. The uneven numbers reflected the relative superiority in air power of the Iraqi military during the conflict due to its ability to obtain weapons easily from several international sources.² Scenes of chaos unleashed by these aerial attacks feature prominently in the literature that takes place on the home front.³

Although a small body of fiction highlighting civilian experiences was written during wartime, stories of soldiers dominated each side's war literature during those years. As Chapter 2 demonstrated, home front stories began to appear with greater frequency in the postwar years, and it emerged as the site of some of the first serious critiques of the war's official narratives. The texts presented in this chapter complement and expand upon the home front narratives featured in Chapter 2 but are distinct. On the one hand, they create a greater distance between the war front and the home front by taking the latter as their point of departure, never venturing toward the battlefield where soldiers killed each other. On the other, there was a greater distance between the war and the time of their publication. The texts I analyze in this chapter were published between 1999 and 2015. They represent another wave of engagement with the Iran-Iraq War on the part of writers who chose to continue grappling with the civilian experience of the war. By keeping the battleground in the background and focusing on various aspects of home front life, these writers demonstrate how some civilians attempted to resist being consumed by the overpowering nature of the state-sponsored war cultures.

The first half of this chapter examines how two postwar writers transformed the home front into a starting point for a completely different kind of war story. The 1999 novel *Kam Badat al-Samā' Qarība* (translated as *A Sky So Close*) by Iraqi author Betool Khedairi (b. 1965), and "Naqqāsh-e Bāghāni" ("The Painter of Baghan"), a short story by Iranian author Hushang Golshiri (1938–2000), create discursive confrontations between the official war culture and the very personal act of writing fiction. These war narratives never engage in direct confrontations with the governments' discourse. Instead, stories of civilian wartime life represent struggles between the independent artist and the attempt by official discourses to overrun civilian and artistic life. The second half of the chapter analyzes two short novels that take place on the home front: *I'jām* (*I'jaam: An Iraqi Rhapsody*) by Iraqi author Sinan Antoon (b. 1967), and *Divār* (*The Wall*) by Iranian writer 'Alireza Gholami

(b. 1978). The antihero protagonists of these two novels represent writers' struggles to rebel against states that have transformed the home front into a prison, by mocking the state and its discourse in a manner that reflected contemporary reality for Iraqi and Iranian writers. In both cases, however, the protagonists and their attempts to resist fail and they are assumed to be killed by the state.

WRITERS' WARS
Art and Resistance on the Iraqi Home Front in Betool Khedairi's A Sky So Close

In 1999, Amman-based Iraqi writer Betool Khedairi (Arabic: *Bitūl al-Khidayrī*) published her first novel, a bildungsroman titled *A Sky so Close* simultaneously in both Beirut and Amman. It has since gone through five printings in Arabic and was translated and published in English in 2001. The novel mirrors several aspects of Khedairi's life. It is narrated by an unnamed young woman who grows up with her English mother and Iraqi father in a small village outside Baghdad called al-Zaʿfraniyya, before moving to Baghdad and finally leaving the country for the U.K. Throughout the novel, she is torn between the clashing values and mores of her mother, who feels increasingly estranged in Iraq, and her father, a chemist who creates flavors for a large food company and dies during the narrator's teenage years. Its ten chapters take readers through a period that begins in the late 1960s and ends just after the 1990–91 Gulf War.

The narrator's childhood in the village, her early teenage years in Baghdad, and her parents' increasingly fraught relationship dominate the novel's first three chapters. The memoir-like narrative recounts a world through the eyes of a child who associates far more with her Iraqi father than her English mother, who is portrayed as cold and insensitive to local culture. More than just two adults who have fallen out of love with one another, the parents' rocky relationship plays out as a clash of civilizations between an occasionally cliched "East" and "West," and complicates the narrator's understanding of her own identity. Despite the slow disintegration of the parents' marriage, the novel's first section, with its focus on the slow passage of time in a bucolic Iraqi village and the sensual vibrancy of sounds, colors, and tastes experienced for the first time by a child, gives the novel a sense of an idyllic life in 1970s Iraq, a time now sometimes referred to as "the days of plenty" (*ayyām al-khayr*). Despite an increasingly tight political environment and rising xenophobia, it was a time when the country experienced no wars with foreign states, and for those who did not criticize the regime, there were opportunities for economic advancement.[4] In the late 1970s, the family moves to Baghdad after the father has a heart attack and the narrator's best friend, a coeval girl from the village named Khadduja, dies from bilharziasis.[5] For her part, the mother had always wanted to work outside the home and insisted that her daughter grow up in a more cosmopolitan environment, get a better education, and learn ballet, all of which were possible in Baghdad. The move, however, exacerbates the parents' marital problems, leading the mother to ask for a divorce. Meanwhile, ballet becomes the focus of the narrator's life.

With the outbreak of the Iran-Iraq War the novel's narration changes abruptly. The fourth chapter opens with a radio broadcast of one of the ubiquitous songs of Saddam's Qadisiyya. A "Bedouin voice," the narrator writes, sings *"Oh mother, on my wedding night the cannon sings throughout the night.../ Oh mother, whoever smells the gunpowder, smells cardamom."* She continues:

> A few months after the full mobilization, our lives are transformed into mere fragments of the lives we had before the war. They soon became a series of days that resembled memories. The events that followed started sliding into each other, like drops of mercury, slowly blending into a gelatinous ball, growing and growing. As the number of military communiques from the government increases, the misty undulations of the mercury ball become distorted in our dreams, and our days are trapped between two questions: Why and until when?[6]

The militarization of society is a watershed moment in the novel and the narration is quickly caught up in it. The Ba'thification of Iraqi society takes center stage, prominently depicted through the government's incessant messaging of victory that punctures the narrator's personal journey. In this way, the Iran-Iraq War creates a palpable background throughout the entire second section of *A Sky So Close*, consisting of chapters 4-6. The war is told through intertextual descriptions of the home front images and sounds of Saddam's Qadisiyya, and through the songs and the televised broadcasts of *Images from the Battlefield*. The narrator writes, "We became acquainted with the events of the battlefield through news bulletins about military clashes that flared up at Zayn al-Kaws and Saif Sa'ad. We learned new terms like 'usurped territories,' 'regaining Arab rights,' 'protecting the homeland,' and 'repelling aggression.'"[7] Meanwhile, the narrator's life is upturned: her father dies from a heart attack, her ballet lessons are canceled because of the war, she falls in love with a sculptor, Salim, whom she meets through her ballet instructor, "Madam," and her mother is diagnosed with breast cancer. All throughout, military communiques constantly break the flow of the narrative. The narrator finds herself unable to escape them, as in the following scene when she first walks into Salim's studio during a social gathering. She admires his sculptures, but her attempt to appreciate them is interrupted as "reports of the military analysts circulate among the works of art, like disembodied voices swirling around each other in the ether." We read:

> Waves of men flowed down onto the battlefield. Our forces repelled the attack by these infinite hordes, preventing the enemy from achieving his dream in reaching the border. They were attempting to create a breach in the front over a small distance. To this end they gathered in exceptionally large numbers. Our forces in that area, the al-Sheeb Pass, which is eleven kilometers wide, remain steadfast and brave.[8]

These interruptions continue until the war concludes near the end of the novel's sixth chapter. Despite their damage to the novel's flow, the narrator never dwells on them. Instead, she ignores them or, at most, treats them as a nuisance. The passage below illustrates this. After a short-lived relationship develops between the narrator and Salim, she receives a letter from him informing her that he will be unable to return on his scheduled leave and that he will likely be assigned to deliver soldiers' corpses to their surviving families. She attempts to read the letter but writes that "the voice of the newscaster follows me like a nightmare: In the battles that the enemy embarked upon, several enemy soldiers were taken prisoner. It has emerged that among those prisoners are several children whose age does not exceed sixteen years old..."[9]

A second letter arrives two weeks later. The narrator attempts to read it amid the cacophony of official media, a voice speaks of "economic growth alongside the rifle" and the imperative of fighting the war on all fronts, including "civilian institutions, schools, hospitals and governmental offices." Salim's letter contains echoes of her own experience while describing a hellish ride to deliver the body of a former soldier:

> *Attempting to switch the radio station is pointless. All I get are verses from the Koran, a military communique, greetings from the soldiers at the front to their families, a patriotic song, or the hissing of a station that has gone off air. . .I delivered the martyr, or what remained of him, to his family. Nights without end have gone by and I remain unable to sleep, so I write to you. Forgive me if I've become a different person.*[10]

Shortly after that he returns on leave, internally broken, and "in a moment of despair and frustration" destroys his own sculptures.[11] The narrator's relationship with him quickly falls apart and she soon leaves the country accompanying her ill mother to receive cancer treatment in the U.K. From there, the novel enters a third and final phase that focuses on the difficulties of integration into British society and the experience of watching the U.S. bombings of Iraq during Operation Desert Storm.

During the significant portion of the novel that dwells on life during the Iran-Iraq War, the narrative deftly navigates the ubiquitous official war discourse of Saddam's Qadisiyya. It avoids confrontation by never condemning the war outright, even if it often presents the official war discourse as a caricature of itself. Its approach is similar to Muhsin al-Ramli's in *Scattered Crumbs* or Sinan Antoon's in *I'jaam*, albeit less blatantly confrontational than either of those novels. Rather, *A Sky So Close* uses the home front experience of the Iran-Iraq War to expose another battle taking place within Iraqi society during the 1980s: a battle over expression and individuality between the regime and the artists it sponsored and the artists who wished to remain independent. This battle plays out in several moments throughout the novel: Salim's sculpture studio, Madam's ballet recital, and the narrator's strict unwillingness to engage with the discourse of Saddam's Qadisiyya. Read in this light, such scenes emerge as sites of struggle between regime partisans and those who attempted to resist.

In all three cases, the artists lose these battles, but in doing so they highlight attempts to resist submitting to the production of official war culture.

For Salim, he tells the narrator that the tortured sculptures he produces "express what is happening outside [...] and the outside is killing what is inside me."[12] Similar to how the military communiques force themselves into civilian life, the war forces itself onto his sculptures, as in one of his works that is described as a "life-size sculpture of a newborn baby [whose] umbilical cord extends from his abdomen to a placenta in the shape of a combat helmet." Or another of "a woman breast-feeding her baby. A pair of khaki helmets protrud[ing] from her chest wall where her breasts should be."[13] Salim ultimately finds himself unable to produce more sculpture, and his experience in the war drives him to destroy his art.

In a second case, the narrator's ballet instructor, "Madam," whose school is shut down during the war, accepts "the constraints of the current circumstances" to direct and star in a performance by the National Youth Theatre titled "Light." The narrator and Salim go to see it and realize that, without making explicit reference to it, the performance is profoundly antiwar. It portrays two peoples, separated by a river, who go to war over access to the sun. At one point during the performance, Madam, in character, tells the young actors that "light entered the eye and did not leave it. Were it not for this fact, we would be unable to see each other. If the warfare continued, the sun would be angered, and the curse of darkness would ensue." Hearing those words, the narrator realizes that this would be her former ballet instructor's final performance:

> I admired her beauty from afar. I wasn't sure whether she was dancing for her dream or for her mother, who hadn't left their house since the day of her divorce. Her father was of Iranian extraction. When they separated, he'd taken his son with him and headed to Tehran; her mother had kept her here. Maybe she was dancing for her only brother, who was fighting in the Iranian army. She hadn't met him for several years; the Shatt al-Arab had become a barrier between them.[14]

The novel stages the performance as a postwar depiction of what al-Musawi calls "indirection" during the 1980s, an approach to cultural production that avoided censorship through "suggestion, implication, juxtaposition, and gaps that involve the reader in comparisons."[15]

The artistic battle against state war culture is waged most prominently by the narrator herself whose testimony of middle-class civilian life during wartime focuses solely on what the war has tragically done to Iraq. Told from this angle, the Iran-Iraq War becomes a personal tragedy, a pointless war consisting of seemingly interminable acts of violence, each more barbaric than the last. The narrator refrains from ever mentioning Saddam Hussein's name or the war's epithet of Qadisiyya, even though the book was first published outside Iraq ten years after the war with Iran ended, and the author also resided in Jordan at the time. While this might be part of the author's "desire to locate her work within a unique framework of Iraqi literary convention"[16] that purposely avoids mention of the dictator, it can also be seen as a concerted effort on the part of the narrator (and author) to wage her own personal literary defense against the project of Saddam's Qadisiyya literature and to keep the war and its ideology at a deliberate distance.[17] Viewed from this angle, my reading of the novel concurs with that of Masmoudi, who sees it as "a form of cultural resistance criticizing the damage done to cultural and social life in Iraq"—and that dance, sculpture, and the author's writing itself, "not only provide testimony but make it their cultural and ethical obligation to stand against the censorship and co-optation of art."[18]

In the final third of *A Sky So Close*, the narrator's mother has a mastectomy in Iraq, is given permission to leave the country, and decides to pursue further treatment in the U.K. Once there, however, it becomes clear that she will soon die. The narrator decides to accompany her and leave Iraq forever. This part of the novel tells the story of the mother's chemotherapy, the narrator's frustration with life in the U.K., and the experience of watching Operation Desert Storm on television. In connecting the experience of the Iran-Iraq War to the next war in Iraq and the ensuing sanctions against the country, *A Sky So Close* is an early example of Iraqi literature that periodizes the contemporary history of Iraq through wars, now a hallmark of contemporary Iraqi fiction, and particularly novels written after 2003.

In *A Sky So Close,* the 1990–91 Gulf War quickly overshadows the war with Iran and reinforces the narrator's status as an outsider in the U.K. This war, like the previous one, is in the background, although more physically distant than before, viewed from the mother and daughter's new lives in London. For the narrator, the frustrations of life in the new city are amplified by witnessing the world's first major war that was televised in real time, with the bombing of Iraq broadcast worldwide like a video game. The narrator watches American pilots reflect on their recent bombing missions. "It was like lighting up a Christmas tree!" exclaims one, while another says it was "like a game of football. At first, a player hesitates because he's afraid and hasn't got the self-confidence, but after you press the button for the first time, you get into the game and start attacking."[19] Outside Iraq, the war appeared as a simulacrum of a real war, with the sides so unevenly matched and the bombing so crassly displayed in major media outlets that Jean Baudrillard famously declared it to be the "war that did not take place."[20]

In the meantime, the mother's cancer rapidly worsens, and her condition becomes an allegory for Iraq as the country buckled under the allied bombardment and the ensuing sanctions, which have been called "the cruelest [. . .] in the history of international governance."[21] The narrator's life in London is now besieged by news from her disintegrating homeland and the rapidly dying patients in her mother's cancer ward. Madam sends her a letter, writing, "[C]arbonated drinks have become items from another planet, they are so expensive. . .Cultural activities are headed for extinction. Hunger and culture compete with each other and we've come to know boredom well [. . .] Depression is available to everyone, free of charge."[22] *A Sky So Close* concludes with the narrator's abortion after a brief affair with a French man in London, followed by her mother's drawn-out death. She decides to stay in London, with the situation in Iraq so dire that the thought of returning is all but impossible. The novel's hopelessness finds parallels in texts by other contemporary Iraqi women writers who witnessed Iraq become a hollowed-out shell of itself throughout the 1990s. Examples include, among others, Dunya Mikha'il's poetry collection *al-Ḥarb Taʻmal Bijadd* (*The War Works Hard*, 2000), Hadiya Hussein's *Mā Bʻad al-Ḥubb* (*Beyond Love*, 2003), and Iqbal al-Qazwini's *Mamarrāt al-Sukūt* (*Corridors of Silence*, 2006). That several Iraqi women writers rose to prominence in the first decades of the twenty-first century by publishing these types of novels has not gone unnoticed. Using Iraqi author Inaam Kachachi's term, "the granddaughters of Scheherazade," to describe these writers, Masmoudi writes that "these novels portray women as witnesses and survivors of different calamities, be they war, detention or economic hardship. The task of bearing witness is specifically incumbent upon women, who as survivors speak up for themselves but also [. . .] for those who disappeared, whether inside the dictator's jails, in mass graves or in successive wars."[23]

Despite its multiple intertextual references to state war culture, *A Sky So Close* displays a remarkable lack of direct engagement with the Iraqi state's war narrative of the Iran-Iraq War. Instead, it plainly presents the state's version of the war and invites readers to see it at face value as propaganda. At times, the narrative hints at events during the Iran-Iraq War that other authors and filmmakers have blatantly criticized, such as the Iraqi military's use of gas or Madam's father being kicked out of the country for allegedly having an Iranian background. However, it offers no judgment or analysis of such things, instead pushing forward and focusing almost solely on the narrator's personal life. By conspicuously avoiding any direct engagement with the Ba'athist regime's politics and policies, Khedairi offers a belated resistance to the efforts of the regime to control all aspects of cultural production that deal with the war, and highlights a form of civilian resistance to the state's attempt at controlling the entire cultural field. The intense focus on the individual civilian allows for the development of an alternative war narrative that reorients the experience of the Iran-Iraq War around writerly and artistic attempts to resist being swallowed by state discourse.

When Writing is Futile: Hushang Golshiri's "The Painter of Baghan"
Writing and publishing from outside Iraq facilitated the critical way that Khedairi and others wrote about the Iran-Iraq War in the 1990s and early aughts. Her transformation of the conflict into individualistic resistance to state war discourse also has counterparts among contemporary Iranian writers who gave voice to the perspective of the home front. One of the finest examples of this can be found in the late Hushang Golshiri's short story "Naqqāsh-e Bāghāni" ("The Painter of Baghan"). Golshiri is widely recognized as one of Iran's foremost literary innovators in the twentieth century. Between the early 1960s and his early death in 2000 in Tehran, he published several short story collections and novels, alongside numerous essays of

literary and cultural criticism. "The Painter of Baghan" first appeared in his 1994 short story collection *Dast-e Tārik, Dast-e Roshan* ("Dark Hand, Light Hand"), which was published before his death. The entire collection is marked by its simple language and style compared to the complicated prose and sometimes flowery language with which he had previously become associated. Some critics have seen "The Painter of Baghan" as one of his best works, with Iranian writer Amir Hasan Cheheltan, for example, calling it not only a masterpiece of Persian fiction, but of world literature.[24]

The story begins with a family's departure from Tehran during a period of Iraqi bombing which destroys buildings in their neighborhood. "When, three alleys over, a missile directly landed on a three-story building that now no longer exists, we decided to hit the road," says the unnamed narrator, who also happens to be a writer.[25] Their car contains six people: the narrator and his wife, Parichehr, who is a painter and whom he calls "Banu," their two children, and Parichehr's maternal uncle, "the Engineer" (*Mohandes*), and his wife, Mehri, who is seven months pregnant. They set off toward Alamut, northwest of Tehran, for a village called Baghan, where they have a house to stay in and will presumably be far from Iraqi missiles. The story's opening gives readers the impression that it will be engaged with the war, but it takes a very different path, meandering through the family's trip to the area around Alamut and their stay in the village, Mehri's obsession with the landscape paintings that adorn the house where they stay, and the narrator's return to Baghan a few years later to find the painter of the landscapes.

Aside from the first reference to the Iraqi bombardment of Tehran and a few passing references to the conflict, there is no mention of the war in the story. On the second night after arriving at their destination, the Engineer tells the narrator "Last night a missile struck close to the Alstom power plant." The narrator brushes his comment aside and quickly responds, "We came here so that we wouldn't have to think about that anymore."[26] Like the narrator of *A Sky So Close*, the narrator of this short story tries to ignore the war, despite it being the very factor that creates the conditions for the story to exist. Once the immediacy of the war is pushed aside, two other elements of "The Painter of Baghan" are developed. The first is the narrator's frustration over his inability to complete any of his writings for the past few years—which correspond to the years since the revolution and war—and the second is Mehri's fixation on the landscape paintings adorning the house they stay in, which appear to be exact replicas of the landscapes as she saw them on their way to the village. She is consumed by a desire to discover who the painter is and how she can acquire one of the paintings. Her fascination with them leads her to behave strangely, almost as if a sort of metaphysical connection existed between her and the painter. She is seemingly struck by a sense of confusion and an inability to distinguish between what she has seen in real life and what the paintings depict.

Once Mehri's fascination passes, the story's narrative gently shifts to the narrator's inability to produce new writing and the creative process of writing itself. On four occasions in the story, the narrator states that before going to Baghan he had suffered from writer's block, rendering him unable to write or publish. The story itself seems to mark a new beginning for him as a writer. "I write," he says in the opening paragraph. "That's clear. I write fiction. But it had been a while that I hadn't written anything new. A few years, I think. I'll tell you why later. What I'm writing right now is a personal report."[27] While not mentioned directly, the narrator's creative block clearly occurred during the war years. And, like Mehri, it seems as if he, too, was enamored by something magical in Baghan. There, he twice experienced a charmed state, "as if he found himself in the fog suspended over the valley," where his creativity was once again reborn.

The inability to write has affected the narrator, but in conversation with the Engineer it emerges that certain conditions have also made writing impossible. Chatting beside a late-night fire, the narrator tells him that it is not that he has not written at all; rather,

> I wrote things that are all sitting, half completed. Then, I also told him that there was a time when I thought that one could change the world through writing. Now, though, I know that an artistic work doesn't even have an effect on its own writer, let alone society. That's why I think the social function of art is a long-term matter and so politics and social issues can't be the sole motivation for the writer to keep working, and I'm not talking here about political writing.[28]

Unable to sleep, Mehri, who has overheard the conversation between the two men, emerges and interrupts them. While her husband goes to get her another blanket, a conversation ensues between her and the narrator:

> "Isn't writing like childbirth, in that one is absolutely forced to write at a particular moment?"
>
> "Sometimes things like that happen, but honestly, the end product doesn't have any relationship to a child except that one can point to it and say 'that's it, it is what it is.'"
>
> "If it's not an obligation, why does a person have to break his back to create a few paintings that will outlive him?"

Mehri then observes how the painter of the landscapes seemingly created his works effortlessly, "without the slightest sign of pain or pressure, as if his hand had painted it on its own."[29] It becomes apparent in the story that this level of artistry can only come from that very state of "suspension" (*taʿliq*) that the narrator feels in Baghan and which Mehri recognizes in the paintings, a state that can only appear far away from Tehran, which was being bombarded and was the epicenter of the state's war messaging.

The family returns to Tehran soon afterward, and the story skips ahead. Some three years later, the narrator tells the Engineer that he would like to go to Alamut and that he would like to try to locate the landscape painter who lives in Baghan. The following morning, he sets off with a photographer friend. They easily locate the man and approach him. He is seventy-two years old, has lived in the village for twenty-two years and does nothing but paint landscapes from his verandah. He invites the narrator into his home and tells them a little about his life, while beginning to create another landscape. He survives from the food and other items the villagers and travelers give him in exchange for paintings and wants nothing else. His wife is dead; his daughters are married and have what they need. He has devoted his life to painting. Watching him, the narrator writes, "Once again, I felt like I was suspended between the sky and the ground. I held my breath so that he wouldn't realize I was watching him paint from behind his back."[30]

"The Painter of Baghan" offers yet another postwar account of creating art during wartime. It treats the war with Iraq as first and foremost a disruption to peaceful civilian life and its creative potential. In this sense, it relates to the narrative of the war put forth in *A Sky So Close*, although as a professional writer, Golshiri's protagonist finds more in common with the secondary characters of Khedairi's novel—Madam and Salim—than with the narrator herself. The narrator's inability to write occurs during a time when cultural producers felt compelled to address the war in a limited way through in their writing. For Golshiri's narrator, that task was impossible. The reason lies in one of the quotations cited earlier. While in Baghan, the narrator tells the Engineer, "[T]there was a time when I thought that one could change the world through writing. Now, though, I know that an artistic work doesn't even affect its own writer, let alone society. That's why I think the social function of art is a long-term matter, and so politics and social issues can't be the sole motivation for the writer to keep working."[31] The environment for cultural producers within Iran during the war was especially oppressive, aside from being obviously dangerous due to Iraqi bombing. The government tried to compel writers to produce war literature in service of the state and supportive of the state's war story. These were fundamentally part of the "politics and social issues" that constrain the narrator. It also seems to mirror Golshiri's personal predicament for part of the 1980s. After publishing prolifically and to much acclaim in the late 1960s and 1970s, he published only a few short stories in the early 1980s before publishing a short story collection, *Panj Ganj* (*Five Treasures*), in Sweden in 1989. For him, too, the establishment of an Islamic Republic and the strict censorship it brought, alongside the seemingly endless war, prevented his creative state from flourishing. Golshiri's engagement with the war in "The Painter of Baghan" and his depiction of the narrator represent the overall situation of Iranian writers within Iran at the time vis-à-vis the war. Publishing in the mid-1990s, Golshiri's reflective, postwar resistance to the state's attempt at overpowering its writers and intellectuals entirely avoids mentioning its wartime or postwar discourse. Instead, his critique of the wartime environment hints at what the state took away: the ability for certain writers to publish and, in some cases, to even find their own voice.

Ex post facto, *A Sky So Close* and "The Painter of Baghan" depict the frustrations that independent writers on the home front had during the war and the difficult conditions that the wartime governments created for them. They do so in ways that reflect the contemporary publishing environments for both Iranian and Iraqi writers and, of course, the personal literary styles of these two distinct authors. With *A Sky So Close*, Betool Khedairi joined a larger chorus of Iraqi writers in the 1990s who were publishing from abroad and using the freedom from the extant Iraqi Baʿthist state to directly address and subtly attack the symbols of what remained of that regime. Nowhere is this clearer than through her critical references to the audiovisual media that bombarded the home front. She and others did this in a way that writers inside Iraq could not do—both because of fear of government reprisals and because of the devastating effect the sanctions had on Iraq and the ability of Iraqis to obtain basic writing and publishing supplies. Iranian writers, like Hushang Golshiri, who resided in the country and who were both unaffiliated with the state's cultural producers and seen as dissident intellectuals by the state, had to tread more carefully. His choice to treat the war as an impediment to the craft of fiction was likely a result of both his style and his personal status in Iran. He stands in contrast to a writer like Ahmad Dehqan, who was his contemporary, but who was a war veteran and despite his critical depiction of the war, came from among the state's cultural producers.

THE HOME FRONT AS PRISON
Language as Resistance in Sinan Antoon's Iʿjaam

The postwar home front fiction of Hushang Golshiri and Betool Khedairi, published roughly in the first decade after the conclusion of the war, presented latent narratives of frustration on the part of writers who were marginalized, discouraged, or prohibited from publishing by the state during wartime and who found a space to express their criticisms of the state in the mid- to late-1990s. But the trend of rewriting the war years has continued well into the twenty-first century as Sinan Antoon's *Iʿjaam* (2004) and Alireza Gholami's *The Wall* (2015) demonstrate. In both of these novels, the Iran-Iraq War home front is depicted as a prison—literally and allegorically. Reading these two works side-by-side reveals the frustrations and limits of linguistic and literary resistance to the official war cultures in both countries.

The Iran-Iraq War's home front appears throughout Sinan Antoon's oeuvre, but features most prominently in his first novel, *Iʿjaam*, published initially by Dār al-Ādāb in Beirut in 2004 and later acquired by

Dār al-Jamal. In 2007, Antoon co-translated the English translation with scholar and translator of Arabic literature, Rebecca Johnson. It was printed with an introduction by Elias Khoury, who situated the novel within other works of modern Arabic prison literature. *I'jaam* is presented as a manuscript found by a Ba'thist security officer on August 23, 1989, a year after the Iran-Iraq War ended. A note by the officer opens the novel wherein he states that he found the manuscript while preparing to move documents to a newly built complex in Baghdad. It was handwritten in Arabic, with the letters undotted, and so another officer, named Talal Ahmad, is tasked with deciphering the text, adding a brief report, and typing it out. Ahmad's report, dated September 1, 1989, makes up the book's final pages. According to him, "The text appears to be a record of a prisoner's unrelated thoughts and illogical recollections." He adds:

> I have deliberated over the manner of rendering the frequent profanity [*al-wisākhāt wa-l-badha'āt*] occurring in the manuscript, but have preserved it as it occurs in the original text, despite the abundance of detestable images and profanity used by the writer to deride the sayings of our Father Leader (may God preserve him), the values and achievements of the party, and our just battle with the tyrannical enemy.[32]

What is bookended by the two officers' notes are the fragmented memories of a young man named Furat, a university-aged student who lives in Baghdad and who is imprisoned during the Iran-Iraq War. Both of his parents are deceased, he lives with his grandmother, and is exempt from military service due to a benign tumor. Although not a political activist in a formal way, he is vehemently anti-Ba'th and has a personal history of making jokes and snide comments to his friends and family about the regime. He is eventually reported to the internal security services. In the opening pages of the manuscript, he describes being picked up by a security officer at the university and driven to a detention center. From that point on, the novel quickly shifts between recounting the present moment in the custody of Ba'thist agents and moments in the author's recent past in Baghdad, usually spent with his girlfriend, Arij, or conversing with his grandmother at home. In prison, Furat is isolated, tortured, and raped. He is given paper and told to write, and an officer calling himself Ahmad, posing as a friend, promises to bring him reading materials. The authorities know he is a writer and want him to record his transgressive thoughts about Saddam Hussein and the regime. Furat uses the paper he receives to create the manuscript that is found later by the security officer but does so by writing a barebones Arabic script without the dots that distinguish the letters or other diacritical markings. Talal Ahmad, the security officer, renders it readable by adding dots and diacritics (a process known as "*i'jām*" for which the novel is named). The resulting novel tells of Furat's horrific experiences in prison, his life in Baghdad, and his dreamlike visions where he interacts with the Arabic letters and their occasionally anthropomorphized dots. His memories make up the novel's fragmented scenes that are broken with the recurring line, "I woke up to find myself (t)here" (*istīqayẓtu l-ajad nafsī hunā(k)*).[33]

Outside prison, Furat's experiences in the novel can be read as an Iraqi civilian's experience of the war. The first and most obvious way is how the novel depicts the militarization of everyday civilian life. For Furat, his life is under siege from constant surveillance by the regime and exposure to its incessant messaging, much of which has to do with the necessity of civilians in supporting the efforts of the troops. It is ubiquitous, appearing in the university, the football stadium, and even at home, through the relentless hum of war talk on television, to which his grandmother is constantly listening. In this way, both *I'jaam* and *A Sky So Close* intertextually engage with Iraqi wartime media, the songs of Qadisiyya, and the omnipresent sayings of the always unnamed leader, Saddam Hussein.

I'jaam also speaks to the impossibility of creating art under the wartime regime. However, it distinguishes itself from the previously covered texts as a novel published outside Iraq after the fall of Saddam Hussein's regime. Rather than hint at the battle at home between writers and the regime's proponents and censors—as Golshiri's story does in the Iranian context, and Khedairi's novel does even more directly in 1999—Antoon's novel bluntly tackles the issue in the Iraqi literary sphere. The following scene clearly illustrates this. In it, he first recalls a conversation with his grandmother wherein she relates to him how, earlier that day, a father acted out hysterically in church over the death of his son, who was killed in combat and whose corpse was brought to the church for a pre-burial prayer service. A marching band made up of Baʿth Party members accompanies the corpse, beating drums and singing the choral song "'Urs al-Gāʿ" ("The Land's Wedding"), one of the nationalist songs made famous during the war. The mother can only recall the song's line "*Āni ummak, gālat al-gāʿ*" (I'm your mother, said the earth), which triggers the rest of the song's lyrics in Furat's head, before he abruptly switches to writing about his experience trying to publish his own short stories before he was imprisoned:³⁴

> Khalid had once convinced me to submit some of my stories to *Jumhuri-yya*, and he even offered to take them himself to the editor of the cultural review, whom he happened to know at the time. I wasn't very hopeful—most of what they published were stories by authors like themselves, who wrote celebratory prose in the meter beat out by the war drum. But Khalid insisted, and I agreed. I gave him a story about the delirium of a grief-stricken mother who waits for the body of her only son to return from the war. The editor rejected it, of course, on the grounds that it was not useful for "mobilization purposes" [*wa-rafaḍa al-muḥarrir al-thaqāfī an yanshurahu liʾannahu lam yakun "taʿbawīyyan" ʿalā ḥadd qawlihi*]. The mother of a martyred son should be proud and greet the body of her martyred son with songs of joy, he told me. For were not the "martyrs nobler than us all?"*
>
> ———
>
> *A saying of our great Leader (may God preserve him).³⁵

The transitions are abrupt, but the fragments are clearly connected. They harshly critique civilian life during the war years. On the one hand, the father's hysterical mourning in church violates the state's code of correct behavior in receiving a martyr—the grandmother describes him saying, "He was dancing and singing, 'My son's not dead. He's not dead!'" On the other, the narrative of heroism that the regime wanted to impose on the people is depicted through the marching band made up of Baʿth party members, which is sent to drown out any other noise that might distract from the idea of a heroic death for the fallen soldier. This scene forces Furat to recall one of the many war songs that flooded the airwaves at the time and that were impossible to ignore, something *A Sky So Close* also attests to by opening its fourth chapter with the same tune: "Oh Mother, on my wedding night, the cannon sings / Oh Mother, the gunpowder smells like cardamom."[36] The quotation by Saddam Hussein and the father's mourning over his son's corpse come together in the final fragment where Furat guesses that the editor of the cultural supplement of the state-run newspaper, *al-Jumhūriyya*, would reject his story. The "meter of the war drum" refers to the literature and other forms of Saddam's Qadisiyya cultural production, as witnessed in the song and the editor's stiff response, literally calling on the mother of "the martyr to be happy and ululate when their son's corpse returns" (*yajib an* [...] *tuzaghrida 'andamā ta'ūd juthat ibnahā al-shahīd*).[37]

If *I'jaam*'s depiction of civilian life under a wartime regime is comparable to the two texts analyzed in the first half of this chapter, its representation of civilian resistance is where it stands out and, in the context of contemporary Iraqi literature, it is the strongest indicator that it was published after 2003. Late in the novel, Furat takes Arij to a soccer match. The newspaper he is holding is confiscated upon entry to the stadium. The reason for this, he claims, is that it was forbidden to disrespect the Leader by sitting on his photo, something the fans might do over the course of the game. The absurdity of the rule prompts him to think about his other uses for the newspaper and leads him to recall how he would occasionally take personal revenge on Saddam and the Ba'th:

> I decided it was better not to expose her [Arij] to my obscenities too early and wait to tell her that I broke the law on a regular basis, taking revenge against the regime in my own personal way. Whenever there was a toilet paper shortage, we were forced to use newspapers, and I would always choose the front page—crowded with photos and inaugurations—as a substitute. I reversed my fortunes: I would be the one sitting on the throne, and he would be sat upon, his thick mustache buffing my anus. Of course, there was always the possibility, even if it was a remote one, that a nosy trash collector would discover clues to my crime. Therefore, I decided to be careful and began to send the leader (and sometimes his guests, too) on a free tour of lower Baghdad, saying farewell with a stream of water. We all knew the tradition of spraying water on whoever leaves us in order to ensure their safe return![38]

I'jaam's mode of condemning the regime in such passages is reminiscent of other contemporary Iraqi novels in the years following the Iran-Iraq War, particularly al-Ramli's *Scattered Crumbs*. The two texts published from outside Iraq rely on a combination of irony, dark humor, and horror to critique Saddam's regime. At the same time, they refuse "to send out any clear ideological message" and are concerned with "the role of literature in a life dominated by everyday repression, degradation, and paralysis."[39] However, Antoon's novel diverges from al-Ramli's in two important ways. Firstly, in its depiction of the Iraqi prison during the 1980s, which constitutes a "strategic critique of the dominant discourses" of the Ba'thist regime from "the perspectives of those who have been coerced, silenced, marginalised, abandoned and tortured."[40] Secondly, and more significantly, in its much more sophisticated relationship to the very act of writing and the (im)possibility of resistance throughout those years. Here, Anna Ziajka Stanton aptly observes that "[t]he principal target of the novel's subversive energies is not the regime as such, but the forms taken by the regime's language: orthographic and phonetic, morphological and visual."[41] The novel's critiques, which are often inserted into the text through the very process of dotting (*i'jām*) the undotted Arabic text, "recast parodically the official terminology of the Ba'athist regime," striking a series of ironic linguistic and literary "blows" against the regime that had fallen just prior to the novel's publication.[42] Since they are often impossible to directly translate between Arabic and English they appear differently in the original and English translation.

Yet, whatever belated resistance the novel offers to the discourse of Saddam's Ba'th Party and by extension, to its war project, it cannot go beyond the "inability of a work of art to address materially or in any way make up for pain's effects on the body that experiences it, or to alter the political realities that caused this body to suffer."[43] In this way, it recalls the sentiments expressed openly in "The Painter of Baghan" and presumed in *A Sky So Close*. In those two cases, the only way to resist the atmosphere created by the war is to flee the sites of attacks against civilians. Furat, however, stays in Baghdad, resists through writing but ultimately dies in a regime prison. Thus, to the extent that literature can be seen as a form of resistance in *I'jaam*, it is bound to the linguistic level.

War in Raw Language: Alireza Gholami's The Wall

Writing nearly a decade after Antoon, Iranian writer Alireza Gholami—the youngest writer I have included in this study thus far—provides yet another narrative of wartime civilian life. His slim novel, *The Wall*, was published in 2015 by Morvāred, a longstanding independent Tehran-based publisher. The novel freshly presents some of the traits of the texts previously treated in this chapter, and demonstrates a continued interest on the part of Iranian writers in returning to this setting, developing it, and turning it into a space for critique. After publication, *The Wall* quickly garnered interest from critics and went through two rounds of printing before being banned by the MCIG. While it is debatable whether or not the superlative title of "most unique war novel" (*motafāvet-tarin romān dar howzeh-ye defāʿ-e moqddas*) is deserved, it is undoubtedly a very different war novel for several reasons.[44]

The Wall takes place in a small, unnamed Iranian town that is the target of heavy Iraqi bombings over a period of twenty-four hours during the winter of 1986 or 1987. Like the somewhat anonymous setting, the antihero narrator, a fourteen-year-old boy who moved there from Tehran about a year earlier, also goes unnamed. His parents both work for the national postal service and their new appointments in the town brought them there. The entire novel is narrated in the past tense from the boy's perspective. As a character, he is uncharismatic, a serial liar, and exhibits both a naivety about the events taking place around him and an emotional detachment to the people who care for him.[45]

The novel opens with a scene of the narrator's midday school assembly in the schoolyard where attendance is about to be taken. The school's principal, Mr. Rasuli, arrives on the raised platform in front of the students, who line up in front of him. The students sing the anthem of the Islamic Republic, raise the flag, and chant slogans. One student recites the Quran, followed by all the students recitation of the opening chapter of the Quran in unison, and they end the assembly by citing three salutations to the Prophet Muhammad and his family (*salavāts*). The narrator says that "the first had no specific reason, but Mr. Rasuli wanted us to say it loudly, the second was for the health of the Imam [Khomeini], and the third was for the victory of the warriors of Islam at the front."[46]

During the second salutation the first of several Iraqi rockets suddenly hits the town. Shattered glass rains down from the second floor of the school building, slicing the principal's neck open. He dies while some of the students and teachers stare at him, and others struggle to open the school's massive door to escape into the town that has quickly been transformed into a giant scene of chaos and mourning. The narrator also leaves, but before exiting the schoolyard, he passes by a room that contains several awards for high-achieving students and steals two of them, hiding them in the yard so that he can pick them up later. Chapters 2–13 of the novel follow the narrator as he wanders the town after the initial attack and during the subsequent bombs. His younger brother, Jamshid, who attended a different school, is killed in the first missile attack, which demolished his school. The narrator finds Jamshid's body, including his leg that was blown off, and calmly takes his remains in a wheelbarrow to the cemetery, where he runs into his mother and a neighbor, *Khāleh* ("auntie") Nahid, whose son was also killed in the attack. They bury the corpses with their hands. The mothers are completely distraught, but the narrator remains emotionally flat, plainly narrating the events and continually thinking about when he can sneak back to the school to collect the awards he had stashed away.

The narrator and his mother eventually return to their house but don't tell the father that Jamshid has been killed. The father, for his part, had recently lost his legs in a separate bombing of the town and is now essentially confined to the top floor of their house. He spends his days in bed, drinking tea and occasionally watching television. He and the narrator say very little to each other; their interactions are confined to the father ordering him to pour tea or turn on the television and the narrator quietly obeying. During the rest of the first day, the narrator wanders around his neighborhood and spends time in the corner store of a man called Mr. Farzaneh, who can only seem to think about marrying the boy's neighbor, Khaleh Nahid. A few other characters are also introduced in passing, such as a neighborhood boy, Mohammad, who tells the narrator about a "Pakistani woman who recently arrived in town and shows you stuff for free,"[47] and a man called Mr. Ranjbar who sits on the corner of their street greeting passersby, about whom nothing is known. The descriptions of the narrator's interactions with these characters and what he observes in the streets are given in simple, short sentences and often dwell on seemingly irrelevant details of the characters' appearances. Aside from periods, the novel has no punctuation, which adds to the narrator's cold, emotional indifference, as seen in the following passage, which takes place just after the first bombing when the narrator is heading in the direction of his brother's school. He plainly describes a scene that he passes:

> I saw a woman who was searching through a few corpses. She had a small boy in her arms and was tapping his back, singing a lullaby to him. The woman, who was wearing a dirty flower-print veil over her head, walked in my direction, trying to put the baby boy to sleep. The boy's clothes were dusty and bloody, and he was quiet. For a moment, the woman stood in front of me. When she turned around, I saw that the boy had no head and his neck was bloody. A few of the men in khaki overcoats were trying to take the corpse out of her hands, but she said she was looking for the head [. . .] An ambulance arrived and three medics whose white uniforms were bloodied stepped out to collect the corpses on the ground [. . .] I saw the medics go towards the woman and try to take the boy out of her hands. A nearby middle-aged man loudly asked the medics not to separate the boy from his mother. He had a bloody plastic bucket in his hand that was full of hands and feet, and he handed it to one of the medics, who rushed it to the ambulance before coming back and telling the mother that what she was doing was weakening people's morale and that they had to take the boy from her. The woman screamed, pounded her chest, and said she wanted the boy's head. Then she kneeled and asked God why he did this to her and her boy.[48]

On the novel's second day, the narrator lies to his mother about having left his bag at school and goes to retrieve the awards he had stolen. He later returns to his house to find his mother and Khaleh Nahid both killed in another missile strike. Practically ignoring the incident, he enters his house, pulls out a packet of letters that he had found and hidden when they first came to the town the previous year, and he begins burning them. The contents of the letters reveal that his mother had had a relationship with another man who was a revolutionary in the 1970s and who had been arrested by SAVAK, the ousted regime's notorious intelligence service, for passing out anti-Shah flyers. He was executed in January 1978, shortly before the revolution. That man, whose name was Amir, is revealed to have been the narrator's biological father. The letters also reveal that the narrator's mother's current husband, who is now legless and homebound, is actually the narrator's stepfather and the biological father of Jamshid. The letters give glimpses into the mother's past life, her separation from her first husband, and her difficulty in convincing her new husband to keep her son, the narrator, in their care. With no one willing to take him, the narrator became tolerated in the couple's home. Meanwhile, the stepfather calls downstairs to ask who has entered the house, where his wife is, and why there is the smell of something burning. Eventually, realizing it is the boy downstairs, he asks him to come up to help him down the steps. The boy remains silent until he leaves the house and yells upstairs to his stepfather, whom he now refers to as "Jamshid's dad." Like the rest of the novel, it is plainly related in the past tense: "I told him that his son Jamshid was killed yesterday and today his wife also died under the rubble. Then I immediately reminded him that he could no longer hurt anyone." Before leaving, he adds a rare moment of insight into his emotions, saying, "At that very moment I realized that sometimes, when we are terrified of someone, we never realize that we actually hate them. Then, a time comes when that fear no longer exists and it's only then that we realize how much we've always hated that person."[49]

The narrator then leaves the house and goes to meet Mohammad, the neighborhood boy. The two go to see the "Pakistani woman" who, according to Mohammad, lives in a storage cube that sits on land surrounded by barbed wire that once belonged to a rich man who fled the country at the outbreak of the war. Mohammad has the narrator enter first through a hole in the fence. He knocks repeatedly on the doors of the cubes, but no one answers. Suddenly, two IRGC officers appear and quickly take the narrator away to be questioned. Mohammad is nowhere to be found. The narrator, unable to defend himself or explain his actions, is repeatedly asked by a higher-ranking officer about whom he works for. Near the end of the quick interrogation, Mr. Ranjbar, who turns out to be an undercover informant, enters the room and explains that the boy ignored his mother's death, went into his family's house, started a fire, and nearly killed his legless father. The boy is handed over to Mr. Ranjbar and taken out of the room. The narrator gets a glimpse of the signed piece of paper in Mr. Ranjbar's hand, which simply says "In the name of God. He is an antirevolutionary." In the penultimate scene, Mr. Ranjbar asks the boy what he feels about what has just happened. The boy responds with one word: "hate" (*nefrat*). The novel ends with the boy being led into a jeep to be driven to a Revolutionary Court for what can only be assumed to be a tragic ending.[50]

On the surface, based on its language, length, and content, *The Wall* appears to be a simple and unsophisticated text, but such a reading ignores the context in which it was published, its deceivingly complex formal characteristics, and the way the novel's language challenges and mocks the official discourse of the Sacred Defense. In her thorough analysis of the novel, Goulia Ghardashkhani keenly notes how the novel is a "geometrical narrative" based on various repetitive elements, ranging from the simple, hand-drawn map of the city that opens the novel to the illustrated clocks that appear on the first page of each chapter. These repeated elements are also reflected in the novel's opening scene (e.g., 13 lines of students), contained in the dialogues (the narrator repeatedly comes back to the awards he stole and tells readers whether another character refers to him as a "good" or "bad" boy), and both the narrator's vocal and physical language, like his constant mention of shifting his winter cap up or down on his head.[51]

The narrator's simple descriptions are themselves transgressive when viewed in the context of Iranian Sacred Defense culture and recall the narrative strategy of subversive affirmation that characterized parts of Muhsin al-Ramli's *Scattered Crumbs*, and which Friederike Pannewick uses to describe the actions and words of Antoon's protagonist, Furat, in *I'jaam*.[52] However, if we are to understand the ways in which Iraqi and Iranian authors have critiqued the Iran-Iraq War and the regimes responsible for perpetuating it through Arns and Sasse's concept of subversive affirmation, *The Wall* actually provides a better example of the technique than either of the aforementioned Iraqi novels. This is because Gholami's novel was written and published from inside Iran, where the author still lives. The material and intellectual conditions for war-related cultural production for a Persian language writer residing in Iran under a regime that is still investing in maintaining the hegemony of its war narrative, are distinct from that of a writer who writes and publishes from exile and/or in the wake of the ancien regime. Thus, the concept of "subversive affirmation" is not only more applicable to Gholami's novel, but the stakes of employing it are significantly higher. Instances of subversive affirmation can be read at various moments throughout the novel, but perhaps the best example is found in the eighth chapter, which begins at 8:45 PM on the first day. The narrator pours his stepfather a cup of tea and sits next to the space heater to watch the nightly news broadcast, while the distraught mother tries to hide the fact that their son had been killed earlier that day. The narrator says,

> [T]he announcer said our fearless warriors struck the criminal enemy forces and were advancing into Iraqi territory. Then he said that the popular forces have been transferred to the Battlefield of Truth vs. Falsehood, and the nation of the Party of God [*Ommat-e Hezbollah*] has provided them with inspirational leadership. Then, the TV showed parts of Qom that had been bombed by Iraq. People were pulling the dead out from beneath the rubble and shouting slogans. The attack took place on the day commemorating Saint Fatemeh's martyrdom and for that reason people were even angrier [...]
>
> I turned around and looked at my father. He was watching the tv and drinking tea.
>
> When the war news ended, the television displayed the picture of a man for a few moments and then announced that his name was Nazar'ali. The news anchor said that he had admitted to being involved in anti-revolutionary activities. Then, Nazar'ali himself spoke. First, he sent his greetings to the leader of the revolution and then offered a prayer for the soldiers at the front. He said that because of his mistakes and wrongdoings, he had been arrested a few days prior and that he deserved it. I looked at my father again. He had placed the teacup beside the cushion, leaned back on the pillow, and pulled the blanket up to his neck.
>
> Nazar'ali [...] said after a few days in prison and his good treatment at the hands of the people in charge, that he had thought about everything and realized that prison was a really positive experience. Then he said he was ashamed and explained that he had taken advantage of the people's naivety and the regime's benevolence [...] Then he said that the Islamic Republic was a good system since it was kind to everyone. For a few moments, Nazar'ali did not say anything and looked down at the floor. Then

> he brought his eyes up again and looked at us. To me, he looked sorry and repentant. I don't exactly remember the last thing I heard him say, but, in my opinion, he said that he had done what the enemies of Islam had wanted.[53]

It is impossible to read passages such as the one above and not sense the narrative's condemnation of the regime through the plain presentation of its own rhetoric, which is so absurd that it works against itself without commentary. The clearly forced televised confession of Nazar'ali combined with the nonchalant behavior of the father work in tandem to defamiliarize the quotidian horror of the broadcast. While televised confessions existed in the 1970s under the Pahlavi state, they became a hallmark of the Islamic Republic's treatment of political opponents in the post-revolutionary state. Such confessions were (and are) often obtained through torture. According to Abrahamian, they serve as "grand theater staged by the authorities as positive propaganda for themselves and as negative propaganda against their real and imagined enemies." He writes:

> [T]he recanters submit to the authorities and recognize their legitimacy by meticulously citing their honorific titles, grand claims, and historic achievements. They reaffirm the official version of reality, of Truth, and of History. [. . .And] proclaim on high their own and their colleagues' utter depravity. They come onto the stage to humiliate, dehumanize, and demonize themselves as well as their associates. Repeating official accusations, they depict themselves as criminals, saboteurs, conspirators, traitors, scoundrels, deviants, degenerates, vermin, mad dogs, and even the Devil's sexual partners."[54]

Moments such as Nazar'ali's confession and the radio broadcasts throughout the novel are where the narrative approach of subversive affirmation shines in *The Wall*. These, combined with the barrage of exaggerated tragedies that befall the narrator and his plain, emotionless mode of storytelling, produce a palpably "ironic and at times sarcastic style of narration." They "reveal the unjustifiable absurdity of the war and its meaninglessness for civilians."[55]

THE HOME FRONT AND THE WAR OVER POETICS

The works of fiction that I have highlighted in this chapter take an approach to writing the Iran-Iraq War that recalls Viet Thanh Nguyen's "panoramic optics" of war and expands the very notion of war literature that underscores the non-combat(ant) side of the conflict. They focus on elements of wartime life that differ significantly from the killing and violence that raged on the war front, and they elevate voices that had been ignored or silenced by official discourses during the conflict. In writing from this angle, these stories offer a counternarrative of the Iran-Iraq War that frames it through artists' frustrations, wasted lives, and political oppression.

Chapter 2 showcased earlier works that were set away from the battlefields. Those texts stress the mournful aspects of postwar life to proffer a critical narrative of loss because of the Iran-Iraq War that stands in contrast to the celebratory tone of official wartime discourses. The texts treated in that chapter work around the war's official narratives and generally occupy an ambivalent space vis-à-vis the state discourses of the conflict that had recently concluded. They expose what was left behind in the war's aftermath and focus on remains, but stop short of directly criticizing the government and never directly mention the state discourses. The more recent texts of this chapter similarly move the war to the background and use it as a starting point for a different type of war literature. However, they produce a different effect that reveals both the changing permissibility of discourse on the Iran-Iraq War, and the different levels of engagement with the "discursive debris" of the war with which Iranian and Iraqi authors were left to contend over the passage of time.[56]

In "The Painter of Baghan" and *A Sky So Close*, Hushang Golshiri and Betool Khedairi put into writing their criticisms of the war years and the war's negative effects on literature and the arts, exposing an internal war for every writer: publish or stay silent. They did so directly (Khedairi) or indirectly (Golshiri). This goes further than the allegorical relationship seen in Muhsin al-Ramli's *Scattered Crumbs* in Chapter 3, where through the character of Qasim "art" is posited against "war," with the former passive and the latter aggressive. In Golshiri's and Khedairi's stories, the war is shown to have damaged language and art itself, concurring that "[d]uring war, the effect of violence upon language is amplified and clarified: language is censored, encrypted, and euphemized [. . .] As war reveals, violence harms language; it imposes silence upon groups and, through trauma and injury, disables the capacity of the individual to speak effectively.[57]

Writing later, Sinan Antoon and Alireza Gholami pick up the threads of critique started in the texts of the first half of the chapter. Khedairi published *A Sky So Close* in the shadow of a waning Ba'thist government in Baghdad, and the novel's nameless narrator largely refrains from commenting on the incessant messaging of Saddam's Qadisiyya broadcast over the radio and television, instead choosing to brush it aside. By contrast, the narrator of Antoon's *I'jaam* takes on the culture and rhetoric of Saddam's Qadisiyya and attacks it, cleverly playing games with the government's own words, even if his resistance is destined to end in his own death. Antoon's direct critiques of the regime and the war appeared just after the fall of Saddam Hussein in 2003, at a time when threats of the Ba'thist regime had been rendered irrelevant to Iraqi exilic and diasporic writers. As a text of that moment, it is also unique in that it limits its focus to the years of the Iran-Iraq War, as opposed to the myriad works of post-2003 Iraqi fiction that explore a longer historical scope.[58] Similarly, in *The Wall* Gholami replaces the subtle suggestive critique of the war made by the narrator of "The Painter of Baghan" with raw, emotionless prose. The novel's young narrator presents the horrid face of the civilian's experience of the war, unfiltered and without a moment of reprieve from the horrors of bombs raining from the sky. The style of writing in *The Wall* can be read as a response to the Iranian government's continued interest in and support of literature that promotes its narrative. Its characters never criticize the government or the ongoing war but simply observe what they see around them and juxtapose the state's war discourse with the routine horror of bombings civilians, exposing the utter disconnect between the two. For the censor, the book initially might have been a representation of the home front written without the proper ideological framing. For the reader, the critique is evident.

With distance from the end of the conflict, writers like Khedairi and Golshiri in the 1990s, and later Antoon and Gholami in the first two decades of the twenty-first century, articulated how the war was an attack on the very act of writing itself. Just as the war silenced some with physical violence on the battlefront, it silenced others through the imposition of its ideological occupations of both countries' cultural spheres. The comparison of these writers and their texts also illuminates how the passage of time has created more differences in the ways Iraqi and Iranian writers have dealt with this war's legacy. The removal of Saddam Hussein's regime brought down the proverbial "war of fear" among writers and allowed them to freely address issues from the previous two and a half decades about which many writers had previously remained silent, particularly those who remained on the inside. Hillawi's *Night of the Lands* was an early example of an Iraqi exilic novel that openly took the Iraqi Ba'th Party to task for its crimes against the Iraqi people in the 1980s. Blatant denunciations of the party like those that appeared in *I'jaam*, especially from the civilian perspective, were far more common after 2003, and Antoon's novel remains one of the first well-known examples of this wave of writing. The Iranian literary reflections on the war since its end still must contend with a MCIG that is invested in maintaining the hegemony of the Sacred Defense narrative. There are still limits to what can be written about the war and published in Iran, evidenced by the banning of Gholami's *The Wall* after its second printing. The next and final chapter will explore how Iranian and Iraqi writers continue to write about this conflict, expanding the war's fictional afterlives. Their return to this period demonstrates the continued entanglements of writers with the legacy of the Iran-Iraq War and ways in which some of the fictional narratives of the conflict now manifest themselves in wholly unique ways.

Five
GHOSTS OF A VIOLENT PAST

THAT WRITERS FROM BOTH IRAN AND IRAQ HAVE CONTINUALLY dealt with the legacy of the war between their two countries is testament to the length and brutality of the conflict, its unsettled legacy, and the need felt by many writers to revisit its various consequences that have affected the region until today. Most of the works covered in the previous chapters have dealt with the war through portrayals of the human consequences of violence. More recently, writers from the two countries have taken up the afterlives of the Iran-Iraq War beyond the world of humans. Within their fictional texts, animals, the earth, and even the undead reveal themselves to be manifestations of the Iran-Iraq War's lingering effects. These nonhuman representations of the Iran-Iraq War are further evidence that time has allowed writers of fiction to approach the catastrophe of this war more creatively, in addition to more clearly seeing its long-term ramifications. The texts dealt with in this final chapter, published between 2008 and 2018—twenty to thirty years after the war ended—both transcend "the real" world of humans and investigate the war's consequences beyond its effects on people, revealing how it left myriad, ruinous consequences in its wake.

Within Arabic fiction, this chapter treats short stories and novels written by Iraqi writers Ahmed Saadawi, Hassan Blasim, and Diaa Jubaili. Unlike the previous chapters that largely featured writing about the war produced in the shadows of both wartime regimes, all the Iraqi writers treated in this chapter published their texts well after the U.S.-led toppling of Saddam Hussein's regime in 2003, when the dynamics between state, society, and the production of fiction fundamentally changed for Iraqi writers. Gone were the governmental censors that limited or fully discouraged writers from treating the war, a regime that threatened the safety of its critics everywhere, and the devastating economic effects of the sanctions of the 1990s and early aughts. In their place, however, was a new chaotic present inside Iraq. Within this environment, these three writers have risen to local and global prominence as part of the explosion in popularity of Iraqi fiction after 2003 that has continued until today.

As several of the texts in the previous two chapters demonstrate, Persian fiction about the Iran-Iraq War has continued in Iran, in both its state-sponsored and non-state-sponsored iterations. While 2003 was a clear breaking point for Iraqi fiction, it did not influence Iranian writers in a comparable manner, and Iran has not experienced any singular moment since the war's end that brought with it a similarly drastic shift in cultural representation of the war like the fall of the Ba'th in Iraq. My focus on one specific text in this chapter is not meant to suggest that fewer Iranian novels about the war have been written in the period under question. On the contrary, many works of fiction have been published that deal with the war, but Nasim Marashi's 2017 novel *Haras* (*Pruning*) is the best example of an Iranian novel that has attained a comparable level of critical attention as the Iraqi texts I reference, while also exhibiting strikingly similar thematic intersections with them. Putting these works of Persian and Arabic fiction into conversation with one another exposes yet another way in which Iranian and Iraqi writers find themselves entangled by circumstances that have prompted comparable approaches to writing about the Iran-Iraq War and its afterlives.[1]

IRAQI FICTION AND THE GHOSTS OF WAR

The end of Saddam Hussein's rule and the elimination of the Ba'th Party in 2003 tore down the proverbial "wall of fear" that constricted many Iraqi writers across the globe. The U.S.-led invasion of the country, which ushered in the chaos that would lead to a civil war and the disintegration of a troubled but somewhat peaceful normalcy for Iraqi civilians, became, along with the recent past, the main subject for dozens of Iraqi writers working and publishing from both inside and outside the country. The result has been a post-2003 Iraqi literature that reckons head-on with the violence of political oppression and wars of the recent past, written amidst the violence of the post-2003 era that has plagued the country until recently. Within this corpus, several writers have chosen to portray the almost incomprehensible levels of violence that followed the invasion through decidedly unreal depictions of violence. Writing about this period, Haytham Bahoora rightly notes that "literary recourse to the metaphysical, whether through the subconscious, nightmares, or the supernatural, are frequent stylistic conventions [. . .] narrating a terrain of unspeakable violence and its many afterlives."[2]

Within this context, and despite the passage of fifteen years since its conclusion—a period that contained two more major wars and twelve years of brutal sanctions—the Iran-Iraq War frequently appears in post-2003 Iraqi fiction. It is often woven into longer narratives of war that encompass the 1980s and end sometime after 2003, with a number of Iraqi writers addressing the Iran-Iraq War as the first of several consecutive cycles of war that have affected the country since 1980. In prominent works such as Muhsin al-Ramli's *Ḥadāʾiq al-Raʾīs* (*The President's Garden*) or Sinan Antoon's *Waḥdaha Shajarat al-Rummān* (*The Corpse Washer*), for example, the war with Iran exists as a distinct episode with far-reaching consequences that continues to affect Iraqis into the present. Even novels that have a clear focus on the 1990s or post-2003 eras—prominent examples include Shahad al-Rawi's *Sāʿat Baghdad* (*The Baghdad Clock*) or Inaam Kachachi's *al-Ḥafīda al-Amrīkīyya* (*The American Granddaughter*)—inevitably reference the war with Iran. The length and brutality of that war as well as its long-term effects on Iraqi society leave no other choice. Despite their stylistic differences and varied levels of attention devoted to the war, these stories are all, to different degrees, "haunted" by the Iran-Iraq War. In using that term, I rely on the work of Avery Gordon, who writes that haunting

> is an animated state in which a repressed or unresolved social violence is making itself known, sometimes very directly, sometimes more obliquely [. . .] haunting describe[s] those singular yet repetitive instances when home becomes unfamiliar, when your bearings on the

world lose direction, when the over-and-done-with comes alive, when what's been in your blind spot comes into view. Haunting raises specters, and it alters the experience of being in time, the way we separate the past, the present, and the future. These specters or ghosts appear when the trouble they represent and symptomize is no longer being contained or repressed or blocked from view. The ghost, as I understand it, is not the invisible or some ineffable excess. The whole essence, if you can use that word, of a ghost is that it has a real presence and demands its due, your attention. Haunting and the appearance of specters or ghosts is one way [. . .] we are notified that what's been concealed is very much alive and present, interfering precisely with those always incomplete forms of containment and repression ceaselessly directed toward us.³

The Iran-Iraq War's presence in the novels cited above leaves a variety of traces on the novels' characters and in many ways can be considered a social "specter" felt long after the war has ended. A strain of post-2003 Iraqi fiction also treats the Iran-Iraq War as something literally much more "ghost-like." Here, characters from the war appear in the years after it ended in a state that is neither that of the living nor the dead, but rather a third category of undead being.⁴ These undead figures that represent the Iran-Iraq War are supernatural manifestations of a past that was never truly dealt with. For some writers, these are also smoothly woven into the "terrain of unspeakable violence and its many afterlives" to which Bahoora refers. Among the Iraqi writers who have employed this approach when weaving the Iran-Iraq War into their now globally well-known works of fiction are Hassan Blasim (Arabic: *Balāsim*; b. 1973), Ahmed Saadawi (Arabic: *Saʿdawī*; b. 1973), and Diaa Jubaili (Arabic: *Diāʾ Jubaylī*; b. 1977). All three, and especially Blasim and Saadawi, have become among the most well-known Iraqi writers of fiction globally after being shortlisted for, or winning, high-profile awards in the Arabophone and Anglophone literary worlds and having their works translated into several languages, sometimes with major literary presses. Blasim, for example, won the PEN Writers in Translation prize in 2009 for his short story collection *The Madman of Freedom Square* and the Independent Foreign Fiction Prize in 2014 for another collection titled *The Iraqi Christ*. The same year, Saadawi became the first Iraqi writer to win the International Prize in Arabic Fiction ("IPAF," often called "The Arabic Booker"), and in

2018, Jonathan Wright's translation *Frankenstein in Baghdad* was shortlisted for The Man Booker International Prize. For his part, Jubaili's short story collection *Lā Ṭawāhīn Hawā' fī al-Baṣra* (*No Windmills in Basra*) won the 2017–2018 Kuwait-based Al-Multaqa Prize for the Arabic Short Story. Their works reveal how some Iraqi authors have employed uncanny, ghost-like creatures to show how the Iran-Iraq War has haunted Iraq in the years since its conclusion.

Revenge of the Dead in Ahmed Saadawi's Frankenstein in Baghdad
The 2013 novel *Frānkshtāyin fī Baghdād* and its English translation, *Frankenstein in Baghdad*, has become the most well-known Iraqi novel today. Aside from the major awards and critical praise that it has garnered, it has gone through several printings in both Arabic and English and has been translated into 25 languages. The novel channels Mary Shelley's *Frankenstein* through an undead monster (referred to as *al-Shismuh* or the "Whatsitsname") and a gothic ambience, to treat the violent chaos unleashed in Iraq in the aftermath of U.S.-led invasion. The novel is framed as a top-secret report from the fictional "Tracking and Pursuit Department" of the Iraqi government that contains the text of a story based on materials collected and emailed to an author. The novel weaves together a wide cast of characters to tell the story of the Whatsitsname, a monster in the form of a living corpse whose body parts are sewn together from the victims of explosions in Baghdad and who is animated by the soul of a security guard recently killed by a suicide bomber. After being completed as a conglomerate of body parts by his creator, a junk collector named Hadi al-'Attag, the Whatsitsname embarks on a revengeful killing spree in Baghdad. First, like a vigilante, he kills the murderers of the victims whose body parts he now consists of. He prowls the streets of Baghdad at night, eluding authorities and journalists, and brutally murdering his victims. His need to seek vengeance and kill on behalf of the victims whose body parts now make up his own causes him to be caught up in an endless spiral of death.

Frankenstein in Baghdad has been the subject of dozens of scholarly and popular reviews and articles.[5] However, the fact that its main character—the Whatsitsname—is directly linked to the Iran-Iraq War, has received almost no attention.[6] Although the Whatitsname may consist of the flesh and soul of post-2003 victims of militias, car bombs, and the collateral damage of the coalition forces in Iraq, he is also connected to another character's memory of the Iran-Iraq War. The first person whom he sees after coming to life is an elderly, senile woman who is the neighbor of Hadi the junk collector, Elishva Umm Daniel (Arabic: *Ilīshūā Um Dānīāl*). Years prior, Elishva's two adult daughters emigrated to Australia, but she chose to stay in Iraq despite the violence, because she is convinced that her son Daniel (Arabic: Dānīyāl), who disappeared twenty years prior during the Iran-Iraq War, will return. As the novel begins, we are told that Elishva no longer has anyone who will listen to her longing for her son and her belief that he is alive and will return. Among the neighbors, "some of them couldn't remember what Daniel looked like [...] he was just one of many who'd died over the years." Thus, "Elishva no longer shared with anyone her belief that Daniel was still alive." The only people with whom she still talks about her missing son are her daughters who now live in Australia and who call her weekly, knowing that their "mother clung to the memory of her late son in order to go on living."[7]

Shortly after coming to life, the Whatsitsname wanders into Elishva's house and she nonchalantly recognizes him as her son. Attributing his arrival to the miracle promised to her by the icon of Saint George on her wall (with whom she also converses), and his hideous physical appearance to the fact that "not many people came back looking the same as when they left,"[8] she immediately addresses him as Daniel and even brings out her son's old clothes, which conveniently fit the monster perfectly. She then pours her heart out to him about all that has happened since his disappearance twenty years prior, while he sits and silently listens. In the process, she remembers one of the few people she hates: Abu Zaydun, a neighborhood barber, and ex-Baʿthist "who was responsible for forcibly enlisting Daniel in the Iran-Iraq War. . . [He] took Danny away by the collar. From the training camp, Daniel went straight to the front and never came back."[9] As night falls and Elishva finally tires of telling Daniel/Whatsitsname her stories, he manages to hoarsely utter his first words to the old woman, telling her he needs to go out but would return soon. That night he begins his vengeful killing spree and among those he kills early on is Abu Zaydun. The now frail old man is found stabbed to death with the scissors from his own barbershop. When the news of his death spreads the next day, his neighbors recalled "how he had been responsible for sending so many young men off to war [and] had been active in Baʻth Party organizations, doggedly pursuing all those who deserted from the army or tried to avoid military training."[10] Thus, in Saadawi's novel, the Iran-Iraq War is intricately connected to the violence of post-invasion Iraq. The war haunts Elishva through the disappearance of her son and practically opens the Whatsitsname's cycle of revenge killings. Before he can take retribution on those responsible for the present violence, he has to purge one of the perpetrators of past violence who had not been held to account. The brutal act demonstrates how the ghosts of the violent past have remained with Iraqis in the violent present.[11]

The Dead Don't Lie: Hassan Blasim's "An Army Newspaper"

Even if the war with Iran forms an essential background to the events of Saadawi's novel, its primary focus ultimately remains the post-2003 violent landscape of Baghdad. By contrast, "Jarīda ʻAskariyya" ("An Army Newspaper"), a short story by Hassan Blasim, summons the undead to squarely focus on the time of the Iran-Iraq War. Like most of Blasim's early short stories, it was originally published online on the author's blog, first in 2008.[12] Later, it was collected and published in his second short story collection that appeared first in book form in English translation and later in the original Arabic.[13] His writings have since gathered more attention in English than in Arabic across both scholarly and popular platforms. His reception in Arabic has also been largely positive, but critics have abstained from the hyperbolic claims that have been made by some critics writing in English, such as calling him "the best writer of Arabic fiction alive."[14] Much of Blasim's oeuvre focuses on the difficulties of everyday life for Iraqis after the 2003 invasion and the challenges and absurdities of migrating to Europe. "An Army Newspaper" explicitly breaks from those thematic preoccupations and remains focused on the 1980s, even dedicating its cover page "To the dead of the Iran-Iraq War." Despite the thematic shift to the recent past, the story remains consistent with his other works of fiction by employing his macabre, fantastic, and experimental approach.[15]

"An Army Newspaper" begins with a narrator declaring his intention to speak to a dead man:

We will go to the cemetery, to the mortuary, and ask the guardians of the past for permission. We'll take the dead man out to the public garden naked and set him on the platform under the ripe orange sun. [. . .] We'll implore him to repeat the story to us. There's no need to kick him in the balls for him to tell the story honestly and impartially, because the dead are usually honest, even the bastards among them.[16]

The story then passes the narrative to the dead writer, who immediately recognizes his interrogator as a living writer and a judge—whom he addresses as "your Honor" (*Sayyidī al-Qāḍī*)—and proceeds to offer a testimony-like account of his time working as the editor of the cultural section of an army newspaper ten years prior, during the Iran-Iraq War, before committing suicide. During his years at the paper, he "would make modest interventions" to submissions, and "add imaginative touches to the written images that would come to us from the front." He speaks frankly of his role during the production of the literature of Saddam's Qadisiyya, telling the writer,

> They were not so stupid as to send in pieces that were plaintive, or full of whining and screaming. Some of them wrote because it helped them believe that they would not be killed, or that the war was just an upbeat story in a newspaper. Others were seeking some financial or other benefits, period. There were writers who were forced to write, but all that doesn't interest me now because at this stage I have no regrets and I am not even afraid. The dead, Your Honor, do not agonize over their crimes, and do not long to be happy, as you know.[17]

The now-dead editor's job progresses successfully until one day he receives a box of five stories written in student notebooks from a soldier who claims to have composed them in a month.[18] The stories are outstanding, but not at all about the war. They are written in "a surprisingly elevated literary style" and deal with reluctant soldiers who went on sexual escapades with women. The editor describes them as "a transparent and cruel exploration of sexual beings from a point of view that was childlike and satanic at the same time." As an editor, he is immediately intrigued and decides to write to the soldier, threatening him with interrogation by the Baʿth Party for transgressing from the party's line on the war and its acceptable cultural representation, a crime that could lead to his execution. He relies on "the perpetual fear of a soldier" to convince the writer to renounce the stories, apologize, or beg for forgiveness for having ever written them.[19] A week later, the editor is overjoyed to discover that the soldier has been killed at the front. He quickly publishes the stories in his own name and receives international acclaim.

Some months later, after the Ba'thist newspaper editor has also become a famous writer, more and more parcels of phenomenal stories begin to arrive at his door, landing daily "like a storm of locusts: today a hundred, tomorrow a hundred, and so on."[20] The stories drive the writer to madness. He hunts down the family of the supposed writer of the stories, confirms that he is dead, finds his grave, exhumes the corpse, and burns what remains of it. Yet, the stories keep arriving, causing the writer to leave his editing job, transport the storerooms of stories at the ministry to a rural farm where he installs an incinerator to burn them and any new stories that arrive thereafter: "[F]rom the morning of the first day at the farm, I was working hard day and night, burning the colored exercise books [. . .] in the hopes that the war would end and this madness of khaki sperm would also stop."[21] Of course, the war eventually stops but the editor tells his writer-judge "a new war broke out. The only option left to me was the incinerator fire." Before the story concludes, he asks the living author if he "also once worked for an army newspaper?"[22]

"An Army Newspaper" goes directly back to the years of the Iran-Iraq War with a damning indictment of both the propaganda literature and the people who facilitated its production. It does so through a ghoulish exploration of madness and war, two recurring motifs in Blasim's writing. War occurs throughout his short stories, not with stories of soldiers or militiamen, but more typically in reference to contemporary events related to the consequences of the 2003 invasion on all parts of Iraqi society. Madness, in Blasim's stories, is "a trope to question interior and external perspectives of war and [. . .] complicate linear narratives that fail to portray the experiences and consequences of war adequately."[23] War and madness are simultaneously present and intricately connected in Blasim's fiction.

Additionally, there is often an element of the uncanny in Hassan Blasim's short stories, even if his stories are usually underpinned by realism and reference points to historical events. The stories contained in *The Madman of Freedom Square*, for example, are often set in realistic settings and contain realistic characters but are then dragged through extraordinary circumstances into the realm of the uncanny and fantastical.[24] "An Army Newspaper" combines these elements to address the production of official war fiction in the 1980s and the people killed in that wave of cultural production during Saddam's Qadisiyya. To do so, it stages a conversation between a dead writer, who went mad during the process of publishing war fiction, and another writer, who is potentially going through the same process in the present. The questions that the story leaves to speculation are also important. There are few indications of the living writer's motives for exhuming the dead writer, and no real clues as to who the living or dead writers are. The living writer never speaks, save for the opening lines that suggest a disdain for the dead writer, and an enthusiasm for disinterring a corpse to do a type of autopsy-cum-testimonial extraction. The dead writer pleas to allow readers to make up their own minds. Before the story ends, he inquires about whether the living writer also works for an army newspaper and if he now also has an incinerator for his novels' characters.

Without a clear motive for digging up the dead writer, readers are left to speculate about why this happened in the first place. The story's dedication to the dead of the Iran-Iraq War implies that the story is a commentary on the horrific process of mass-producing war literature—what the dead editor himself calls "khaki sperm"—and the power and corruption of the state-sponsored writer/editor during wartime. The story's final lines suggest the living author might also work for some type of "army newspaper" sometime around the year 2000 or 2001—based on the dead author's comment that he killed himself some "10 years ago," just after Operation Desert Storm.[25] A good example of such a state that sponsored writers at that time could be Iran, which has preserved a robust culture of state-sponsored literary production about the war since the conflict ended. Read in this manner, "An Army Newspaper" can be seen as a writer's reckoning with the parallel cultural horrors of the Iran-Iraq War that took place in both countries by forcing a generation of cultural producers—many of whom have died—to testify to their crimes: the living, state-sponsored, and possibly Iranian writer, editor, or intellectual is hearing directly from his

Ba'thist predecessor about the dangerous consequences of promoting an authoritarian state's literature: madness that eventually leads to suicide.

Blasim's "An Army Newspaper" has been righty identified as a story of "ghosts and haunting that interrogates the past and the genealogy of the cultural production during the war years."[26] It also shows how "memory is haunted, not just by ghostly others but by the horrors we have done, seen, and condoned, or by the unspeakable things from which we have profited," as Nguyen writes.[27] It finds a parallel in *Frankenstein in Baghdad*, by implying that Iraq's recent past contains an unfinished chapter about its Iraqi victims that has never properly been treated, buried instead under more wars. The undead in both these stories "appear when the trouble they represent is no longer being contained or repressed or blocked from view."[28] Each use the monstrous undead to put on trial (and convict) members of the Ba'thist war machine, whether it is the home front party apparatchik like Abu Zaydun, or the cultural producers who were part of the home front war effort. The additional presence of madness in both stories, be it Elishva's dementia or the editor's slide into insanity via the "khaki sperm" he helped create, critique the supposedly "'sane' discourse of cultural and political authority" forced on a population by the Iraqi (and perhaps Iranian) wartime state(s).[29] The elimination of these remnants of the Ba'th show how the violence of the past is intricately linked to the violence of the present.

Diaa Jubaili's Flash Fiction and the Salty Taste of Death

A more recent take on the theme of the undead in relation to the Iran-Iraq War comes from Diaa Jubaili, whose 2018 collection of short stories and flash fiction, *No Windmills in Basra*, was his first book-length work to appear in English translation. Since 2007, Jubaili has been one of the most prolific Iraqi writers of fiction, with nine novels and novellas and three short story collections to his name. *No Windmills in Basra* is the author's closest engagement with the Iran-Iraq War. The 76 stories in the collection of less than 175 pages in Arabic touch on a variety of topics and are divided into six mostly thematic sections (Wars, Love, Women, Children, Mothers, and Miscellaneous). In the following pages, I limit my readings to three of Jubaili's stories that explicitly treat the Iran-Iraq War. These micro-stories combine Jubaili's close attention to the human senses and the natural environment of the Iraqi south around Basra, and showcase the tendency for the human characters in his stories to physically transform into non-human beings. Like Saadawi and Blasim, they also involve elements that range from the fantastical to the uncanny, which place the stories firmly outside the realist vein that still dominates most Iraqi fiction. Their brevity gives them the flavor of puns, short folktales, or even short prose poems.

"Al-Mamlaḥa" ("The Saltworks") tells the story of a boy named Jamal who develops a skin condition that resembles psoriasis (al-ṣadafiyya), but his legions are actually pure, edible salt. As a child, after the bizarre condition is identified, his mother begins to scrape the salt from her son, using it in her cooking, and sharing it with her family. She never buys the seasoning again. "Life was good for his family [. . .] until the war broke in 1980. Jamal was conscripted into the grind of war, in a cursed spot in the Basra region known as "the Saltworks" [. . .] west of the city of Faw [. . .] where the bloodiest battles took place."[30] That is where Jamal disappears, and his body is never recovered. Years pass without a trace of him. Everyone gives up or stops caring about his return, save for his mother "whose life and cooking lost all flavor" and who continues to visit the Red Cross to see if there is any evidence of her salt-shedding son, dead or alive, who disappeared in Faw's "Saltworks." He is never found, and the story ends with her exclaiming "My son, Jamal! He [was] a lump of salt and he dissolved!" (Ibnī Jamāl. . .faṣṣ milḥ wa dhāb!).[31]

"The Saltworks" contains the tropes that reappear in subsequent stories in the collection: the sense of taste, the earth, physical transformation, and the disappearance of conscripts. Another piece of flash fiction, "Ṭʻam al-Mawt" ("The Taste of Death"), takes readers to the same setting: the Faw Peninsula, just twenty kilometers south of Basra. Two years after the Iran-Iraq War, a farmer named ʻAtwan, who hails from a village in the area, returns to see his land transformed into a brackish bog with nothing able to grow in the earth. With his sons, he cleans the salt off the top of the soil and brings in fresh water to restore the land to what it had previously been. Some days later, "at sunset [. . .] a platoon of fourteen soldiers that had been buried beneath the earth since the war rose up and started walking away."[32] Shocked but feeling guilty that he disturbed the dead soldiers, whose bodies are weighed down with mud and literally falling apart, ʻAtwan stops them to say that he did not mean to disturb them and to ask where they are going.

One of the undead soldiers replies "After you leached the salt out of the topsoil, with all that massive amount of fresh water that you poured over our bones, we felt our deaths had lost their taste [. . .] It's because of you that our death will never have a taste again!"[33] The dead soldiers leave and the story ends.

A third micro-story in the collection that directly references the war with Iran and takes place in the same area is "al-Ḍifdaʿ" ("The Frog"). Here, a man named ʿAlwan discovers that there is a local clientele for frog meat, which is consumed by the East Asian workers who labor in surrounding oil fields. Frogs are among the most common animals in this part of Iraq's marshlands and ʿAlwan comes up with the idea of selling fresh frog meat to these workers.[34] He discovers that the frogs are a great business opportunity, and he starts making money from catching and selling them. But one day while fishing for frogs in the one of the Shatt al-Arab's tributaries, he catches a giant frogman (*isṭāda ḍifdaʿan bashariyyan*) "who had been hiding there beneath the algae since the Iran-Iraq War."[35] He immediately starts addressing ʿAlwan: "'Who are you? Iraqi or Iranian?' the frogman asks, wheeling around in all directions. He shades his eyes with his algae- and wart covered hand, to shield them from the burning midday sun. 'Is the war over?'"[36] Like Jubaili's other works of flash fiction, the story comes to an abrupt and poignant conclusion.

The three stories I cite here share a preoccupation with the afterlives of the Iran-Iraq War in the Iraqi south, and they combine the uncanny and fantastical elements of Saadawi's and Blasim's fiction with an attention to the flora and fauna of the marshlands, now damaged by the eight years of brutal warfare that took place upon them and that left behind polluted ground and water, as well as soldiers' dead bodies buried beneath the muddy earth. And this is before the mass American bombing of Iraq between 1990 and 2003, which included the use of depleted uranium. Jubaili's approach to the Iran-Iraq War does more than write back to the previous dominant narrative of the war, the way that Saadawi's and Blasim's undead characters do. His undead characters are ephemeral snapshots that expose an intimate connection between those killed in the Iran-Iraq War and southern Iraq's marshy no-man's land that was once the site of some of the most ferocious battles between the two militaries.

The undead soldiers buried in the mud around the Faw Peninsula and rising out of the earth recall the horrific battles that took place in 1986 and 1987, as Iranian forces briefly occupied the peninsula, and then approached and were pushed back from Basra. In particular, the undead frogman in "The Frog" evokes Iran's catastrophic Karbala 4 Operation. The Iranian assault was led by amphibious soldiers whose surprise attempt to cross the Arvand Rud/Shatt al-Arab was an utter failure that led to the deaths of thousands of soldiers between December 25 and 27, 1986. The Iraqi side had been tipped off prior to the surprise attack and suffered significantly fewer casualties. This operation is often overshadowed by the massive Iranian offensive known as the Operation Karbala 5/Great Harvest (see Chapter 3) that took place between January and early April of 1987.[37]

In Iran, memory of Karbala 4 was revived in 2015 when the bodies of 175 Iranian divers who disappeared during that operation were recovered. Some of them appeared to have had their hands bound and were either shot execution style or weighed down to drown to death.[38] While this was the largest of such events in Iran in recent years, the government has continued to organize ceremonies and publicize the return of MIA soldiers' remains, which are not rare events since a 2008 agreement brokered by the International Red Cross and Red Crescent Movement on the exchange of soldiers' remains between the two countries.[39] As of writing, the most recent high-profile event occurred in May 2023 when Iranian state television station IRIB TV3 broadcast the ceremonial return of the body of a missing soldier to his parents, thirty-one years after he had disappeared. Replete with theatrical weeping and reverberating sounds of Shi'i mourning rituals, the emotionally distraught parents of the MIA soldier were brought to the event and touched the shrouded body on a red stage. Soon afterwards, however, it was revealed that the body was fake. The program garnered sharp criticism on social media and Persian language news outlets both inside and outside of Iran.[40] Although it lacks the enormous ceremonial return and media coverage, the search, recovery and return of Iraqi dead bodies from these areas also continues. As recently as February 2022, the Iraqi Red Crescent Society called on Iraqi families to retrieve the remains of 629 martyrs identified and waiting for collection near Basra.[41] Since then, there have been several instances where both governments repatriated the remains of soldiers from the other side.

In Jubaili's writing, the land that was a former war zone between the two countries is haunted by the specter of war and is one of the sites of the Iran-Iraq War's afterlives. In his micro-stories, the land, its mud, and the Shatt al-Arab and its tributaries, seem to have no shortage of bodies willing to rise to the surface, if only they are called forth. This haunted geography preoccupies writers on the other side of the war, too, with Iranian writer Nasim Marashi employing ghost-like figures to highlight a haunting presence left in the wake of the Iran-Iraq War, linking it to the environmental degradation left in its aftermath.

WAR'S HAUNTING AFTERLIVES IN NASIM MARASHI'S *PRUNING*

In 2017, Iranian writer Nasim Marashi (b. 1984) published her second novel, *Pruning*.[42] It depicts the dark consequences of the Iran-Iraq War for the parents of a child who was killed in the initial Iraqi bombardment of Khorramshahr and portrays some of the bitter afterlives of the war as experienced by Iranian civilians of the city. It does so by connecting the violence and personal losses of the conflict to the haunting consequences of slow, long-term violence felt within Khuzestan in the years following the war's end. This postwar reality is more than the melancholic memories of wartime deaths, though. It includes the psychological consequences of war on the families of those who lost loved ones, especially mothers, who are presented as constant mourners both for people and places forever lost. This includes the destruction of the natural environment of the country's southwest region, and significantly, its marshlands located between Abadan and Ahvaz, an area referred to as the Shadegan Ponds (*Tālāb-e Shādegān*), further within Iranian territory but part of the same natural environment featured prominently in Jubaili's work. *Pruning*, which is set in 1997, is built on a fragmented narrative that suspensefully unfolds as the author rapidly plays with both the progression of time and narrative point of view. Uniquely within Persian literature, *Pruning* draws a throughline from the moment of a mother's despair during the Iran-Iraq War, to postwar processes of mourning, the 1990–91 Gulf War, the slow violence of war's environmental ruin, and a narrative of ecological and personal survival and renewal.

Pruning revolves around Rasul and Naval (*Navāl*), a husband and wife from Khorramshahr, and their five children. The children's births, and in two cases, deaths, span a period that begins in 1978 and ends nearly twenty years later. These births and deaths punctuate the storyline, creating seminal moments around which the parents form their happiest and darkest memories that reappear several times over the course of the novel. Structurally, the novel uses Rasul and Naval's married life, along with Rasul's search for Naval in the present moment, as a type of frame story to unfold layers of the couple's backstory that contains moments of joy, unspoken memories of death, and the seeds of haunting traumas.

The novel opens with an image of Rasul, a once tall, strong, and proud father, now aged and haggard after losing two children over the previous decade, and having taken on the role of single father of the three remaining children for the three years before the novel's opening scene. Of the five children whom he fathered with Naval, their firstborn son, Sharhan, is killed in 1981 during the first year of the war. His daughter Tahani, the youngest of all five children, dies shortly before the novel begins, quietly choking to death on a jujube fruit in the family's backyard. Among Rasul's three remaining children are his two daughters, Anis and Amal, each born shortly after Sharhan's death, and his son, Mahziar, now aged six. In the novel's opening scene Mahziar accompanies Rasul who is driving along the Ahvaz-Abadan Highway in the sweltering heat to the nearby marshlands where he has recently learned that Naval—who disappeared approximately three years earlier—is now living. In the novel's first chapter, the father and son, with the help of a local man who has a boat, arrive at their destination, a fictional island village in the marshes called Dar ol-Talʿeh (*Dār al-Ṭalʿeh*), where Naval is now said to live. The island is inhabited only by women; outsiders, especially men, are not supposed to enter. The rest of the novel takes place there, where a few of the island's elderly women insist that Naval is no longer the woman Rasul once knew and that he should avoid contact with her and go home. Meanwhile, Rasul and Naval's backstory is revealed in the form of the husband's flashbacks, or moments in the narrative that loosely connect an occurrence in the present to a point in the previous two decades.

At the heart of Naval's disappearance are two incidents involving her children. The first is the death of their firstborn child, Sharhan, who was only three years old when he was killed in a missile strike on Khorramshahr, nearly sixteen years before the story's present moment. His death traumatizes the couple and despite the birth of two girls shortly after, Sharhan's loss casts an irreparable shadow over them. The second incident happens ten years later when Naval becomes pregnant again, with what would be a fourth child, who, she claims during the pregnancy, will be a boy. From this pregnancy comes Mahziar, Rasul's son (or so readers are led to believe). However, the true story is more complicated. Toward the end of the novel, it is revealed that shortly after Mahziar's birth, which happens while Rasul is away working as a contractor in Kuwait putting out oil well fires, Naval, despondent, paid a nurse at a hospital to "ensure" she would have a boy. To do so, the nurse paid a local Arab family and traded them the girl whom Naval had just birthed in exchange for their newborn son. Rasul returns home a few weeks later and realizes what has transpired in his absence. Enraged, he finds out who has his biological daughter and buys her back, while also keeping Mahziar as an adopted son. By that time, Naval has already left, both out of disgust for herself and, as revealed in the novel's penultimate chapter, at Rasul's behest. From that moment onward, Rasul is essentially left on his own to raise four young children: Anis, Amal, Mahziar, and Tahani, his youngest biological daughter who dies shortly before the novel begins. Despite the hardships that the family endures, *Pruning* offers no cathartic denouement. The trip to the island does not end successfully for Rasul, and he must come to terms with the fact that his wife is now transformed forever and will stay on the island.

Pruning's most direct references to the Iran-Iraq War take place through Naval's flashbacks to the war years, and the most important of those takes readers back to Khorramshahr in the early days of the war. The references to the war are moments that civilians experience—never direct references to frontline combat or the street-to-street fighting that took place in Khorramshahr and some of the country's southwestern cities. Unsurprisingly, the most memorable example of these is Sharhan's death in a missile attack on the city, which appears in the book's third chapter It repeatedly refers to the sensorial markers that surround Naval during the moments when Sharhan is killed; the sounds, sights, and smells that stick to her memory afterward. Naval, who is in the kitchen at the time hears "that sound" and runs outside to find Sharhan in the alley beside the house. The boy is sitting on the street, stunned. People are running frantically in every direction, screaming. Naval grabs her son and carries him into their home, still fixated on what she heard. As she brings him inside, her attention shifts to his heavy breathing that turns into wheezing. Then she feels a "warm liquid dripping down the bump of her stomach" and sees her yellow and green shirt, now colored red.[43] Rather than refer directly to rockets and bombs, the passage instead makes repeated references to Naval's sensorial memories: the sounds of the rockets, women screaming, her son's final breaths, the smell of dates left burning on the stove, the weight of her body from a second pregnancy, and the warmth of the fluid she feels drip on her leg, the first sign that her son has been fatally injured in the attack and is bleeding to death. She embodies the consequences of her son's death and the first days of war. To read the Iran-Iraq War in *Pruning* is less about reading what happened during the eight years of conflict and more about how the effects of the war, and especially how the death of Naval' son consumes her and leads her to the island.

The first indication that the consequences of war are too much for Naval to bear appear some three years after the war ends, and nearly eleven years after Sharhan's death. By that point, the couple has relocated to Ahvaz, she has had two more children and is pregnant with a third. Here, the novel takes a sudden turn toward the uncanny. For ten years since Sharhan's death, Naval claims, literally, to have been unable to see men or boys with the exception for Rasul. Visually, she only registers women. Rasul, rather than recognizing a deeper problem, only insists that she must move on. He tells her that she ought to "snap out of it because the war is over. [. . .] if she would just take a proper look around, she would see men in the streets. Men who were POWs are being freed. Men who left cities are coming back and boys are being born one after another." None of that matters to Naval as she continues to be haunted by the war:

> [O]n the many nights that Naval couldn't sleep, she wouldn't count sheep, but instead would count Khorramshahr's dead men. She would start with her family and those close to her: her son; then her father and her cousins who, prior to Sharhan and her father, had died, their bodies blown into bits and pieces. Then she moved on to her neighbors, then her childhood

playmates, then the other folks who used to live in town, then the people whose names she saw on television, on the *hejlehs* at the end of the alleyways, on the headstones at Jannat-Abad Cemetery, names that she just couldn't forget and which Rasul ordered her to never again mention.[44]

Within the larger context of Iranian literature of this war, *Pruning* stands out by creating a transnational connection between Iran and Iraq by depicting Iranian civilians' experiences of the 1990–1991 Gulf War. Parts the novel go back to January and February 1991 and the Iraqi retreat from Kuwait. At that time, the Iraqi military set fire to over 700 Kuwaiti oil wells and storage tanks, dumped massive amounts of oil into the Persian Gulf, and created trenches and man-made "oil lakes" in an attempt to stop the potential advance of coalition troops into Iraq.[45] The massive fires created billows of black smoke that choked the skies for months, with the first fire put out in April and the last on November 6, 1991.

Pruning brings together these distinct wars in two ways: via Naval's memories of chemical weapons during the Iran-Iraq War, and later through Rasul's journey to Kuwait as part of one of the international firefighting crews that helped put out the oil fires—an effort that American firefighters dubbed "Operation Desert Hell."[46] Naval's haunting memories of the Iran-Iraq War meld with how she comes to experience the 1990–1991 Gulf War from afar. The oil fires caused what was referred to as "black rain" to fall on the surrounding region, spreading out for hundreds of kilometers from the fires' epicenters, which included large parts of Iran.[47] Some three years after the Iran-Iraq War ends, Naval "suddenly sees the sky go black as if it were night." She hears thunder and lightning and feels drops on her hand. "It was black [. . .] as if there was ink on it, something greasy and dirty that couldn't be shaken off. It occurred to Naval that war had started again. This black ink was [a sign of] chemical weapons." Convinced that Iraqi planes are dropping chemical weapons and that she and everyone around her will die there and then, she thinks "How good it is that Sharhan has already died. He won't burn to death from these chemicals."[48] The black rain, infused with oil debris from the burning wells, brings to the fore all of Naval's embodied trauma from the Iran-Iraq War. She collapses in the street, only to be revived after a neighbor shakes her back to reality.

But if the burning oil fields from the environmental fallout from the 1990–1991 Gulf War are a source of trauma for Naval, for Rasul they become a means of income, revenge, and pride. He joins the well-paid effort to put out the fires and returns from Kuwait "darkened, fattened, wearing jeans and a golden American watch."[49] A flashback takes us to that time, as he fights the fires with ferocity, with almost superhuman qualities. Others pass out from the intensity of the heat, but the fires had no effect on Rasul:

> He was Abraham. Strong and full of hope. While facing the fires and the terrifying sounds of the roaring flames that sucked up the air from every direction and sent plumes of black smoke into the sky, he would hear the intermingled laughter of Naval and his son together. Those were the sounds that got him through his days in Kuwait. He would stand in front of the fires and listen, allowing those otherworldly sounds of the fires to enchant him [...] They came from another world and brought with them sounds of laughter. The sounds of Sharhan in Khorramshahr, sounds that were supposed to come back with the birth of Mahziar."[50]

The passage weaves memories of the death of the couple's firstborn in the Iran-Iraq War into their attempts to get on with their lives in the postwar era, connecting that era to the next regional war that happens so quickly and takes place so close to their home.

The Environment, Loss, and the Living Dead

Rasul will never hear the imagined sounds that carried him through his experience in Kuwait. Instead, he returns home to the realization that his biological daughter had been traded (along with a large sum of money he had saved for the family) for a local family's newborn son. After he kicks Naval out of the house, she goes first to their old and now destroyed home in Khorramshahr. She is found by one of the women from the island community of Dar ol-Tal'eh, who takes her there.

While Naval and Rasul's backstory frames and animates the novel's plot, the women who reside on the island, along with the natural environment that surrounds it, give *Pruning* another rich level of engagement with the various afterlives of the Iran-Iraq War. From the time that Rasul and Mahziar step onto the narrow canoe-like boat that takes them to the island, the novel emphasizes the ecological setting of the marshes, stressing the tragic beauty, power, and suffering of the giant, ubiquitous palm trees—often headless and burnt, a sign of a tree that has been killed but stands while dying from within—and the water buffaloes who appear repeatedly throughout the passages that take place on the island. But just as trees bear the scars of war and the slow environmental decay that follows, the buffaloes also show signs of pain and suffering:

> Rasul looked at [the women's] black water buffaloes that stood taller than him. Seven enormous buffaloes, all of them injured and deformed. Up close they appeared as huge, black, demon-like beasts that only resembled something of a water buffalo. Each one was now incomplete. The one standing in front had two wooden sticks tied with a rope to what remained of its front legs. To move, it would press the two sticks to the ground and spring its giant body forward with its back legs. Another had a triangular chunk missing from its back hump that left a shining wound in its place. For another, a bone covered by loose skin stood in place of its leg [. . .]. Finally, the last buffalo was missing the entire upper half of its face. What remained was a mouth with two large holes above it, which it kept close to the front buffalo, smelling her and using the scent to guide herself forward. What was left of the creatures' udders were crumpled pieces of skin that sagged between their legs and as they walked, while their flesh slipped in and out from between bones of their rib cages.[51]

The headless palm trees and wounded water buffaloes of the marshes are signs of what Rob Nixon has called "slow violence." As opposed to violence that "is customarily conceived as an event or an action that is immediate in time, explosive and spectacular in space, and is erupting into instant sensational visibility," slow violence "occurs gradually and out of sight," it is a "violence of delayed destruction that is dispersed across time and space, an attritional violence that is typically not viewed as violence at all."[52] Despite over forty years of attention given to this war and its consequences in Iran through research and cultural production, its environmental and ecological impact has received relatively little attention, and much of that has gone to the analysis of oil spills in the Persian Gulf. This is likely because the Iranian government's immediate attention was focused on rebuilding cities, the economy, and the military, and because unlike the 1990–1991 Gulf War, "the international community did not monitor environmental effects of the Iran-Iraq war."[53] Yet, some facts are known. For example, more than three million date palms and five thousand hectares of orchards were destroyed in the Iran-Iraq War. Additionally, nearly 130,000 hectares of natural forests and 753,000 hectares of pastureland were made unusable in the provinces most affected by the war. Iran's southwestern provinces, where *Pruning* is set, "experienced extreme environmental damage" with its residents reporting a higher incidence of a variety of health problems "possibly as a result of war-induced toxins in the environment."[54] Researchers have also concluded that water and land in the areas hit hardest by the war are still polluted by its effects, including those caused by chemical weapons.[55]

Aside from the ecological ruin of an isolated island community and its slow ecological renewal, Dar ol-Tal'eh is also depicted as a place surrounded by a magical and mysterious aura.[56] The women whom Naval joins there are all widows and/or mothers who have lost children, a category of person for whom neither English nor Persian has a single word, as they do for "widow" or "orphan."[57] Together, they form a community based on having experienced irrevocable loss that holds deep connections to the island's natural surroundings. For Naval, her losses are compounded: in addition to the loss of her home, and the deaths of her family members in Khorramshahr, she must contend with her initial refusal to leave that city, which resulted in her son Sharhan's death; as well as the loss of her daughter whom she traded away to appease her husband and try to make up for Sharhan's death. She is now made up of all these losses; they keep her on the island.

In going to Dar ol-Tal'eh, Rasul naively thinks he will find his wife and bring her home, fixing his family's dire circumstances. After arriving, however, his attempts to see her fail. For days he is stalled by a few of the island's old women, namely Umm 'Aqil and Umm Ziya, who aside from knowing him from when they all lived in Khorramshahr, also refer to him by a name he has not heard in years: Abu Sharhan, or "Father of Sharhan."[58] At first Umm 'Aqil and Umm Ziya are adamant that he and Mahziar cannot be there, as the island is strictly for women who have lost loved ones in the war. After a couple of days of insisting, though, he breaks free from them to approach the house where he believes Naval resides, but is stopped by strong winds and choking sandstorms that seem to be controlled by a supernatural force. Before finally coming face-to-face with her, Umm Ziya tries to kill his hopes once and for all, telling him that the women on the island are not simply hiding their past lives. He tells him:

> You want too much from this life, Rasul. We're cursed. There are some things that people shouldn't see. A woman shouldn't see her children die, her home destroyed, her land blown away. If she sees those things, she shouldn't remain here. She should die. Life isn't supposed to be like this—that children die and mothers live, that fathers die and their land remains. We're not humans, Rasul. They dragged us into the lowest depth of hell and pulled us back up. We've come back from hell. Look at us. We're dead. Our land, our water buffaloes, us; we're all dead. We only walk. What did I tell you before? Don't think that Naval is the same Naval that you had before. Don't think you'll take her hand, leave, and it'll be over. Go see her, then go make up a story to tell for the rest of your life. I'm telling you this for your own sake, Rasul. It's going to be hard.[59]

This scene sets the stage for an intense meeting that soon takes place between the couple. Umm Ziya takes Mahziar aside so Rasul can meet Naval. She is now a barely recognizable shell of her former self: frail, hunched over, and ghost-like. Her voice at first is strange and almost inaudible.

> Naval was not the person who used to walk the earth, she was a ghost, lethargic, slow. She didn't walk but hovered just above the ground. She wore a black shirt, her long, gray hair was pulled behind her head. She sat on a rock in front of Rasul [...] He could not stop staring at her, at the shadow of what Naval once was. He looked at her for a sign of the Naval who was once his wife and could not find her. She looked up at him. He shivered. Her eyes were no longer dark. They had turned gray. She had become the same Naval from years ago in Khorramshahr, but now colorless. And her body now consisted of all the bodies of those who had died in the war and afterward: her father, Sharhan, and more than anyone else, Tahani. Her sickliness was Tahani's. The paleness of her face, too. She was Tahani, alive and old, now looking at Rasul. A long time passed this way, enough that Rasul could think of a thousand things to say but

couldn't bring himself to mutter one. "You gave her [Tahani] a beautiful name," Naval said.

Rasul was stunned. It wasn't Naval's voice. It was hoarse and scratchy. It was the voice of her father coming out of Naval's mouth. "I read it on her gravestone," she said.[60]

These ghostly descriptions of Naval in the novel's penultimate chapter depict her as the embodiment of the condition in which she now lives, a fantastical state of permanent mourning for her family and her city, recalling what Žižek has called "the monstrous living dead."[61] In this form, Naval represents what Gordon considers "a loss [...] of life" or "a path not taken." She embodies features of her dead family members while still fleetingly manifesting parts of her old self. At the same time, however, her existence on the island also "represents a future possibility, a hope."[62] Naval's new state of being and presence on Dar ol-Taʻleh grants her supernatural powers. Namely, after Umm ʻAqil brings her to the island from the site of her destroyed house in Khorramshahr, Naval acquires healing powers and a new maternal role, this time for the dead and dying palm trees, claiming to the other women soon after she arrives that she is "the mother of anything that has died in the war."[63] Indeed, Rasul finds himself in front of a barely recognizable being that resembles Naval, but this new Naval can bring back to life the burnt, headless palm trees of the island that were badly damaged in the Iran-Iraq War. This is what gives the women on the island hope and her presence and powers are what sustains the community.

Her inability to return to society and the women's need for Naval ensure that she will never leave the Dar ol-Taʻleh and its marshes. In this sense, Naval's loss, which originated in the war, is the starting point for an entirely new life. Judith Butler's observation on the political possibilities of loss is instructive here. She writes:

> Places are lost—destroyed, vacated, barred—but then there is some new place, and it is not the first [...] [T]here is an impossibility housed at the site of this new place. What is new, newness itself, is founded upon the loss of original place, and so it is a newness that has within it a sense of belatedness, of coming after, and of being thus fundamentally determined by a past that continues to inform it. And so this past is not actually past

in the sense of "over," since it continues as an animating absence in the presence, one that makes itself known [...] We could say [...] that this new place is one of no belonging, where subjectivity becomes untethered from its collective fabric, where individuation becomes a historical necessity. But perhaps this is a place where belonging now takes place in and through a common sense of loss [...] Loss becomes [a] condition and necessity for a certain sense of community, where community does not overcome the loss, where community cannot overcome the loss without losing the very sense of itself as community. And if we say this second truth about the place where belonging is possible, then pathos is not negated, but it turns out to be oddly fecund, paradoxically productive.[64]

It is precisely this mode of productivity that Rasul realizes in his final moments on Dar ol-Tal'eh. He watches Naval rub burnt palm trees, bringing them back to life, and slowly realizes that he and Mahziar will return to Ahvaz without her. After their initial meeting, and still dumbfounded by the site of Naval, Rasul wanders into the nearby palm grove hoping to speak to Umm Ziya, whom he had just seen enter it. She disappears and he suddenly finds himself stunned, in awe of the palms' trunks "which seem to have existed forever and which will remain forever. [...]. Burnt, dead, but standing. These trees were the guards of this village. Eternal soldiers. Just like the men for whom Naval once searched. The men whom she did not see."[65] Rasul finally comes to the realization that "the palms did something to Naval that he never could have done. Now she belonged to them. She belonged to those dead dishdasha-wearing men."[66] He quickly leaves after telling Umm 'Aqil that Naval should stay for the palms and that he will bring their daughters another time to see her.

Although *Pruning* uses the war as a starting point to which it constantly refers, it stands out as singular story in the context of Iranian war literature. Not only does it eschew the prominent features of both Sacred Defense literature and general war literature in the Iranian context, it also sheds light on silenced narratives of the war's afterlives, such as the incurable melancholy of the mother who loses a son and the war's destruction of the natural environment. The novel offers no solution for bringing back what the war took away. The dead are forever dead, and the living must learn to move on. By leaving Naval on the island, in a liminal state of being that is neither fully with the living nor with the dead, Marashi's novel proffers a conclusion to the war that skirts around the official governmental script of Sacred Defense, as well as more straightforward attempts at criticizing the government's handling of the conflict. Instead, it highlights a quiet counternarrative to the war that is completely devoid of the tired clichés that have dominated war literature since the 1980s: there are no heroes, no martyrs, no stories of the war front or the lives of veterans.[67] Indeed, *Pruning* does not even celebrate any of its own characters, choosing to leave them all as highly imperfect victims. The novel is simply not interested in treating the war in such a way, even though its storyline cannot exist if not for the war. Instead, the Iran-Iraq War and its consequences become an entirely personal tragedy for their protagonists, and the starting point for wholly different types of stories. These stories are what call attention to the haunted remains of postwar life that are neglected by the Sacred Defense narrative: the destruction of the earth, the permanent loss of a city and home, and the loss of loved ones who had no interest in a war between good and evil. Furthermore, the novel's engagement with war is even more general than the Iran-Iraq War. By tying the effects of that war to the 1990–1991 Gulf War, *Pruning* reframes Iran's war with Iraq as part of a chapter of entangled violence that crossed borders, connecting the effects of Iraq's second major conflict in the late twentieth century to the lives of Iranians who inhabit the same geography.

WRITING THE SPECTERS OF WAR

For all their engagement with the consequences of the Iran-Iraq War, none of the texts treated in this chapter are conventional pieces of "war literature," even if they are stories that have been shaped entirely by, and in fact owe their complete existence to, that war. By reading them as part of the Iran-Iraq War's literary afterlives, I am again invoking Nguyen's notion of a "panoramic optics" to show how broad the effects of war are on literature and to expose the wide range of engagements that writers have had with the Iran-Iraq War. These panoramic optics allow us to include Iraqi fiction that is ostensibly about the post-2003 period (Saadawi's *Frankenstein*); or which is entirely about fantastical, undead victims of the war who exist outside the immediate context of the war front or the home front (Blasim's "Army

Newspaper"); or whose deaths at the front seem to have very little to do with the states' narratives of the war (Jubaili's micro-fiction); alongside an Iranian novel about civilians living through the tenacious consequences of home front violence (Marashi's *Pruning*). In all these works, written decades after the conflict ended, by a younger generation of writers, specters of the Iran-Iraq War are palpably present.

The question of generation, which I have brought up only minimally until now, is worth considering, if only briefly. The writers in this chapter were all born between 1973 and 1984. Their personal experiences of the war varied, but none of them fought at the front or were older than fifteen when the war ended. Saadawi and Blasim hail from Baghdad and experienced the war as adolescents and young teenagers there. Jubaili is younger, from Basra, and was only three years old when the war broke out and twelve when it ended. Marashi is younger still; she was born in 1984 and thus barely capable of remembering the war. That all these authors—who are at least a generation younger than the writers who addressed the war in the 1980s and 1990s—have chosen to do so through ghosts and the uncanny, signals a new approach to this war across both national literatures. Their relationship to the war and representation of it is different from that of earlier generations. If it is not too early to draw conclusions, it seems clear that some writers of this generation are willing to make a strong break with realism's dominance of the war's literature in both Persian and Arabic literary traditions, and to draw clearer connections between the war and the slow violence left in its wake. Moreover, the tropes of Iranian and Iraqi literatures of this war, which were covered repeatedly in the previous chapters of this book, are transformed by the authors of the texts covered in this chapter. Among others, the absence of soldiers gone missing in action, mourning mothers, headless palm trees, symbolic animals, and soldiers returning from the front, all appear in these works but do so in new ways that defy the older modes of representation and gesture towards the creation of new horizons of expectation for readers. These texts more fully integrate the Iran-Iraq War into the longer histories of contemporary Iran and Iraq, while also calling for a more complicated understanding of the war, its afterlives, and the war's literature.

Conclusion
CULTURAL AFTERLIVES OF 1979

THE CONTINUED INTEREST BY WRITERS IN ADDRESSING THE IRAN-Iraq War seems unlikely to disappear anytime soon. Nearly four decades have passed since the Iran-Iraq War ended, and the conflict is still being addressed in fictional works that achieve high-profile status, written by a broad array of writers, across multiple generations of men and women who bring different perspectives, styles, and ideological orientations to their war stories. Writers who were already established when the war began addressed it early on; another group—including some writers from the same generation—gained a name for themselves with the financial opportunities that writing for the state afforded them; other writers grew up in the shadow of the war, as both young soldiers and civilians, and began writing about it, often highly critically, in the 1990s and early 2000s; and in the past decade and a half, writers who were too young to remember experiencing the war firsthand have also begun writing about it. Taken together, these writers have produced an enormous body of fiction about the Iran-Iraq War, primarily written in Arabic and Persian and aimed at readers of those languages. If one looks beyond fiction to consider poetry, theatre, cinema, and the visual arts, the number of cultural texts that address this conflict grows exponentially. All this points to the fact that Iranians and Iraqis themselves see the war years as a pivotal period in their modern history. It set the stage for much of what has come afterward and, in many ways, continues to be felt until today.

The comparisons made in this book between Iranian and Iraqi literatures highlight how mutual entanglements with the Iran-Iraq War have pushed some writers from both sides of the conflict to address its legacy and use fiction as a vehicle to rewrite the wartime states' narratives. Bringing together the literatures of this war also calls attention to the ways that the war has affected the trajectories of each national literature since 1980, both of which go beyond the borders of the Iraqi and Iranian states. Reading these contemporary literatures alongside each other and in relation to the war reveals how this event altered the trajectories of Iranian and Iraqi fiction, coincidentally making some of the analytical frameworks first used to read one country's literature now just as applicable to the other. By way of example, the fissure between writers producing outside and inside Iraq during the years of Ba'thist rule that Fatima Mohsen and others have highlighted, now seems to be more applicable to the publishing ecosystem of Iranian Persian language writers than that of Iraqi Arabic language writers. Since the fall of the Iraqi Ba'thist regime, Iraqi readers and writers inside and outside the country are no longer cut off from each other. Some censorship still exists in Iraq, but it is neither as strict nor as systematic as it was under Saddam Hussein. Instead, vague laws allow the government to prohibit the distribution of books that are deemed politically or religiously sensitive at any given moment.[1] More importantly, digital publishing, the ability to publish with Arabic language presses outside Iraq, and the widespread presence of literature available for free (and often illegally) online, has eroded divisions between writers and readers located within the country and abroad. Iraqi writers on the inside and outside now both participate in a global Arabic literary ecosystem, perhaps best evidenced by the presence of Iraqi writers from across the globe on the same lists of international Arabic literary prizes, such as Gulf-based prizes like the International Prize for Arabic Fiction, the Katara Prize and AlMultaqa Prize, for the Arabic Short Story. Of course, some important differences among Iraqi writers themselves remain, not least between those who left the country between the 1970s and 1990s and those who worked with the Ba'thist regime during the same time, as well as between those who supported the 2003 invasion and those who opposed it. Nevertheless, the ability of both texts and writers to enter and exit Iraq is significantly easier today than at any point since the years of Baʻthist rule.

By contrast, one cannot speak of a similarly coherent publishing ecosystem of Persian literature today. Writers working in Iran are still subject to the Islamic Republic's strict censorship laws and infamously laborious process of obtaining permission for their books to be published. Works of Persian literature published by presses outside the country rarely, if ever, receive permission to be distributed within the country, which is often the reason why they are published abroad in the first place. Digital publishing and even the free availability of works of contemporary Iranian literature online has not successfully bridged the divide, either. Recently, Laetitia Nanquette has noted that despite the generally well-connected nature of the Iranian diaspora, large-scale transnational literary exchanges have not developed between the Iranian literary communities inside and outside Iran, due to "[d]istrust between the diaspora and Iran, [...] heavy sanctions, and restrictions on cultural exchange."[2] The result is a discernable Iranian "literature of the outside" and a "literature of the inside," that is reminiscent of Iraq's Baʻthist era. A once useful framework for reading the literature of Iraq, this bifurcation is now arguably more useful for reading the literature of Iran.

The dynamics of writers among themselves and their relationships to their places of residence both inside and outside Iran and Iraq, also affect how these different groups have addressed the war. As this book has demonstrated, Iraqi writers publishing outside the country have been writing about the war with Iran since the 1980s. This is likely to do with the wave of Iraqi intellectuals and artists who fled the country during the war with Iran, and who brought their experiences of the war and Baʻthist oppression into their literary works. Successive wars and crippling sanctions after 1990 created new waves of Iraqi exiles and refugees. The writers among them wove the story of the Iran-Iraq War into Iraq's longer experience with war going well into the twenty-first century. With the fall of Saddam, Iraqi writers across the globe began addressing the war in a similar fashion, almost universally critiquing it and condemning the wartime government.

On the other hand, exilic and diasporic Iranian writers have not demonstrated as much interest in writing about the experience of war with Iraq, opting instead to focus on the 1979 Revolution and political oppression within Iran, as well as the difficulties of assimilating into European and North American societies. Like the Iraqi case, this has much to do with the timing of Iranian emigration, with the greatest wave occurring shortly after the Revolution. It seems that relatively few of these writers experienced the war in ways that would make it into their literary works. By contrast, the war with Iraq has remained one of the most prominent topics in Persian literature produced within Iran, with the state capitalizing on it as much as possible, others using it as a point of contention with the state, and others still only mentioning it as an unavoidable part of life for most of the 1980s with consequences that reach into the present.

Thus, nearly four decades since the end of this conflict, the stakes of writing about this war remain much higher in Iran than they do in Iraq, and to differing degrees, they have been since 1988. The Islamic Republic remains invested in its war narrative and the production of literature and other forms of cultural production that reinforce it. Alongside the Iranian novels I have treated here, the majority of which are not considered "Sacred Defense literature" by critics of Persian literature, there are a plethora of war memoirs, films, novels, short stories, works of literary criticism, and poetry that reinforce the narrative of the Sacred Defense. At this point, Sacred Defense cultural producers, writers or otherwise, are far more professionalized than they were during the war, but at its core, the war narrative is the same as it was during wartime: a religio-nationalist narrative of "resistance" that supports the Islamic Republic of Iran. When considered alongside state funding and support for national and local prizes for the best works of Sacred Defense cultural production, one sees that the "Sacred Defense cultural industry" is alive and well, even if its base of consumers remains limited.

THE WAR'S OTHER CULTURAL AFTERLIVES

Looking beyond the literary sphere can help illustrate how Iranian and Iraqi cultural producers' relationships to the war differ today. Since the early 2010s, Iranian state-sponsored cultural producers have expanded Sacred Defense culture to encompass and represent the Islamic Republic's new challenges. For example, as the Syrian Revolution surged in 2011, Iran swiftly came to the assistance of the Bashar al-Assad regime, a fellow member of the so-called regional "Axis of Resistance," which includes Lebanon's Hizballah and Iraqi Shi'i paramilitary organizations. By 2012, Iran began sending units of the IRGC along with groups of volunteer Iranian, Afghan, and Pakistani Shi'i fighters, known as "Shrine Defenders" (*Modāfʿeān-e Haram*), to Syria ostensibly to protect the Shi'i shrines from destruction at the hands of the so-called Islamic State (IS or *Daesh*). In doing so, they also provided critical support for the Syrian army and state-sponsored militias in their crackdown on civilian protestors and a range of anti-Assad militants operating in the country. As the recruitment efforts in Iran ramped up and the bodies of these fighters began coming back in larger numbers, regime-affiliated cultural producers increasingly tied the war effort to the visual, sonic, and literary iconography of the Sacred Defense. By the mid-2010s, pro-regime social media and online news outlets were spreading images that clearly linked this new resistance operation to the legacy of the Iran-Iraq War. One such video from 2015 features Sadeq Ahangaran, the Islamic Republic's panegyrist (*maddāh*) and dirge reciter par excellence, who rose to fame for his emotional recitations preparing Iranian soldiers to fight and die at the Iran-Iraq War front. He recites several dirges in the presence the Supreme Leader Ali Khamenei and a hall full of tearful members of the IRGC, including Qasem Soleimani, then leader of the Quds Force, the IRGC division primarily responsible for foreign military operations, at the time the most important of which was in Syria.[3] Ahangaran, who among the living cultural producers who were active during wartime, has the most recognizable and powerful voice of the Iran-Iraq War, the sound of which immediately conjures images of frontline soldiers preparing for combat. Since at least the mid-2010s, he has appeared repeatedly at events that evoke the war's memory and connect it to contemporary events, such as the war in Syria or Soleimani's assassination by the U.S in 2020.[4] Even more recently, images of Iranian soldiers from the Iran-Iraq War have also been incorporated into state messaging on the Coronavirus pandemic, visually connecting "the soldiers of the Sacred Defense with the Health Defenders [*Modāfeʿān-e Salāmati*]."[5] At the same time, the production of Sacred Defense literature, especially in the form of memoirs issued by state-sponsored publishers, remains constant. The most prominent example of this is the memoir of Seyyedeh Zahra Hoseyni, titled *Dā* (the Kurdish word for "mother") which is marketed by Sureh-ye Mehr as a must-read and is currently in its 159th printing, although the number of actual book purchases, let alone readers, is highly debatable and likely far less than that number suggests.[6] These are just a few ways in which the war with Iraq continues to be upheld as a fundamental pillar of the current Iranian regime and appears in the greater contemporary Iranian cultural landscape.

Broader Iraqi cultural memory of the Iran-Iraq War is distinct from its Iranian counterpart, despite its recurring appearance in Arabic fiction. Since 2003, the absence of the Iraqi wartime government and a near nonstop cycle of other wars and forms of violence from 1980 to at least 2017, have stripped away the once great political importance that representation of this war had for Iraqi writers. Long gone are the days when Iraqi writers felt threatened for writing against the war or Saddam Hussein. Almost since the time the Iran-Iraq War ended, the Iraqi state lost interest in investing in cultural production praising Saddam's Qadisiyya. Furthermore, the post-Saddam iterations of the Iraqi government, which generally have had much friendlier relations with Iran, have never assigned much symbolic importance to this war either. As this book shows, however, that does not imply that writers (or scholars) are not interested in the war with Iran or the variety of ways it has made itself felt for Iraqis until today. The presence of the Iran-Iraq War in many works of Arabic fiction, as well as scholarship on contemporary Iraqi history, society, and culture, tells a different story. In these cases, the Iran-Iraq War—the actual "First Gulf War"—is consistently portrayed as the start of a decades-long sustained experience of varying levels of warfare, and one of the root causes of post-1988 wars and violence. Iraqi fiction written since the 1990s often portrays this war as the source of long-term pain, buried traumas, and the basis of many present-day unsettled scores.

Nonetheless, other aspects of the Iraqi ancien régime's official war culture have lived on outside the literary realm. Today, among some Iraqis both within the country and abroad, there is nostalgia for Saddam's rule, which despite nearly ten years of war and authoritarianism, some now retrospectively view as an era less mired in governmental corruption and sectarianism. This feeling is even held by many Iraqi Arab youth who carry "feelings of nostalgia for a time that they did not live through but that they feel symbolized Iraqi national unity and strength."[7] This sentiment has perhaps contributed to the recent spread of some once popular "songs of Saddam's Qadisiyya" that flooded the airwaves during the 1980s. Today, these songs occupy a niche but well-visited corner of the Arabic language internet, with dozens of social media accounts devoted to keeping alive the memory of these songs and all they represent. The wartime song "*Yā Gā', Turābich Kāfūrī*" ("Oh Homeland, Your Earth is my Camphor") is an interesting example. The lyrics in Iraqi colloquial Arabic were composed by the popular poet Kazim al-Isma'il al-Kati' and then put to music and sung by musician 'Ali 'Abd Allah, "appearing [on radio and television] almost daily during the eight years of the war."[8] One video that exists on several social media sites today features 'Abd Allah during the 1980s leading a chorus of dozens of vocalists in civilian and military garb enthusiastically singing this song, while a conductor energetically manages a massive orchestra of strings, wind instruments, and drums. An audience of men, women, and children, dressed in clothing marking them as Iraqis from across the ethnically and culturally diverse country, clap their hands and sing along, even if several of them also look utterly bored, likely a testament to the staged and forced nature of the entire event.[9]

After the war, the song lay dormant for some time before reappearing in the context of the Syrian Civil War. A video of it with updated, synthetic music and modified lyrics, now dedicated to the Free Syrian Army, appeared first on YouTube in 2014.[10] A few years later, the song was redone by other singers in support of the uprisings and demonstrations that occurred across Iraq from 2019 to 2021, known as *Thawrat Tishrīn*.[11] Although the lyrics were modified every time, Iran remained the target. Syria and Iraq are the two countries outside Iran where the Islamic Republic has leveraged the most influence since the early twenty-first century, namely through trade, sending a steady stream of Iranian Shi'i pilgrims, and propping up politicians and silencing local opposition. Thus, the Iran-Iraq War has not just played a part in shaping the present, but as a song like this demonstrates, the memory and tropes of the decade-long war continue to be revived. As the song is transformed to fit the needs of new political contexts, more cultural afterlives of the Iran-Iraq War are created.

WRITING THE FUTURE

Whether it is in literature or within other cultural media, the use and representation of the Iran-Iraq War remains controversial to differing degrees. To breathe life into the narratives of the wartime states is to endorse the regimes' politics of an unsettled, violent past. To contest those narratives is to write back against the wartime states and the sentimentalization of one of the twentieth century's bloodiest conflicts. But recent works of fiction also use the Iran-Iraq War to call attention to other ongoing catastrophic consequences of the conflict for both countries: the effects of war on the natural environment.

In this way, it is useful to go back to the novel with which this book opened: *The Corpse Washer* by Sinan Antoon. Although it only briefly deals directly with the Iran-Iraq War, it does so poignantly and provides one of the finest examples of how Iraqi novelists have treated the war within the longer durée of Iraq's modern history, with the war against Iran forming just one of several chapters of violence that have plagued the country since 1980. Midway through the novel, the protagonist, Jawad, receives a letter from his uncle Sabri, a former communist who fled Iraq in the early 1980s, going first to Beirut and then Berlin, where he remained. Shortly after the U.S.-led invasion and following Jawad's father's death, Sabri returns to Iraq for a short visit for the first time in two decades. Upon his return to Berlin, he publishes his reflections on the visit online, an excerpt of which he includes in a letter he sends to Jawad. Titled "A Lover Pauses before Iraq's Ruins" ("Iṭlāl al-Mushtāq 'alā Aṭlāl al-'Irāq"), he writes:

> Iraqis and palm trees. Who resembles whom? There are millions of Iraqis and as many, or perhaps somewhat fewer, palm trees. Some have had their fronds burned. Some have been beheaded. Some have had their backs broken by time but are still trying to stand. Some have dried bunches of dates. Some have been uprooted, mutilated and exiled from their orchards. Some have allowed invaders to lean on their trunk. Some are combing the winds with their fronds. Some stand in silence. Some have fallen. Some stand tall and raise their heads high despite everything in this vast orchard: Iraq. When will the orchard return to its owners? Not to those who carry axes. Not even to the attendant who assassinates palm trees, no matter what the color of his knife.[12]

The passage does not name the Iran-Iraq War directly, but its mournful framing of what Iraq has become after more than two decades of relentless warfare and sanctions speaks directly to the legacy of the conflict and gestures toward the ways other Iraqi authors allude to the war. In particular, the passage's references to resilience, exile, death, and silence, all symbolically articulated through the palm tree—itself a trope from both sides of this war's literature—point to the themes that have been explored in the post-Iran-Iraq War literature throughout this book. At the same time, by not mentioning any specific war, Sabri presents an allegory of all that the Iraqi people have experienced since the mid-1970s, as the Ba'thist regime tightened its grip around the country and Iraq barreled from one war to another. The Iran-Iraq War was just one part of this story.

In using the palm tree and orchard as an allegory for Iraq and Iraqis, Antoon also calls attention to the environmental fallout from war. The Iraqi date palm, which once numbered over thirty million, with large groves in the areas that were hardest hit by the Iran-Iraq War, has been reduced to less than half that amount.[13] Cutting the trees during war, combined with Saddam Hussein's draining of the Iraqi marshlands following the 1991 uprising, as well as the effects of climate change, have made the country's date palms more than a metaphor for Iraqis' pain, but rather a physical symbol of country's present-day struggles. It is possible that this signals a transformation in the war's representation, in other words, an "environmental turn." This book's final chapter shows how recent prominent works of fiction by Diaa Jubaili in Iraq and Nasim Marashi in Iran, focus on the slow violence and environmental ruin left in the aftermath of wars. In Iran, war fiction has mostly focused on the physical violence faced by humans. But like Antoon and Jubaili, Marashi also sees traces of that violence on the earth. Her focus on the scars of war literally left on the palm trees and water buffaloes of Iran's marshlands shows a broader understanding of violence than what Iranian authors had previously presented.

Marashi's 2017 novel, *Pruning*, appeared while Iranian consciousness of climate change and the Anthropocene was on the rise, and public concern for the issue has only grown since then. The well-known Iranian climate activist, Mohammad Darvish, recently called attention to the Iranian government's persistent summoning of the Iran-Iraq War and simultaneous enforcement of conservative social norms while utterly neglecting of the country's environment, which in recent decades has succumbed to desertification, incredibly high levels of air pollution, and a sharp rise in the number of animal species that are now critically endangered or extinct. In an interview with the Iranian media site *Bāzār o Mā* (The Market and Us), he connects the state's exploitative memory of the war with the current environmental decay, noting that during the war:

> Around 500,000 [soldiers] were martyred, taken prisoner, or injured in combat [but] we didn't give up a bit of land. Now, however, we've lost 50,000 square kilometers of Iran's soil [to desertification]. What's even sadder than that—the ruling powers of this country don't even see these 50,000 square kilometers. If you take your headscarf off, they [the government] will see you but they don't see these 50,000 square kilometers. This is all incredibly sad.[14]

Darvish's comments highlight a growing frustration toward a government whose priorities no longer align with a large segment of society. He alludes, on the one hand, to the recent uprising in Iran in opposition to the government's "morality police" (*gasht-e ershād*) and imposition of forced hijab since 1979, with the slogan "Woman, Life, Freedom" (*Zan, Zendegi, Azādi*), and on the other, to the government's incessant messaging and reminders of the sacrifices made by Iranian soldiers during the Iran-Iraq War. If Iraqi writers include the war with Iran as an integral part of recent Iraqi history that calls for literature's interrogation, we might read contemporaneous Iranian writing on the war as an effort to highlight aspects of the conflict that continue to be censored by the same regime that existed during wartime.

CULTURAL AFTERLIVES OF 1979

Whether it is debating the war wounds of the past or connecting those unhealed wounds to other issues, the ways in which Iranian and Iraqi writers continue to address the war between the two countries recalls the notion of "writing back" that I allude to in this book's introduction. Iranian and Iraqi writers have written against the official stories of the Iran-Iraq War by creating a variety of counternarratives that, with the passage of time, have become increasingly critical of the war and the wartime regimes. As the literature of this war demonstrates, Iranian and Iraqi writers of fiction remain invested in writing their countries' recent, unsettled history, channeling many of the committed principles of previous generations of writers but combining them with increasingly complex literary styles and aesthetics.

An examination of Arabic and Persian fiction of the Iran-Iraq War demonstrates how multilingual, relational comparison informed by literary history and sociopolitical context can help understand, periodize, and even canonize these two literatures. The historical and political circumstances in which Iraqi and Iranian writers found themselves during the 1980s create the first basis for contemporary comparison between the literatures of Iran and Iraq. These writers' textual strategies for dealing with their mutual entanglements with the war and its afterlives since 1988, opens another space for the comparative study of war and literary production between the two countries. This approach hints at considering the pivotal year 1979 and the era that it inaugurated not only as a historical and political turning point but a cultural one as well, particularly for a region that stretched from North Africa to South Asia.[15] A post-1979 literature might be a body of texts produced in response to, and in the aftermath of, the political and social changes that occurred in or around the year 1979, including the Iranian Revolution, the peace treaty between Egypt and Israel, the seizure of the Grand Mosque in Mecca, Saddam Hussein's full ascent to power, and the Soviet invasion of Afghanistan. It would encompass not only the Persian and Arabic literatures of the Iran-Iraq War, but also literature written in Kurdish and other regional languages. A regional post-1979 literature might also consider the rich literary legacies of the wars in Lebanon, Algeria, and Afghanistan, the 1980 Turkish Coup, and the first Palestinian Intifada, among other contexts.

In examining how writers and other cultural producers have responded to this historic shift, which included new waves of war and political oppression, and how they have looked back at these violent pasts, including the Iran-Iraq War, we are given a way to rethink cultural comparison within a regional framework, unrestricted to national and linguistic borders. This approach suggests another model of South-South (or East-East) literary comparison, where, in this case, we engage with modern literatures written in Arabic and Persian on their own terms, and through a recent historical context that informs the material conditions for cultural production across the region. Such an approach might start to give real meaning to a term like "Middle Eastern literatures," which is used all too often without defining how literatures like Arabic, Persian, Turkish, Kurdish, or Hebrew are, or are not, related to one another.

Acknowledgments

I'm indebted to many mentors, friends, and colleagues who, over many years, several places, and very different stages of my life, helped me write this book. The research and writing of *Dust That Never Settles* was mostly done in two phases. The idea of bringing together the Arabic and Persian literatures of the Iran-Iraq War first occurred to me while studying both languages and literatures at NYU's Department of Middle East and Islamic Studies, a place that proved to be both a fertile intellectual environment and a home away from home for nearly a decade. I'm immensely grateful to both Mehdi Khorrami and Hala Halim, who were early supporters of this project and provided invaluable assistance and advice on it. Alongside them, Sinan Antoon was generous with his time and knowledge of Iraqi literature as I began my research. I hope he can still stand by it, now that it's changed quite a bit and also treats some of his own novels. Others faculty members who were, and in some cases still are, part of the NYU-MEIS community encouraged this project, broadened my horizons, and helped me secure funding to carry out my research and writing. Among them, I'm especially grateful to Shiva Balaghi, Zvi Ben-Dor, Peter Chelkowski, Khaled Fahmy, Arang Keshavarzian, Elias Khoury, Zach Lockman, Ella Shohat, and Nader Uthman.

In the process of writing this book, several people kindly supported my work. I'm grateful to Georges Khalil at the Forum Transregionale Studien and the EUME program for hosting me as a fellow of the Volkswagenstiftung in 2016–17. I'm also much obliged to Elias Muhanna and Beshara Doumani at the Center for Middle Eastern Studies at Brown University for supporting my research through a visiting assistant professorship the following academic year. Along the way, Christoph Werner, Goulia Ghardakhshani, William Granara, Ali Mirsepassi, Olmo Gölz, Kevin Schwartz, Timothy Nunan, Asghar Seyed-Ghorab, and Lara Harb each invited me to present work through talks or workshops where I received useful feedback on various aspects of this project. In 2018, I was lucky to land at Rutgers University-Newark, where I'm still based. I can't imagine being there without the support of colleagues who have made the place enjoyable and interesting: Sadia Abbas, Zahra Ali, Belinda Edmondson, Laura Lomas, Jack Lynch, Wendell Marsh, Mayte Green-Mercado, and Alex Seggerman. It's rare to find academic administrators who are genuinely supportive of critical work in the humanities, but Nancy Cantor, who was Chancellor of RU-N while I wrote this book, and Jacqueline Mattis, Dean of the School of Arts and Sciences, truly were, and I'm grateful for their support. I'm also thankful to Maddy Munoz-Bertram for making the process of dealing with university bureaucracy as simple and painless as possible.

Just as important in many other ways have been scholars, peers, friends, and fellow travelers (in every sense) from New York, Berlin, Tehran, Istanbul, Beirut, Cairo, Providence, London, and other places (including over Zoom). I've learned a great deal from all of you who have patiently listened to my half-baked ideas, given advice, read works-in-progress, been writing partners, answered random questions, helped with translations, provided company at libraries, invited me to participate in workshops and on conference panels, kindly sent me materials that I didn't have access to, and put up with my complaints, dourness, bad jokes, and occasionally inappropriate dry humor. I'm grateful (alphabetically) in so many different ways to Refqa Abu Remaileh, Dena Al-Adeeb, Ali Akhtar, Yvonne Albers, Michael Allan, Rumzi Araj, Qusay al-Attabi, Negar Azimi, Haytham Bahoora, Narges Bajoghli, Ryvka Barnard, Shahzad Bashir, Nadim Bawalsa, Asef Bayat, Orkideh Behrouzan, Michael Beard, Zeynep Bilginsoy, Omar Cheta, Elliot Colla, Siad Darwish, Sheida Dayani, Arash Davari, Sam Dolbee, Emily Drumsta, Tarek Elariss, Alex Elinson, Özge Ersoy, Firoozeh Farvardin, Samir Frangieh, Nizar Ghanem, Omar al-Ghazzi, Zeina Halabi, Mimi Hanaoka, Bilal Hashmi, Hatim

El-Hibri, Elizabeth Holt, Peyman Jafari, Joshua Jordan, Pamela Karimi, Alya Karame, Arta Khakpour, Roya Khoshnevis, Justine Landau, Sean Lee, Patricia López-Gay, Shamiran Mako, Shervin Malekzadeh, Anne-Marie McManus, Fredrik Meiton, Jessica Metz, Amin Moghadam, Amy Motlagh, Suneela Mubayi, Laetitia Nanquette, Harry Neale, Frederike Pannewick, Haley Peele, Matt Powers, Dina Ramadan, Haidar Saeed, Khaled Saghieh, Ozen Nergis Seckin Dolcerocca, Setareh Shahbazi, Fatemeh Shams, Hoda El Shokry, Ehsan Siahpoush, Nahid Siamdoust, Sayed Elsisi, Naghmeh Sohrabi, Sophia Stamatopoulou-Robbins, Nathan Shockey, Nicholas Simcik, Chris Stone, Azim Tahmasepi, Nader Talebi, Levi Thompson, Hanan Toukan, Ziad Turkey, Merve Unsal, Sholeh Vatanabadi, Max Weiss, Alex Winder, Ekin Yasin, Rayya El Zein, and probably many others who I hope will forgive me for forgetting to mention their names.

Much of the writing and final research for this book took place between fall 2020 and fall 2023. I'm thankful for the time away from teaching and the financial assistance I received from the National Endowment for the Humanities, the American Council of Learned Societies, and Rutgers Research Council. When the pandemic closed most access to libraries, Eileen Gillooly generously accommodated me as an ACLS fellow at Columbia's Heymen Center for the Humanities. Later, a course release from the Rutgers-Newark Institute for the Study of Global Racial Justice allowed me to complete the book's final chapter. I'm obliged to friends and colleagues who read chapter drafts and provided feedback that improved it greatly. Thank you so very much, Sadia Abbas, Patrick Deer, Yasmeen Hanoosh, Hala Halim, Mehdi Khorrami, Sean Lee, Laura Lomas, Amy Malek, Milad Odabaei, Nasrin Rahimieh, Kamran Rastegar, and Samah Selim, as well as two anonymous readers who reviewed the book for Stanford University Press and suggested revisions. Early on, when the writer's block seemed insurmountable, Allison Brown provided necessary developmental editing on the book's first three chapters. During a spring 2024 sabbatical that led me to Finland, Hanna Meretoja kindly offered me space at the University of Turku's Department of Comparative Literature where I finished most revisions.

I am honored to have this book appear with Stanford University Press and its Studies in Middle Eastern and Islamic Societies and Cultures series. I feel especially lucky to have had the chance to work with Kate Wahl whose reputation as an excellent editor is deserved. Her professionalism and speed put me to shame, and her edits and suggestions greatly improved the book. As series editors, I'm also thankful to Laleh Khalili and Sherene Seikaly for their support. Laleh was generous with her time and suggesting ways to reframe the book's arguments early on. I also thank Shiva Ahmadi who graciously allowed SUP's designers to use a portion of "Firecracker," just one of her many heartbreakingly beautiful works.

This book took too long to finish. I don't know when it would have been completed and what it would have looked like if some of the things that slowed me down had not happened, but in the end, it was better for me to put the book, rather than life, on hold. I'm eternally grateful to Ana Ortin Peralta for her support and patience with me as I finished this project. Our children Maya and Gabriel were born at two distinct points when I was supposed to dive into working on "the book." They've been the best things to ever happen to us. I hope they can either forgive me or forget about the excess hours that I spent in front of the computer screen during their first years of life. Finishing this book would have also been impossible without my parents who have been unwavering in their support of my studies, travel, and learning since day one, and who more recently and especially during the COVID-19 Pandemic, helped take care of their grandchildren while I worked on this and too many other things. Similarly, I owe thanks to my in-laws who also took care of us and their grandchildren while we tried to work on scholarly publications over the past few years. I'm indebted to my family in Tehran who, for a decade and a half of trips to Iran before I wrote this book, generously introduced me to the city, made me feel at home, and lovingly received me every time I returned.

In 2015, the day before I was due to defend my doctoral dissertation, my brother Arion unexpectedly passed away, leaving a deep void in the lives of everyone in my immediate family and casting a heavy shadow over everything I did and thought about for years afterward. As I finally reach the point where mentioning his name brings smiles instead of tears, I dedicate this book to his memory.

Notes

Introduction

1. Reprinted with the permission of Yale University Press, from *The Corpse Washer* by Sinan Antoon. Copyright © 2013 by Yale University Press, page 13. Arabic language original found in Sinan Antoon, *Waḥdahā Shajarat al-Rummān* (Beirut: Dār al-Muʾassasa al-ʿArabiyya lil-Dirāsāt wa-l-Nashr, 2010), 22.

2. From Hossein Mortezaeian Abkenar, "Rahman's Story." Translation © 2013 by Sara Khalili. First published in *Words Without Borders*, July 2013. All rights reserved. Persian language original found in Hossein Mortezaeian Abkenar, "*Dāstān-e Rahmān*" in *Konsert-e Tār-hā-ye Mamnuʿeh* (Tehran: Nashr-e Āgah, 1999), 61. See also *Words Without Borders*, July 1, 2013, https://wordswithoutborders.org/read/article/2013-07/rahmans-story.

3. A more literal translation of the Arabic title would be *For the Lone Pomegranate Tree*. The author has explained that the title of the English language translation was changed at the publisher's insistence. See Sinan Antoon, "New Texts Out Now: Sinan Antoon, *The Corpse Washer*," Jadaliyya, September 25, 2013, https://www.jadaliyya.com/Details/29556.

4. Antoon, *The Corpse Washer* 12 (A); 8 (T).

5. See Waïl S. Hassan, "Arabic and the Paradigms of Comparison," in *The 2014–2015 Report on the State of the Discipline of Comparative Literature*, Website of the American Comparative Literature Association, http://stateofthediscipline.acla.org/entry/arabic-and-paradigms-comparison-1#_edn3. For examples of other studies that compare modern Arabic and Persian literatures see Kamran Rastegar, *Literary Modernity*

Between the Middle East and Europe: Textual Transactions in Nineteenth-century Arabic, English, and Persian Literatures (London: Routledge, 2007) and Levi Thompson, *Reorienting Modernism in Arabic and Persian Poetry* (Cambridge: Cambridge University Press, 2022).

6. Many scholars have demonstrated how the term "Middle East" is neither neutral nor accurate and is rooted in a Eurocentric and American military-colonial framing of the world with Orientalist roots. Despite its faults, it is also a term that demarcates for readers the region that encompasses modern Iran and Iraq. Moreover, it exists in both Arabic (*al-sharq al-awsaṭ*) and in Persian (*Khāvar-miāneh*) and is used to refer to the same geographical region, albeit with the same inaccuracies that are found in English. A neutral term like "Southwest Asia" is far more accurate for the area under question in this book, but its use remains comparatively constricted to specialists. For more on the development of this term, especially vis-à-vis the study of the region in the United States, see Zachary Lockman, *Contending Visions of the Middle East: The History and Politics of Orientalism* (New York: Cambridge University Press, 2009), 98–99.

7. Shu-mei Shih, "Comparison as Relation," in *Comparison: Theories, Approaches, Uses*, eds. Susan Stanford Friedman and Rita Felski (Baltimore: Johns Hopkins University Press, 2013), 79–98.

8. Ibid., 79–80.

9. For more on the regional importance of this year, see Hamit Bozarsalan, "Revisiting the Middle East's 1979," in *Economy and Society*, vol. 41, no. 4, 2012; David Lesch, *1979: The Year that Shaped the Modern Middle East* (Cambridge, MA: Westview Press, 2001). Less scholarly but very readable accounts of the period can also be found in Christian Caryl, *Strange Rebels: 1979 and the Birth of the 21st Century* (New York: Basic Books, 2013), and Kim Ghattas, *Black Wave: Saudi Arabia Iran and the Forty-Year Rivalry That Unraveled Culture, Religion, and Collective Memory in the Middle East* (New York: Henry Holt and Company, 2020).

10. For more about Iran's Arab minority, see Rasmus Christian Elling, *Minorities in Iran: Nationalism and Ethnicity after Khomeini* (New York: Palgrave Macmillan, 2013), 100–113.

11. By the end of the war, the Baʻthist government had expelled more than 400,000 Iraqi Shiʻa, the majority to Iran, but also to Syria, accusing them of being of "Iranian origin" and disloyal to Iraq. See Marion Farouk-Sluglett and Peter Sluglett, *Iraq Since 1958: From Revolution to Dictatorship* (London: I.B. Tauris, 2001), 258. See also Zainab Saleh, *Return to Ruin: Iraqi Narratives of Exile and Nostalgia* (Stanford, CA: Stanford University Press, 2020), 150–157.

12. Pierre Razoux, *The Iran-Iraq War*, trans. Nicholas Elliot (Cambridge, MA, and London: The Belknap Press of Harvard University Press), 202–207, 217–218; Javier Perez de Cuellar, *A Pilgrimage for Peace: A Secretary General's Memoir* (New York: St. Martin's Press, 1997), 135.

13. The nearly 124 mile/200 km waterway that is the confluence of the Tigris and Euphrates rivers and forms the border between Iran and Iraq is called the *Shaṭṭ al-'Arab* in Arabic and *Arvand Rud* in Persian. Likewise, the Iranian city Ahwaz has two pronunciations: *Aḥwāz* (Arabic) and *Ahvāz* (Persian).

14. Their presence was limited but some Shi'a Afghan volunteer troops fought alongside the Iranians, particularly in the "Abuzar Brigade" deployed at the Iraqi front, primarily from 1985 to 1986. See Kevin Schwartz, "'Citizen Martyrs': The Afghan Fatemiyoun Brigade in Iran." *Afghanistan* 5, no. 1 (2022), 98. Similarly, Egyptian and Sudanese laborers were recruited to work in wartime Iraq to make up for the labor shortages caused by the high number of Iraqi men serving in the military. When the Iraqi military faced a shortage of soldiers it offered those laborers financial incentives to serve at the front. See Dina Khoury, *Iraq in Wartime: Soldiering, Martyrdom, and Remembrance* (Cambridge: Cambridge University Press, 2013), 95, 103.

15. The reported number of soldiers and civilians killed in this war varies wildly, and it is unlikely that we will ever have an exact death toll. Shortly after the war ended, it was commonplace in the media all over the world to say that over a million were killed, even though both governments claimed significantly lower numbers. Iranian casualties were certainly higher than Iraqi, largely due to military tactics that produced mass casualties on the battlefields. For a sense of the range of numbers given, consider this: the Wikipedia entry for the "Iran-Iraq War" lists 1,000,000–2,000,000 killed (https://en.wikipedia.org/wiki/Iran%E2%80%93Iraq_War#); most scholarly estimates are around 300,000 Iraqi and 650,000 Iranian casualties; and official government numbers in 1988 were 250,000 Iraqi and 155,000 Iranian casualties.

16. Kissinger, who lived to be one hundred years old (1923–2023), was and is widely disdained by critics of U.S. foreign policy and defenders of human rights. To many, his life and legacy mirror the Iran-Iraq War: seemingly interminable, incredibly violent, and largely unnecessary.

17. On the Iran-Contra affair, see Malcolm Byrne, *Iran-Contra: Reagan's Scandal and the Unchecked Abuse of Presidential Power* (Lawrence, KS: University Press of Kansas, 2014).

18. For a concise summary of U.S. involvement in the Iran-Iraq War see Andrew J. Bacevich, *America's War for the Greater Middle East: A Military History* (New York: Random House, 2016, Kindle edition), Chapter 6 "Rescuing Evil."

19. For an account of the military consequences of the downing of Iran Air 655, see Razoux, *The Iran-Iraq War*, 455–462. To understand the impact of the attack on Iranian understandings of U.S. aggression that persist until the present day, see Habib Ahmadzadeh, *A City Under Siege: Tales of the Iran-Iraq War*, trans. Paul Sprachman (Costa Mesa, CA: Mazda Publishers, 2010). The downing of the plane plays a major role in Kaveh Akbar's popular novel *Martyr!* (New York: Alfred A. Knopf, 2024), which is, to my knowledge, the first time the event has appeared in a work of popular American literature.

20. On the demonization of Saddam Hussein in the U.S. media, see "Shaping Saddam: How the Media Mythologized a Monster," *The Yale Review of International Studies*, June 2018, http://yris.yira.org/acheson-prize/2473.

21. Nida Alahamad and Arang Keshavarzian, "A War on Multiple Fronts," *Middle East Report in Print*, Vol. 40, No. 4, Winter 2010, 17.

22. It remains to be seen how the discourse of the Islamic Republic will change vis-à-vis the Kingdom of Saudi Arabia. At the time of writing, the two countries have begun a cautious rapprochement.

23. Laurie Brand, *Official Stories: Politics and National Narratives in Egypt and Algeria* (Stanford, CA: Stanford University Press, 2014), 8.

24. Kamran Scot Aghaie, *The Martyrs of Karbala: Shi'i Symbols and Rituals in Modern Iran* (Seattle: University of Washington Press, 2004), 8.

25. Meir Litvak, "Karbala," *Encyclopædia Iranica* (2012) online edition, https://iranicaonline.org/articles/karbala

26. Peter Chelkowski, "Ta'zia," *Encyclopædia Iranica* (2009) online edition, http://www.iranicaonline.org/articles/tazia.

27. Peter Chelkowski and Hamid Dabashi, *Staging a Revolution: The Art of Persuasion in the Islamic Republic of Iran* (New York: New York University Press, 1999), 273–274.

28. The term "Karbala Paradigm" was coined by Michael Fischer in *Iran: From Religious Dispute to Revolution* (Cambridge, MA: Harvard University Press, 1980).

29. *Āfāq 'Arabiyya*, vol. 5 (October 1980): 160. The town is called "Zayn al-Kash" in Persian.

30. Touraj Daryaee calls the idea that Persian soldiers greatly outnumbered the Muslim army "pure fiction [. . .] which aims to aggrandize Arab Muslim achievement" because so many Sassanian troops had been killed or were not present due to

the Byzantine wars and internal strife. See *Sasanian Persia: The Rise and Fall of an Empire* (London: I.B.Tauris, 2014), 37.

31. Aaron Faust, *The Baʻthification of Iraq: Saddam Hussein's Totalitarianism* (Austin, TX: University of Texas Press, 2015), 9.

32. Ibid., 12.

33. Faust identifies the party's means to Baʻthify society as "ideology, organization, terror, and enticement" (13).

34. Sinan Antoon, "Debris and Diaspora: Iraqi Culture Now," in *Uncovering Iraq: Trajectories of Disintegration and Transformation,* eds. Christopher J. Toensing and Mimi Kirk (Washington, D.C: Center for Contemporary Arab Studies, Georgetown University, 2010), 120; Salam ʻAbbud, *Thaqāfat al-ʻUnf fī al-ʻIrāq* (Cologne: Manshūrāt al-Jamal, 2002), 273.

35. Ervand Abrahamian, *A History of Modern Iran* (Cambridge and New York: Cambridge University Press, 2018), 166.

36. Abbas Amanat, *Iran: A Modern History* (New Haven, CT: Yale University Press, 2017), 778.

37. Ibid., 781. An interesting parallel exists between what Amanat calls Khomeini's "Qomified" style of rule and the Tikriti-dominated ruling cadre of supporters with whom Saddam Hussein surrounded himself.

38. Abrahamian, *A History of Modern Iran*, 173.

39. Although the Islamic Republic expanded it, censorship of the press and literature was also widespread under the Pahlavi regime. See Ahmad Karimi-Hakkak, "CENSORSHIP," *Encyclopædia Iranica*, December 15 (1990), https://www.iranicaonline.org/articles/censorship-sansur-in-persia. See also Abrahamian, *A History of Modern Iran*, 177–182; Amanat, *Iran*, 397–819; Fatemeh Shams, "Literature, art, and ideology under the Islamic Republic: An extended history of the Center for Islamic Art and Thought," in *Persian Language, Literature and Culture: New Leaves, Fresh Looks*, ed. Kamran Talattof (New York: Routledge, 2015), 163–193. Sussan Siavoshi, "Cultural Policies and The Islamic Republic: Cinema and Book Publication," *International Journal of Middle East Studies*, 29 (1997), 509–530.

40. Although he focuses strictly on poetry, Levi Thompson offers the best overview of how commitment was taken up in both Arabic *and* Persian literatures in the mid-twentieth century in *Reorienting Modernism in Arabic and Persian Poetry* (Cambridge: Cambridge University Press, 2022). For an overview of the various ways in which writers and intellectuals manifested political commitment in Arabic literature see Qussay Al-Attabi, "The Polemics of Iltizām: *Al-Ādāb*'s Early Arguments for Commitment," *Journal of Arabic Literature*, v 52, no. 1–2, (2021) 124–146; Verena Klemm, "Different Notions of Commitment (*iltizām*) and Committed Literature

(*al-adab al-multazim*) in the Literary Circles of The Mashriq," *Arabic and Middle Eastern Literatures* 3.1 (2000): 51–62; Friederike Pannewick, Georges Khalil, and Yvonne Albers, eds., *Commitment and Beyond: Reflections on/of the Political in Arabic Literature since the 1940s* (Wiesbaden, Germany, Reichert Verlag, 2015). For similar studies in Persian literature see Wali Ahmadi, *Modern Persian Literature in Afghanistan: Anomalous Visions of History and Form* (New York: Routledge, 2008); Samad Alavi, "The Poetics of Commitment in Modern Persian: A Case of Three Revolutionary Poets in Iran," PhD diss., University of California, Berkeley, 2013; Hamid Dabashi, "The Poetics of Politics: Commitment in Modern Persian Literature," *Iranian Studies* 18, no. 2 (Spring–Autumn, 1985): 147–188; Kamran Talattof, *The Politics of Writing in Iran: A History of Modern Persian Literature* (Syracuse, NY: Syracuse University Press, 1999), 66–107.

41. Alavi, "The Poetics of Commitment in Modern Persian Literature" xiv; Talattof, *The Politics of Writing in Iran* 67–68.

42. Alavi, "The Poetics of Commitment in Modern Persian Literature" vii.

43. Al-Attabi, "The Polemics of Iltizām, 124–125; Klemm, "Different Notions of Commitment" 52–55.

44. Klemm, Ibid., 58.

45. Hala Halim, "The Pre-postcolonial and Its Enduring Relevance: Afro-Asian variations in Edwar al-Kharrat's texts," in *Postcolonialism Cross-Examined: Multidirectional Perspectives on Imperial and Colonial Pasts and the Neocolonial Present,* ed. Monika Albrecht (New York: Routledge, 2019), 84.

46. Thompson, *Reorienting Modernism* 42.

47. Egyptian author and critic, Edward al-Kharrat, is credited with coining the term "al-ḥassāsiyya al-jadīda." See Albers, et al., "Introduction: Tracks and Traces of Literary Commitment—On *Iltizām* as an Ongoing Intellectual Project," in *Commitment and Beyond*, 14.

48. Refqa Abu-Remaileh "The Afterlives of *Iltizām*: Emile Habibi through a Kanafaniesque Lens of Resistance Literature," in *Commitment and Beyond*, 171.

49. Fatima Mohsen, "Debating Iraqi Culture: Intellectuals between the Inside and Outside," in *Conflicting Narratives: War, Trauma and Memory in Iraqi Culture,* eds. Stephan Milich, Friederike Pannewick, and Leslie Tramotini, (Weisbaden: Reichert Verlag, 2012), 11.

50. Yasmeen Hanoosh, "Contempt: State Literati vs. Street Literati in Modern Iraq," *Journal of Arabic Literature*, vol. 43, no. 2/3, (2012): 382. For more on these authors, see Fabio Caiani and Catherine Cobham, *The Iraqi Novel: Key Writers, Key Texts,* (Edinburgh: Edinburgh University Press, 2013).

51. Hanoosh, *Contempt,* 375.

52. Haidar Saeed, "How Small the State, How Grand the Idea: Thoughts on the Relationship between the Intellectual and the State in Iraq," in *Shahadat: Witnessing Iraq's Transformation after 2003*, ed. Angela Wollenberg (Berlin: Driedrich Ebert Foundation, 2007), 95–96.

53. Abrahamian, *A History of Modern Iran*, 110. He aptly calls the Tudeh allies, "fellow travelers." Thompson's observation on Iranian poet Ahmad Shamlu and Iraqi poet Badr Shakir al-Sayyab is also germane. Both were card-carrying Communists in the 1950s but later "distanced themselves from Communism, Sayyāb moving in a nationalist direction and Shāmlū preferring to remain ideologically free but sympathetic to the Left" (43).

54. Alavi, "The Poetics of Commitment in Modern Persian," xvi-xvii.

55. Talattof, *The Politics of Writing in Iran*, 77–81.

56. Shams "Literature, art, and ideology," 169. See also Ali Gheissari, *Iranian Intellectuals in the Twentieth Century* (Austin, TX: University of Texas Press, 1998), 113.

57. For a listing of several memoir-esque writings by high-profile Iraqi authors written since 2010 see Hend Saeed, "Recommendations: On the New Wave of Memoirs from Iraq," *Arablit*, https://arablit.org/2024/05/14/recommendations-on-the-new-wave-of-memoirs-from-iraq/, May 24, 2024.

58. Bradly Epps, *Significant Violence: Oppression and Resistance in the Narratives of Juan Goytisolo (1970–1990)* (Oxford: Oxford University Press, 1996), 2, quoted in Mohammad Mehdi Khorrami, *Modern Reflections of Classical Traditions in Persian Fiction* (Lewiston, NY: Edwin Mellen Press, 2003), 143.

59. Richard Terdiman, *Discourse / Counter-Discourse: The Theory and Practice of Symbolic Resistance in Nineteenth-Century France* (Ithaca, NY: Cornell U Press, 1985), 61.

60. Eric Davis, *Memories of State: Politics, History, and Collective Identity in Modern Iraq* (Berkeley and Los Angeles: University of California Press, 2005), 21.

61. Hanoosh, "Contempt," 374.

62. Khorrami, *Literary Subterfuge and Contemporary Persian Fiction: Who Writes Iran?* (London and New York: Routledge, 2015), 2.

63. Françoise Lionnet, "Postcolonial studies, creolizations, and migrations," in *Postcolonialism Cross-Examined: Multidirectional Perspectives on Imperial and Colonial Pasts and the Neocolonial Present*, ed. Monika Albrecht (London: Routledge, 2020), 68. For original usage see Bill Ashcroft et al., in *The Empire Writes Back: Theory and Practice in Post-Colonial Literatures* (London: Routledge, 2002).

64. There are obvious limits to using the term "postcolonial" for Iran, which was never formally colonized, even though it postures itself politically like other postcolonial states. Iraq by any definition is a postcolonial state.

65. Stefan Meyer, *The Experimental Arabic Novel: Postcolonial Literary Modernism in the Levant* (Albany, NY: State University of New York Press, 2001), 15.

66. Haytham Bahoora, "Iraq," in *The Oxford Handbook of Arab Novelistic Traditions,* ed. Waïl S. Hassan (Oxford: Oxford University Press, 2017), 255.

67. See Khorrami, *Modern Reflections...*, and Arta Khakpour, "Each into a World of His Own: Mimesis, Modernist Fiction, and the Iranian Avant-Garde," PhD Diss., New York University, 2014.

68. Meyer, *The Experimental Arabic Novel*, 2–3.

69. This phenomenon is not limited to this war. For examples in twentieth-century Anglophone contexts see Mark Rawlinson, "War and Civilians," in *War and Literary Studies*, eds. Anders Engberg-Pedersen and Neil Ramsey (Cambridge: Cambridge University Press, 2023), 201–215.

70. For a discussion of how choices over this terminology play out in Iran, see Mehdi Saʿidi, *Adabiyāt-e Dāstāni-ye Jang dar Irān* (Tehran: Pazhoheshgāh-e ʿOlum-e Ensāni va Motaleʿāt-e Ejtemāʾi-ye Jahād Dāneshgāhi, 2016), 15–24. For Iraq, see Ikram Masmoudi, *War and Occupation in Iraqi Fiction* (Edinburgh: Edinburgh University Press, 2015), 13–14.

71. Viet Thanh Nguyen, *Nothing Ever Dies: Vietnam and the Memory of War*, (Cambridge, MA: Harvard University Press, 2016), 224.

72. Tim O'Brien, *The Things They Carried* (New York: Penguin Books, 1991), 76. Quoted in Nguyen, 226.

73. Nguyen, *Nothing Ever Dies*, 226.

74. Ibid.

75. Ibid., 227.

Chapter 1

1. Kaveh Bahman, "Behtarin Dastān-e Jangi keh tā Hālā Khāndeh-id Kudām ast?" *Adabiyāt-e Dāstāni,* no. 23, (September 1994): 152. Cited in Mir-ʿAbedini, *Sad Sāl...*, 891.

2. Warid Badr al-Salim, Hamza Mustafa, Muhammad Hayyawi (eds.) "al-Muqaddama" in *Dhākirat al-Ghad: Shahādāt wa-Ruʾā wa-Tajārib* (Baghdad: Wizārat al-Thaqāfa wa-l-Iʿlām, Dār al-Shuʾūn al-Thaqāfiyya al-ʿĀmma Āfāq ʿArabiyya, 1989), 5.

3. Kadhim Jihad Hasan, "Iraqi Literature: an exemplary multi-millennia continuity," *Banipal,* (Summer 2003): 54.

4. Salam ʿAbbud, *Man Yaṣnaʿ al-Dīktātūr? (Ṣaddām Namūdhijan)* (Cologne: Manshūrāt al-Jamal, 2008), 93–94.

5. Patrick Deer, *Culture in Camouflage: War, Empire and Modern British Literature* (New York: Oxford University Press, 2009), 4.

6. The sonic aspects of war and life during the Iran-Iraq War have not been thoroughly explored. The most in-depth research done on the topic on the Iranian side is in Armaghan Fakhraeirad, Laudan Nooshin, and Anna Rezaie, "A Sonic Tale of Two Cities: Memory, Trauma, and Auditory Scars in Tehran and Abadan-Khorramshahr" *City, University of London Research Online*, https://openaccess.city.ac.uk/id/eprint/30089/. Although focused much more on post-2003 Iraq, Martin Daughtry also treats many auditory aspects of the Iran-Iraq War in *Listening to War: Sound, Music, Trauma and Survival in Wartime Iraq* (New York: Oxford University Press, 2015). For an application of his concept of the "belliphonic" in an Iranian war novel see Amir Moosavi, "Sonic Triggers and Fiery Pools: The Senses at War in Hossein Mortezaeian Abkenar's *Scorpion*," in *Losing Our Minds, Coming to Our Senses*, eds. Mehdi Khorrami and Amir Moosavi (Leiden: Leiden University Press, 2021), 171–194.

7. For more on music in Iran since 1979 see Nahid Siamdoust, *Soundtrack of the Revolution: The Politics of Music in Iran* (Stanford, CA: Stanford University Press, 2017). For music of the Iran-Iraq War specifically, see Sayyed Vahid Husayni, *Bazm-e Razm* (Tehran: Mu'assaseh-ye Revāyat-e Fath, 2016). Far less has been written on music and television under the Iraqi Baʻth; see Amatzia Baram, *Culture, History, and Ideology in the Formation of Baʻthist Iraq, 1968–89* (New York: St. Martin's Press, 1991) and ʻAbbud (2002). The songs of Saddam's Qadisiyya (*aghānī Qādisiyyat Ṣaddām*) are widely available on YouTube and other social media platforms. Songs of both sides have been appropriated and used in support of sectarian militant groups in Iraq and Syria during recent civil wars in those countries.

8. Of these films, the 1981 historical feature-length film *Qādisiyya*, depicting the battle as one between an outnumbered Arab Muslim army and the Persian Sassanian Empire, is the best example. It was funded by the Iraqi state but made by the well-known Egyptian director Salah Abu Seif and starred the famous Egyptian actress, Suʼad Hosni. In Iran, the 1985 action war-film *The Eagles* ('Oqāb-hā), by Samuel Khachikian, was seen by over 10% of the country's population and remains one of the most-viewed Iranian films. See Hamed Yousefi, *Sanʻat Farhang-e Jang*, BBC Persian, 2013.

9. For a succinct examination of this media during the war, see Blake Atwood *Underground: The Secret Life of Videocassettes in Iran* (Cambridge, MA: The MIT Press, 2021).

10. The aesthetic of the Martyrs Monument, built during the first years of the war, differs from that of the other monuments mentioned and does not participate in the glorification of the war or Saddam Hussein. See Kanan Makiya, *The Monument: Art, Vulgarity, and Responsibility in Iraq* (Berkeley: University of California Press, 1991); Sinan Antoon, "Bending History," *Middle East Report*, 257 (2010): 29–31.

11. Marc Santora, "Aftereffects: Basra; Near the Border with Iran, Memories of War Blend with Hope for Better Relations," *New York Times*, May 5, 2003, http://www.nytimes.com/2003/05/05/world/aftereffects-basra-near-border-with-iran-memories-war-blend-with-hope-for-better.html.

12. In recent years these murals have appeared less frequently and are increasingly replaced by different types of murals. See Pamela Karimi, "Imagining Warfare, Imagining Welfare: Tehran's Post Iran-Iraq War Murals and their Legacy," *Persica* 22, (2008): 47–63.

13. Kevin L. Schwartz and Olmo Gölz, "Visual Propaganda at a Crossroads: New Techniques at Iran's Vali Asr Billboard," *Visual Studies*, 36:4–5 (2021): 476–490.

14. Anna Vanzan, "The Holy Defense Museum in Tehran, or How to Aestheticize War," *Middle East Journal of Culture and Communication,* 13, 1 (2020): 63–77.

15. Several collections of pro-regime poetry in Arabic and Persian exist. For critical readings of the Persian poetry of this war see Fatemeh Shams, *A Revolution in Rhyme: Poetic Co-Option Under the Islamic Republic* (Oxford: Oxford University Press, 2021) and Asghar Seyed-Gohrab, *Martyrdom Mysticism and Dissent: The Poetry of the 1979 Iranian Revolution and the Iran-Iraq War (1980–1988)* (Berlin: De Gruyter, 2021). For Arabic poetry see Muhammad Mazlum, *Ḥaṭab Ibrāhīm aw al-Jīl al-Badawī: Shiʿr al-Thamānīnāt wa-Ajyāl al-Dawla al-ʿIrāqīyya* (Damascus: al-Takwīn lil-Taʾlīf wa-l-Tarjama wa-l-Nashr, 2007) and Wiebke Walther, "Between Heroism, Hesitancy, Resignation and New Hope: The Iran-Iraq War in Iraqi Poetry," in *Conflicting Narratives: War, Trauma and Memory in Iraqi Culture*, eds. Stephan Milich, et al. (2012), 75–109.

16. "Avvalin Kārbord-e Vāzheh-ye Defāʿ-e Moqaddas Tavassot-e Cheh Kasi Bud?" *Navid-e Shāhed*, February 11, 2014, https://navideshahed.com/fa/news/315705.

17. See "New Commitments" in this book's introduction.

18. That said, each side avoided explicit sectarian discourse (i.e., Sunni vs. Shiʿi), instead calling the other population to revolt against their "misguided" political leaders.

19. See Morad Saghafi, "Crossing the Desert: Iranian Intellectuals after the Islamic Revolution," *Critique*, no. 18, (Spring 2001): 26, and Masmoudi, *War and Occupation*, 10–14.

20. Muhammad Ghazi al-Akhras, *Kharīf al-Muthaqqaf fī al-ʿIrāq* (Beirut: Dār al-Tanwīr, 2011), 30–49.

21. Hanoosh, "Comtempt" 391; Al-Akhras, *Kharīf al-Muthaqqaf* 38–39.

22. Hanoosh, ibid., 392.

23. Edited versions of the speeches are collected in *Dah Shab: Shab-hā-ye Shāʿerān va Nevisandegān dar Anjoman-e Farhang-e Irān-Ālmān* (Tehran: Amir Kabir, 1978). For a concise history of the Association, see Ahmad Karimi-Hakkak, "Protest and Perish: A History of the Writers' Association of Iran," in *A Fire of Lilies*:

Perspectives on Literature and Politics in Modern Iran (Leiden: Leiden University Press, 2020) 53–84.

24. Karimi-Hakkak, Protest and Perish, 71.

25. Ibid., 74.

26. Kānun-e Nevisandegān-e Irān, *Nāmeh-ye Kānun-e Nevisandegān*, no. 4, (Tehran: Enteshārāt-e Āgāh, 1982), 5.

27. Ibid., 7–8.

28. Ibid. See "Tā Ān Su-ye Arvand-rud," 72–81. Of course, the first invasion commenced with the Battle of Qadisiyya, which Saddam had embraced as an epithet for his war.

29. *Tu-ye Dasht-e Beyn-e Rāh* ibid. *Nāmeh-ye Kānun-e Nevisandegān*, no. 4 146–151.

30. Morad Saghafı, "Crossing the Desert: Iranian Intellectuals after the Revolution," *Critique*, no. 18 (Spring 2001): 25–28.

31. *Komitehs* were "revolutionary committees" that "popped up in every neighborhood, in government departments, airports, factories, and business offices [and] carried out the self-assumed task of 'defending' the revolution." See Amanat *Iran*, 775–777.

32. Karimi-Hakkak, " Protest and Perish," 84.

33. Ali Shariati (1933–1977) was one of the most important oppositional intellectuals in the years preceding the 1979 Revolution. He was well-known for positions that sought to merge Marxist and Islamist strains of thought. See Shams, *A Revolution. . .*, Chapter 2 and Hamid Dabashi, *Theology of Discontent: The Ideological Foundation of the Islamic Revolution in Iran* (London: Routledge, 2017).

34. Gheissari, *Iranian Intellectuals*, 112.

35. Mohsen Makhmalbaf, "Qesseh-ye Maktabi," *Jong-e Sureh*, no. 2, Aban (Nov-Dec 1981): 63–67.

36. For English analyses of this novel and film see Talattof, *The Politics*, 123–125, and Dabashi, *Makhmalbaf at Large: The Making of a Rebel Filmmaker* (London: I.B. Tauris, 2008), 89–105.

37. Mir-'Abedini, *Sad Sāl* 899. These novels were largely written in the form of first-person war stories like the memoirs of fighters whose publication has proliferated since the end of the war.

38. With support from the MCIG's cultural division, the journal first appeared in 1982 and ran until 2013. It featured sections on aesthetics, the Islamic arts, music, plastic arts, cinema, theater, photography, and poetry. Although the war occupied much of its content, particularly during its early years, its scope was much larger than the war and the continuation of the Islamic Revolution which concerned *Sureh* so intensely. See Amir Moosavi "Dust That Never Settled: Ideology Ambivalence and

Disenchantment in Arabic and Persian Fiction of the Iran-Iraq War (1980–2003)," PhD Diss., New York University, 2016.

39. In 2013, the University of Texas Press published *The Neighbors* in English translation by Nastaran Kherad.

40. See Ahmad Mahmud, *Zamin-e Sukhteh* (Tehran: Entesharat-e Mo'in, 2020), 20th ed.

41. Ibid., 179.

42. Ibid., 329.

43. Interview with Ahmad Mahmud in Layla Golestan, *Ḥekāyat-e Ḥāl: Goftegu bā Ahmad-e Mahmud* (Tehran: Ketāb-e Mahnāz, 1995), 157–158.

44. Ibid., 159–160.

45. I refer to these journals by their Arabic names. See Khoury, *Iraq in Wartime*, for a discussion of *Alif-Bā*, along with several daily newspapers.

46. "Fī Dhākirat Tishrīn," *Āfāq 'Arabīyya* 6, (1980): 3.

47. Shafīq al-Kamali, "al-Thaqāfa wa-l-Ma'raka," *Āfāq 'Arabiyya* 6, (1980): 138. Even these crude pronouncements were not enough to save Kamali from a Ba'thist purge. The writer died in 1984, possibly poisoned after a brief imprisonment. See Muhsin al-Musawi, *Reading Iraq: Culture and Power and Conflict* (London: I.B. Tauris, 2006), 79, 81.

48. This is the first issue of *al-Aqlām* that lists Hammudi's name as "secretary editor." The journal's most forceful pro-war years coincide with Hammudi's tenure as its head editor.

49. Editorial Board, *Mawqifunā*," *al-Aqlām* 15, (1980): inside cover.

50. See, for example, Kazim Sa'ad al-Din, "Min Shi'r al-Ḥarb wa-l-Muqāwama fī al-'Ālam," *al-Aqlām* 16, (1981); 86–101; or the second half of the December 1981 issue where the war is referenced throughout in Muhammad Hasan Ibrahim, "Bayn al-'Arabiyya wa-l-'Ibriyya: al-Jānib al-Lughawī min al-Ṣirā'a al-'Arabī al-Ṣuhyūnī fī al-Filisṭin," *al-Aqlām* 16, (1981): 61–72

51. Al-Hassan, *Women, Writing and the Iraqi Ba'thist State* 36.

52. For an immediate assessment of the war's literature from inside Iraq see Badr et al., *Dhākirat al-Ghad*.

53. Salam 'Abbud *Thaqāfat al-'Unf*; Sinan Antoon "Bending History;" Kadhim Jihad Kadhim, *Le Roman arabe, (1834–2004)*, (Arles, France: Sindbad, 2006); 'Abbas Khidr, *al-Khākīyya: Min Awrāq al-Jarīma al-Thaqāfiyya fī al-'Irāq* (Cologne: Manshūrāt al-Jamal, 2005); Fatima Mohsen "Cultural Authoritarianism" in *Iraq Since the Gulf War: Prospects for Democracy,* ed. Fran Hazelton (Fran Atlantic Highlands, NJ: Zed Books, 1994).

54. Achim Rohde, *State-Society Relations in Ba'thist Iraq: Facing Dictatorship* (New York: Routledge, 2010), 156.

55. Al-Hassan *Women, Writing;* Khoury, *Iraq in Wartime.*

56. Khoury, *Iraq in Wartime,* 204.

57. miriam cooke, *Women and the War Story* (Berkeley, CA: University of California Press, 1996), 220–266; Caiani and Cobham, *The Iraqi Novel,* 139–193, and "Autumn Visions: War and the Imagery of Muḥammad Khuḍayyir" *Journal of Arabic Literature* 49, (2018): 243–270.

58. Khoury, *Iraq in Wartime,* 195.

59. 'Abbud, *Thaqafat al-'Unf,* 247.

60. Khoury, *Iraq in Wartime,* 221–233, provides an excellent overview of the "Cult of Martyrdom" in Saddam's Qadisiyya. Writing in the early aftermath of the war, Ervand Abrahamian called the contemporary Islamic Republic a "martyrs' welfare state," *The Iranian Mojahedin,* (New Haven: Yale University Press, 1989), 70. See also Kevan Harris, "A Martyrs' Welfare State and Its Contradictions," in *Middle East Authoritarianisms: Governance, Contestation, and Regime Resilience in Syria and Iran,* Steven Heydemann and Reinoud Leenders, eds., (Stanford, CA: Stanford UP, 2013), 79.

61. Khoury, *Iraq in Wartime,* 166–169.

62. For more on who the Iraqi state currently considers a martyr, see the website of the Iraqi Martyrs' Foundation, http://alshuhadaa.gov.iq/.

63. Saskia Gieling, *Religion and War in Revolutionary Iran* (London; New York: I.B. Tauris, 1999), 56–57.

64. There are a large and ever-growing number of studies of martyrdom in post-Revolutionary Iran, see Seyed-Gohrab, *Martyrdom Mysticism and Dissent,* Chapter 2, for a recent study of martyrdom in Persian poetry.

65. Khoury, *Iraq in Wartime,* 219.

66. Ibid., 220

67. See Baram, *Culture, History, and Ideology*; Davis, *Memories of State*; Faust *The Ba'thification of Iraq.*

68. Baram, *Culture, History, and Ideology,* 41–68; Faust, *The Ba'thification of Iraq* 51–68.

69. Khoury, *Iraq in Wartime,* 223–224.

70. Mir-'Abedini, *Sad Sāl,* 901.

71. Fatima Mohsen "Cultural Authoritarianism" in *Iraq Since the Gulf War: Prospects for Democracy,* ed. Fran Hazelton (Fran Atlantic Highlands, NJ: Zed Books, 1994), ," 16.

72. al-Musawi, *Reading Iraq,* 84.

73. ʿAbd al-Jabbar Mahmud al-Samarraʾi, "Ḥawla Mafhūm al-Istishhād" in *Qādisiyyat Ṣaddām wa-l-Khayār al-Qawmī* (Baghdad: Dār al-Shuʾūn al-Thaqāfiyya al-ʿĀmma, 1986), 101–54.

74. ʿAbd al-Sattar Nasir became one of the most prolific writers of the genre of Saddam's Qadisiyya. He published dozens of short stories, children's stories, and works of literary criticism during the war years. In 1999, he left Iraq and fled to Canada, where he died in August 2013. Once out of Iraq, Nasir wrote a mea culpa and openly attacked Saddam Hussein in his later writings. See his articles compiled in *Maqhā al-Shahbandar* (Cairo: Maktabat Madbūlī, 2005).

75. ʿAbd al-Sattar Nasir, *al-Shahīd 1777* (Baghdad: Dār al-Ḥurriyya li-l-Ṭabāʿa, 1981), 32.

76. Ibid., 35.

77. ʿAbbud, *Thaqafat al-ʿUnf*, al-Hassan, *Women, Writing*, and Khidr *al-Khākīyya* are the most thorough studies of this literature.

78. Khoury, *Iraq in Wartime*, 205–206.

79. ʿAbbud, *Thaqafat al-ʿUnf*, 27–28.

80. Ahmad Khalaf, "Nuqṭat Tamās," quoted in ʿAbbud, *Thaqafat al-ʿUnf*, 28.

81. Khidr, *al-Khākīyya* 54.

82. Al-Hassan, *Women, Writing* 50.

83. "The Mehdi" is a reference is to the twelfth Shiʿi Imam believed to have gone into occultation and who will return at the end times.

84. Reza Sarshar, "Māndāb," in *Khodāhāfez, Barādar* (Tehran: Entesharāt-e Barg, 1989), 143–144.

85. Ibid., 890.

86. See, for example, Amin Khorrami, "Khorramshahr; *Nakhl-hā-ye bi Sar va Qalam Tasvirgar va Sarih-e Qāsemʿali Farāsat*," *Islamic Republic News Agency* (IRNA), Sept. 23, 2019, https://www.irna.ir/news/83043168/.

87. Several of the Persian novels and short stories that I analyze in this book feature protagonists named "Naser," which means "victor." While the choice of name may be intentional on the part of the induvial authors, the fact that these characters all have these names, is, to the best of my knowledge, coincidental.

88. Qasemʿali Farasat, *Nakhl-hā-ye bi Sar* (Tehran: Amir Kabir, 1988), 52.

89. Ibid., 98. Mohammad Jahan-Ara was the actual commander of the Khorramshahr branch of the Revolutionary Guards at the time of the Iraqi invasion. He is hailed as one of the war's early heroes. Now commonly referred to as *Shahid Jahān-Ārā*, he is elegized with the well-known religious song (*sorud*) of Bushehri origin, "Mamad Nabudi Bebini" ("Mohammad, You Weren't There to See It") popularized by Gholam Koveytipur after Iranian forces retook took Khorramshahr. Jahan-Ara's role

in the novel is limited to a few words and scenes. To my knowledge, the insertion of actual historical figures was not common in Iraqi fiction at the time.

90. Ibid.,100.

91. Ibid., 215.

92. Goulia Ghardashkhani, "*Da* and Its Mothers of the Martyred: Meaning and Contest in an Iranian War Memoir," *British Journal of Middle Eastern Studies*, vol. 51, no. 2, (2024): 273–274.

93. Khoury, *Iraq in Wartime*, 204. While her observation is about Iraq, it is also highly germane to Iran. For a commentary on the similar set of circumstances in Iran, see Mir-'Abedini, *Sad Sāl*, 890.

94. For a detailed reading of Fasih's novel, see Saeedeh Shahnahpur, *Writing War in Contemporary Iran: The Case of Esmā'il Fasih's Zemestān-e 62* (New York: Peter Lang, 2019).

95. Mohsen, "Debating Iraqi Culture," 19.

Chapter 2

1. Khoury, *Iraq in Wartime*, 220.

2. For a more comprehensive overview of the literary examples of this phenomenon see Mir-'Abedini, *Sad Sāl*, 931–983; 1,281–1,302. For similar developments in film, see Hamid Naficy, *A Social History of Iranian Cinema: Volume 4, The Globalizing Era, 1984–2010* (Durham, NC: Duke University Press), 1–93.

3. Slavoj Žižek, *Violence* (Picador: New York, 2008), 4–5.

4. Khudayyir's short story collections *al-Mamlaka al-Sawdā'* (1972) and *Fī Darajat Khamsa wa-Arba'īn Mi'awī* (1978) had been met with critical acclaim both in- and outside Iraq.

5. One of these was a short story titled *Wasiyyat al-Jundī* about the final moments of a soldier fighting in the marshes between Iran and Iraq and his (or another soldier's funeral). Although it does not portray combat or engage with the Saddam's Qadisiyya narrative, for Khudayyir its setting and content is uncharacteristically direct about the war front the experience. It was never republished. See the journal *Asfār*, no. 2, (1985): pp 24–25.

6. Creation dates and occasionally places of publication for most of these stories can be found in both story collections. Most of these stories were written in the last two years of the war and were then published between 1988 and 1993 before making it into book form.

7. Chip Rossetti, "A Shared Imaginary City: The Role of the Reader in the Fiction of Muḥammad Khuḍayyir," PhD diss., University of Pennsylvania, 2017.

8. See https://basrayatha.com.

9. Fabio Caiani and Catherine Cobham, "Autumn Visions: War and the Imagery of Muḥammad Khuḍayyir," *Journal of Arabic Literature* 49, (2018): 248.

10. Muhammad Khudayyir, *Baṣrayāthā: Ṣūrat al-Madīna* (Baghdad: al-Amad, 1993), 137 (Arabic). English translation refers to *Basrayatha: Story of a City*, William Hutchins, trans. (New York: Verso, 2008), 147–148.

11. *Basrayatha*, Ibid., 139 (A); 148 (T).

12. See Khoury, *Iraq in Wartime*, 48–81.

13. Khudayyir, *Basrayatha*, 153 (T); 140 (A).

14. "Familiar" [*alīfa*] follows Hutchins' translation. The word can also carry the meaning of "tamed," "friendly," or "intimate." *Thaʿābīn alīfa* could also mean "pet snakes."

15. Khudayyir, *Basrayatha* 154 (Translation modified); 141 (A).

16. Ibid; 142 (A).

17. Bennett Andrew and Nicholas Royle, "Animal" in *An Introduction to Literature Criticism and Theory* (Milton Park: Routledge, 2016, 5th ed.), 177. See also Matthew Calarco, *Zoographies: The Question of the Animal from Heidegger to Derrida* (New York: Columbia University Press, 2008).

18. Hutchins' English translation inserts the word "should" into the Arabic "I Erase and Draw." It adds readability while capturing the self-command that Khudayyir issues.

19. Ibid., 156 (T); 143 (A).

20. Ibid., 156 (T); 143 (A).

21. Ibid.

22. See: Masmoudi, *War and Occupation*, 13–14; Shakir Mustafa, "Genre Negotiations: Review of Muhammad Khudayyir, *Basriyatha: Sūrat Madina*. Baghdad: Manshūrat al-Amad, 1993," *Edebiyat: Journal of Middle Eastern Literatures* 13:1, (2002), 108–109.

23. Caiani and Cobham "Autumn Visions," 247.

24. Ibid., 269.

25. *Censoring an Iranian Love Story* (New York: Alfred A. Knopf, 2010); *Moon Brow* (Brooklyn, NY: Restless Books, 2018); *Seasons of Purgatory* (New York: Bellevue Literary Press, 2022). Since 2009, Mandanipour's works have been translated exclusively by Sara Khalili. *Censoring* has only ever appeared in its English translation.

26. During the twentieth century, land reform took place twice in Iran: first during the Shah's "White Revolution" in the 1960s (see Amanat, *Iran*, 577–581), and then following the 1979 Revolution. In the second case, in 1980 the new government passed Article 49 of the constitution, which stated "The government has the

responsibility of confiscating all wealth accumulated through usury, usurpation, bribery, embezzlement, theft, gambling, misuse of endowments, misuse of government contracts and transactions, the sale of uncultivated lands and other resources subject to public ownership, the operation of centers of corruption, and other illicit means and sources, and restoring it to its legitimate owner; and if no such owner can be identified, it must be entrusted to the public treasury." See "The Constitution of the Islamic Republic of Iran," at *The Constitute Project* (https://constituteproject.org/countries/Asia/Iran_Islamic_Rep_of_?lang=en).

27. Shahriar Mandanipour, "Rang-e Ātash-e Nimruzi" in *Māh-e Nimruz* (Tehran: Nashr-e Markez, 1997), 9. Page numbers refer to the original Persian language text. English translations are slightly modified translations of "The Color of Fire at Midday," in *Sohrab's Wars*, Mehdi Khorrami, trans. and ed. (Costa Mesa, CA: Mazda Publishers, 2008), 68.

28. Ibid.

29. Ibid., 12 (P); 72 (T).

30. Ibid., 8 (P); 69 (T).

31. Ibid., 9 (P); 69–70 (T).

32. Ibid., 10 (P); 70 (T).

33. Ibid.

34. Ibid., 11 (P); 70 (T).

35. Ibid., 15 (P); 75 (T).

36. Ibid., 14 (P) 74 (T).

37. Ibid., 21–22 (P); 80 (T).

38. Ibid., 23 (P); 81 (T).

39. Khorrami, *Modern Reflections*, 110.

40. Mandanipour, "The Color of Fire at Midday," 22 (P); 81 (T).

41. Khorrami, *Modern Reflections*, 126; Mir-'Adedini, *Sad Sāl*, 1059.

42. Efthymia Rentzou, "Animal," in *A New Vocabulary for Global Modernism*, Eric Hayot and, Rebecca Walkowitz, eds. (Columbia University Press: New York, 2016), 40–41.

43. Ibid.

44. See, for example, Husayn Sarmak Hasan, *Ighmāḍ al-'Aynayn al-Mumīt: Dirāsāt fī Adab Lu'ay Ḥamza 'Abbās al-Qaṣaṣī* (Stockholm: Dār al-Yanābīa', 2010), 9–10. See also, Yasmeen Hanoosh, "Two Stories by Luay Hamza Abbas," June 20, 2011, https://www.jadaliyya.com/Details/24115.

45. Lu'ay Hamza 'Abbas, *'Alā Darāja fī al-Layl* (Amman: Azmina, 1997), 19.

46. Ibid., 20.

47. Ibid., 20.

48. For more on these battles see Dilip Hiro, *The Longest War: The Iran-Iraq Military Conflict* (New York: Routledge, 1991), 168–212.

49. Khudayyir, *Basrayatha* 115–116 (A); 122–123 (T). ʿAbd al-Wahab's story was later included in his collection *Rāʾiḥat al-Shitāʾ* (Basra: Ittiḥād al-Udabāʾ wa-l-Kuttāb al-ʿIrāqīyyīn fī al-Baṣra, 2009), 129–142. I am indebted to Haidar Saeed who first brought this to my attention.

50. ʿAbbas, *ʿAlā Darāja fī al-Layl*, 13.

51. Ibid., 40.

52. Ibid., 42.

53. Ibid., 43.

54. Ibid., 44.

55. Khoury, *Iraq in Wartime*, 73–77; 165–172.

56. Hiro, *The Longest War*, 168–170; Razoux, *The Iran-Iraq War*, 463–465.

57. Quoted in Khoury, *Iraq in Wartime*, 75.

58. Human Rights Watch, *Genocide in Iraq: The Anfal Campaign Against the Kurds*, 1993, http://www.hrw.org/reports/1993/iraqanfal

59. Ibid.

60. For more on the massacre see Amnesty International, "Blood-Soaked Secrets," 2017, https://www.amnesty.org/en/latest/campaigns/2018/10/blood-soaked-secrets; Nasser Mohajer, ed., *Voices of a Massacre: Untold Stories of Life and Death in Iran, 1988* (London: Oneworld, 2020); and Shahla Talebi, *Ghosts of Revolution: Rekindled Memories of Imprisonment in Iran* (Stanford, CA: Stanford University Press, 2011). A spectrum of human rights organizations and political groups claim widely different numbers for the massacre, generally ranging from 5,000–12,000 killed.

61. Razoux, *The Iran Iraq War*, 466–467; Hiro, *The Longest War*, 246–247. For a chilling and controversial example of how this battle appears in Persian fiction see Amir Moosavi, "Dark Corners and the Limits of Ahmad Dehqan's War Front Fiction," *Middle East Critique* 26(1), (2016), 45–59.

62. ʿAbbas, *ʿAlā Darāja fī al-Layl*, 39–40.

63. Daftar-e Motālaʿāt-e Adabiyāt-e Dāstāni, *Gozideh-ye Dāstān-hā-ye Kutāh dar Zamineh-ye Jang-e Tahmili va Defāʿ-e Moqaddas az Matbuʿāt-e Irān* (Tehran: Markaz-e Motālaʿāt va Tahqiqāt-e Farhangi, Vezārat-e Farhang va Ershād-e Eslāmi, 1996), 310–332.

64. Razoux, *The Iran-Iraq War*, 222.

65. Amir Hasan Cheheltan, "Munes, Mādar-e Esfandiār," in *Chizi beh Fardā Namāndeh ast* (Tehran: Negāh, 1998), 119.

66. Ibid., 117.

67. Ibid., 126.

68. Ibid., 131.

69. Located in the southernmost part of Tehran, Behesht-e Zahra is the largest cemetery in Iran with over 1.6 million graves. Notably, it has a large section dedicated to martyrs of the Iran-Iraq War.

70. Ibid., 131.

71. In a similar manner, Hossein Abkenar would later also evoke another story of *The Shahnameh* in his novel of the Iran-Iraq War using the character of Siavash. See Chapter 3.

72. Chelkowski and Dabashi, *Staging a Revolution*, 109–112.

73. Jay Winter, *Sites of Memory, Sites of Mourning: the Great War in European cultural history* (Cambridge: Cambridge University Press, 2014), 2.

74. David Eng and David Kazanjian, eds., *Loss: The Politics of Mourning* (Berkeley, CA: University of California Press, 2003), 2.

Chapter 3

1. Michel Foucault, *Power/Knowledge: Selected Interviews and Other Writings, 1972–1977* (New York: Pantheon Books, 1980), 133.

2. This chapter draws from and develops arguments that I originally published in the following articles: "How to Write Death: Resignifying Martyrdom in Two Novels of the Iran-Iraq," *Alif: Journal of Comparative Poetics*, no. 35: 9–31 (2016); "Dark Corners and the Limits of Ahmad Dehqan's War Front Fiction," *Middle East Critique* 26(1): (2017) 45–59; "Desacralizing a Sacred Defense: The Iran-Iraq War in the fiction of Hossein Mortezaeian Abkenar," *Iran Namag* 5(3): (Fall 2020), 158–175.

3. Sarah Cole, *At the Violet Hour: Modernism and Violence in England and Ireland* (New York: Oxford University Press, 2012), 42–43.

4. Ibid., 54.

5. Razoux, *The Iran-Iraq War*, 400.

6. Ahmad Dehqan, *Safar beh Garā-ye Devist va Haftād Darajeh* (Tehran: Sureh-ye Mehr, 2005). Translations refer to *Journey to Heading 270 Degrees*, Paul Sprachman, trans. (Costa Mesa, CA: Mazda Publishers, 2006), 135.

7. Ibid., 125 (T).

8. Ibid., 166 (T).

9. Cole, *At the Violet Hour*, 54.

10. For an analysis of this film and its sociological importance see Narges Bajoghli, "*The Outcasts*: The Start of 'New Entertainment' in Pro-Regime Filmmaking in the Islamic Republic of Iran," *Middle East Critique* (2017): 61–77.

11. Bajoghli, *Iran Reframed: Anxieties of Power in the Islamic Republic* (Stanford, CA: Stanford University Press, 2020), 53.

12. The Foundation's prizes were discontinued in 2014.

13. Ahmad Dehqan, *Man Qātel-e Pesar-e-tān Hastam* (Tehran: Ofoq, 2005), 69.

14. Ibid., 70.

15. Ibid., 75.

16. Ibid., 75.

17. Ibid., 77.

18. For more on the Iraqi Communist Party's opposition to the war and its some of its members' limited participation in the Kurdish resistance to the Iraqi military and Baʻth party, see Tareq Y. Ismael, *The Rise and Fall of the Communist Party of Iraq* (Cambridge: Cambridge University Press, 2008), 197, 200, 266. For perspectives from within Iraq Kurdistan outside of Baʻthist control during the 1980s see the Iraqi exilic journal *al-Badil* that was in print from 1980–1991 and was headquartered in Beirut and later Damascus, with a network of members across the Middle East, North Africa, and Europe.

19. For a succinct summary of this important moment that resulted in the deaths of 30,000–60,000 rebels in the south, and nearly 20,000 in the north see Faleh Jabar, "Why the Uprising Failed" *Middle East Research and Information Project* 176, (May/June 1992), https://merip.org/1992/05/why-the-uprisings-failed.

20. Janan Jasim Hillawi, *Layl al-Bilād* (Beirut: Dār al-Ādāb, 2002), 81–82.

21. Ibid., 166.

22. Ibid., 214.

23. Astrid Ottosan al-Bitar, "Another Story to Be Told: Iraqi Novels of Exile in Sweden," in *Conflicting Narratives*, Milich et al., eds., 209–211.

24. Ibid., 210; Hillawi, *Layl al-Bilād*, 167–168; 213.

25. Hillawi, "Ḥallat Sāʻat al-Masāʼ Ṭāʼiran Ramādīyyan" in *Kul yā Ṭāwūsī Ḥattā Takbar* (Uddevalla, Sweden: Dār al-Manfā, 1999). An English translation of this story by Paul Starkey can be found in *Banipal* 17, (Summer 2003): 42–45.

26. Cole, *At the Violet Hour*, 53.

27. For an analysis of novels by these writers, and especially the role of the war deserter in them, see Masmoudi, *War and Occupation*, Chapter 2. The major difference between Hillawi's novel discussed here and the texts discussed by Masmoudi is that Hillawi's novel was published while Saddam Hussein's Baʻthist regime was still in power, even if it was in its final days.

28. Ahmad Shakeri, "Majmuʻeh-ye Man Qātel-e Pesar-e-tān Hastam Māteriālisti ast," *Farsi News Agency*, September 24, 2006, http://farsnews.ir/newstext.php?nn=8507020264.

29. Moosavi, "Dark Corners." For a more recent discussion, see Sam Farzaneh's interview with Fatemeh Shams on the podcast *Shirāzeh*, Episode 50, May 30, 2024, a transcript of which is available here: https://www.bbc.com/persian/arts-69075151,

30. Mehr News, "Gelāyeh-hā-ye Ahmad Dehqān az Pedarkhāndeh-hā-ye Adabiyāt va Farhang," September 25, 2013, https://www.mehrnews.com/news/2295361.

31. M.R. Ghanoonparvar, "War Veterans Turned Writers of War Narratives" in *Moments of Silence: Authenticity in the Cultural Expressions of the Iran-Iraq War, 1980–1988*, Arta Khakpour, et al., eds (New York: New York University Press, 2016) 88–102.

32. Shahla Talebi, "An Iranian Martyr's Dilemma: The Finite Subject's Infinite Responsibility," *Comparative Studies of South Asia, Africa, and the Middle East* 33 (2), (2013): 177–96.

33. The author has given several interviews that offer details of his personal life. For a relatively recent example see Muthana al-Nahar, "Maḥaṭāt fī Ḥayāt al-Adīb al-ʿIrāqī Muḥsin al-Ramlī. . .al- Ḥayāt wa-l-Barzakh wa-l-Jinna," *Al-Jazīra*, December 16, 2022, https://www.aljazeera.net/culture/2022/12/16/محطات-في-حياة-الاديب-العراقي-محسن.

34. I refer to this character using the spelling found in the published English translation, with the addition of the initial ʿayn. The spellings of other names in quotations reflect the spelling found in the English translation.

35. Muhsin al-Ramli, *al-Fatīt al-Mubʿathir* (Cairo: Dār al-Markaz al-Ḥaḍāra al-ʿArabīyya, 2000), 40. English translation refers to *Scattered Crumbs*, Yasmeen Hanoosh, trans. (Fayetteville, AK: University of Arkansas Press, 2003), 50.

36. Ibid., 27 (A); 34 (T).

37. Ibid., 60 (A); 80 (T).

38. Ibid., 61 (A); 82 (T).

39. Inke Arns, Sylvia Sasse, "Subversive Affirmation. On Mimesis as a Strategy of Resistance," *Irwin: East Art Map*, London / Ljubljana, (2005): 2.

40. Al-Ramli, *Scattered Crumbs*, 66 (A); 87–88 (T).

41. Ibid., 72 (A); 96 (T).

42. Ibid., 89 (A); 122 (T).

43. Ibid., 91 (A); 124 (T). In 2009, the *al-Jazeera* television program *Mawʿid fī al-Mahjar* featured al-Ramli. The biographical information is from that interview. See the transcription here: http://www.aljazeera.net/programs/a-date-in-exile/2009/7/13/محسن-الرملي.

44. Hossein Mortezaeian Abkenar, *ʿAqrab Ru-ye Pelleh-ha-ye Rāh-āhan-e Andimeshk, ya, Khun az in Qatār Michekeh, Qorbān!* (Tehran: Nashr-e Nay, 2006), 36–37. For the sake of readability, I have added punctuation to this excerpt.

45. Scientists have shown that this is not actually suicide but a reaction to the extreme heat, which most varieties of scorpions cannot handle.

46. The decision to ban the publication of the novel came as a surprise to the publisher, who had planned to distribute the already-printed third edition of the book. See "*Enteshār-e Romān-e Toqif Shodeh-ye 'Aqrab dar Farānseh*," Rādio Zamāneh, January 17, 2011, https://www.radiozamaneh.com/30387.

47. The edition published by Naakojaa has dropped the second part of the original title.

48. The choice of name here may be more than coincidence and could be read as a possible combination of the author's middle name and the name of the father of modernist Persian literature, Sadegh Hedayat.

49. Abkenar, *The Scorpion*, 4.

50. IBNA, "*Aqrab Ru-ye Pelleh-hā-ye Rah-ahān-e Andimeshk*: Negāhi-ye Motefāvet-e Defā'-e Moqaddas," October 24, 2007, https://www.ibna.ir/fa/report/9755/.

51. Ibid.

52. "Enteqād-e Shākeri az Dāvari-ye Ketāb-e Sāl-e Defā'-e Moqaddas," *Ketab News*, November 8, 2007, http://www.ketabnews.com/fa/news/1805/ مقدس-دفاع-کتابسال-داوری-از-شاکری-انتقاد.

53. Abkenar, *The Scorpion*, 7–8.

54. Ibid., 24–26.

55. Ibid. 41. The novel concludes with the death of another character who is also presumably Siavash at the hands of an MP.

56. Ibid., 62.

57. Ibid., 77–80.

58. Brian McHale, *Postmodernist Fiction* (London and New York: Routledge, 1987), 90.

59. Ibid., 90.

60. The debate around what constitutes "postmodernist" fiction in the Persian literary context is unsettled. Although *The Scorpion* contains elements that are seen as postmodernist within any world literature, I concur with Khorrami, who writes that critics have still not clearly defined the term despite its "indiscriminate" use in modern Persian literary criticism, to the point that "it has basically lost its meaning and has its own genealogy." See Khorrami, *Literary Subterfuge*, 224 fn. 177.

61. Moosavi "Dark Corners," and "How to Write Death." These articles demonstrate how Dehqan's fiction bears the hallmark of rebellion but does not outright challenge the official record formally or ideologically. Ahmadzadeh's fiction remains even more within the confines of what is acceptable in the context of Iranian war fiction.

62. Abkenar, *The Scorpion*, 31–32.

63. Mohsen, "Debating Iraqi Culture," 10–11.

64. Two very well-known examples emerging from the American- and French-Iranian diasporas are Azar Nafisi's *Reading Lolita in Tehran*, and Marjane Satrapi's *Persepolis*. Although it plays a more important role in *Persepolis*, in both texts the presence of the war, despite it lasting for nearly a decade in the course of their stories, occupies relatively little space. For a comparative example in Persian language exilic literature see ʿAbbas Maʿrufi, *Fereydun Seh Pesar Dāsht* (Berlin: Gardun, 2008, 4th ed.). The novel goes from the events of the Revolution to the life of exile in Germany and barely mentions the war. I am indebted to Christop Werner for pointing this out at the European Round Table on Modern Persian Literature in Bamberg, Germany in July 2024. A recent notable exception to this is Shahriar Mandanipour's *Moon Brow* (Brooklyn: Restless Books, 2018).

65. This trend is explored more in Chapter 5.

66. See Hanoosh, *Contempt*, and al-Akhras, *Kharīf*.

Chapter 4

1. Razoux, *The Iran-Iraq War*, 302.

2. Ibid., 436.

3. Globally, these attacks have been most memorably depicted in Marjane Satrapi's graphic memoir, *Persepolis*. Since *Persepolis* originally appeared in French in 2000, it has been translated into more than a dozen languages and has sold more than two million copies. Wee Kali Faulwetter, "The Graphic Translation of Persepolis," Motaworld Blog, February 17, 2022, https://www.motaword.com/blog/persepolis.

4. Ruth Abou Rached, *Reading Iraqi Women's Novels in English Translation: Iraqi Women's Stories* (Abingdon Oxon: Routledge, 2021), 60. See also, Saleh, *Return*, 30, 180–182.

5. For more on the depiction of Iraqi villagers and class differences in the novel, which Ferial Ghazoul describes as "solidarity among the subaltern" see "Iraq" in Ghazoul et al., *Arab Women Writers: A Critical Reference Guide, 1873–1999* (Cairo: American University in Cairo Press, 2008), 198.

6. Betool Khedairi, *Kam Badat al-Samā' Qarība!!* 4th ed. (Beirut: al-Muʾassasa al-ʿArabiyya lil-Dirāsāt w-al-Nashr, 2007), 91; Betool Khedairi, *A Sky So Close*, Muhayman Jamil, trans. (New York: Anchor Books, 2002), 106.

7. Ibid., 99–100 (A); 121 (T).

8. Ibid., 121 (A); 150 (T).

9. Ibid., 143–4 (A); 178–9 (T).

10. Ibid., 144 (A); 179–80 (T).

11. Ibid., 141 (A); 146 (T).

12. Ibid., 122 (A) 146 (T).

13. Ibid., 120 (A), 143 (T).

14. Ibid., 149 (A), 179 (T).

15. Musawi, *Reading Iraq*, 132.

16. Jennifer Chandler, "No Man's Land: Representations of Masculinities in Iran-Iraq War Fiction," PhD Diss., University of Manchester (2012), 129.

17. Khedairi would hardly be the only author writing from outside Iraq who has done this. Both Sinan Antoon and Muhsin al-Ramli have done the same in novels published around the same time and later.

18. Masmoudi, "Portraits of Iraqi women: between testimony and fiction," *International Journal of Contemporary Iraqi Studies*, vol 4, nos. 1-2, 70.

19. Khedairi, *A Sky So Close*, 160 (A); 200 (T).

20. Jean Baudrillard, *The Gulf War Did Not Take Place* (Bloomington, IN: Indiana University Press, 1991).

21. Joy Gordon, *Invisible War: The United States and the Iraq Sanctions* (Cambridge, MA: Harvard University Press, 2010), 1.

22. Khedairi, *A Sky So Close*, 176–177 (A); 220 (T).

23. Masmoudi, *War and Occupation*, 19.

24. Amir Hasan Cheheltan, "Bāzkhāni-ye Dāstān-e 'Naqqāsh-e Bāghāni' Asar-e Hushang-e Golshiri," BBC Persian, June 5, 2010, http://www.bbc.com/persian/arts/2010/06/100603_l41_golshiri_memory_cheheltan.shtml.

25. Hushang Golshiri, "Naqqāsh-e Bāghāni" in *Nimeh-ye Tārik-e Māh: Dāstān-hā-ye Kutāh* (Tehran: Entesharāt-e Nilufar, 2002), 483. Translations here are my own, but readers can find the whole story translated by Samuel Thrope, "The Painter of Baghan," in *Consequence*, (Spring 2015): 122–135.

26. Ibid., 487.

27. Ibid., 483.

28. Ibid., 488.

29. Ibid. 488.

30. Ibid., 494.

31. Ibid., 488.

32. Sinan Antoon, *I'jām: Riwāya* (Beirut: Manshūrāt al-Jamal, 2013), 125. *I'jaam: An Iraqi Rhapsody,* Rebecca Johnson and Sinan Antoon, trans. (San Francisco: City Lights, 2007), 97.

33. In the published English translation of Antoon's *I'jām*, this line is always written separately from the surrounding paragraphs thus giving it more emphasis than in the Arabic original, which places the phrases at the opening of the paragraph that follows it.

34. The English translation omits the lyrics of the song. Likely because of the difficulty in rendering the colloquial lyrics into English while maintaining its poetic rhyme.

35. Antoon, *I'jaam*, 33–34 (A); 18 (T); The quotation demonstrates some of the ways in which the English and Arabic versions of the novel differ, with the subtitle added for English readers who presumably would not be familiar with the sayings of Saddam Hussein.

36. Khedairi, *A Sky So Close*, 91 (A); my English translation.

37. Antoon, *I'jaam*, 34 (A); 18 (T).

38. Antoon, *I'jaam*, 117 (A); 89 (T).

39. Frederike Pannewick, "Dancing Letters: The Art of Subversion in Sinān Antūn's *I'jām*," in Milich, et. al., *Conflicting Narratives*, 72.

40. Masmoudi, *War and Occupation*, 20.

41. Anna Ziajka Stanton, *The Worlding of Arabic Literature: Language, Affect, and the Ethics of Translatability* (New York: Fordham University Press, 2023), 122.

42. Ibid., 121 and Saad A. Albazei, "Review of *I'jaam: An Iraqi Rhapsody* by Sinan Antoon, trans. Rebecca C. Johnson and Sinan Antoon," *World Literature Today* 82, no. 6 (2008): 58. Quoted in Stanton, 122.

43. Stanton, *The Worlding of Arabic Literature*, 123.

44. See Jām-e Jam Online, "*Yeki Bud va Yeki Nabud:' Nevisandigān*," https://jamejamonline.ir/fa/news/796966/یکی-بود-یکی-نبود-نویسندگان, May 12, 2016; and Goulia Ghardashkhani, "Narrative Geometry in 'Ali Reza Gholami's *Divar* (The Wall): New Developments in Iranian War Literature," *Iranian Studies*, vol. 53, nos. 5–6, (2020): 875.

45. There are hints in the novel that point to a severe case of Asperger's Syndrome in the novel's protagonist.

46. 'Alireza Gholami, *Divār: Romān* (Tehran: Entesharāt-e Morvāred, 2015), 12. Such scenes were common in 1980s Iran. The late Abbas Kiarostami brilliantly captured one such morning assembly in his 1987 documentary *Mashq-e Shab* (*Homework*).

47. Ibid., 76.

48. Ibid., 29–30.

49. Ibid., 125. The narrator's burning of the letters recalls a story by Ahmad Dehqan titled "Tambr" ("The Stamp") when a traumatized, bitter narrator relates a horrific incident during the final days of the Iran-Iraq War. See Moosavi, "Dark Corners." Gholami, on the first page of *The Wall*, lists fifteen famous, mostly European twentieth-century authors, who wrote famous works about the First or Second

World Wars, and to whom he sends respect. At the end of the list, two Iranian writers are named, Ahmad Mahmud and Ahmad Dehqan.

50. Ibid., 142.

51. Ghardashkhani, "Narrative Geometry."

52. See Chapter 3, and Pannewick, "Dancing Letters."

53. Gholami, 85–86

54. Ervand Abrahamian, *Tortured Confessions: Prisons and Public Recantations in Modern Iran* (Berkeley, CA: University of California Press, 1999), 6–7.

55. Ghardashkhani, "Narrative Geometry," 879.

56. Antoon, "Debris and Diaspora."

57. James Dawes, *The Language of War: Literature and Culture in the U.S. from the Civil War through World War II* (Cambridge, MA: Harvard University Press, 2002), 2.

58. This is likely why the book has garnered interest by Persian translators. To my knowledge, *I'jaam* is the earliest post-2003 Iraqi novel to appear in Persian translation, and two translations of it exist. See *Noqteh-hā (I'jām)*: *Ḥamāseh-i-ye 'Irāqi (Dots (I'jām): an Iraqi Epic)*, Mas'ud Yusef Hasirchin, trans. (Tehran: Nashr-e Hamān, 2019); and *I'jām* Hasan Hatami, trans. (Tehran: Rahi, 2020). According to Antoon, Hatami's (authorized) translation is from the Arabic original, while Hasirchin's (unauthorized) translation is from English. (Personal correspondence, July 22, 2023).

Chapter 5

1. This chapter's section on Marashi's novel *Pruning* draws from and develops arguments that were originally published in Amir Moosavi, "Mourning Mothers and Wars That Never End: Reading Nasim Marashi's *Haras* (Pruning) in the Shadow of the Iran-Iraq War," *British Journal of Middle Eastern Studies* 51, no. 2 (2024): 249–63.

2. Haytham Bahoora, "Writing the Dismembered Nation: The Aesthetics of Horror in Iraqi Narratives of War," *Arab Studies Journal* (2015): 185.

3. Avery Gordon, *Ghostly Matters: Haunting and the Sociological Imagination* (Minneapolis: University of Minnesota Press, 1997), xvi.

4. Slavoj Žižek, *The Parallax View* (Cambridge, MA: The MIT Press, 2006), 20–21.

5. See, for example, Bahoora, "Writing the Dismembered Nation;" Drew Paul, "Transmission and Transit in Contemporary Arabic Literature: *Naql* and Its Limits," *Journal of Arabic Literature* 53, 1–2 (2022): 100–131; and Annie Webster, "Writing Urban Warfare: Pedestrian Perspectives in Post-2003 Baghdad," *The Routledge Companion to Literary Urban Studies* (London: Routledge, Taylor & Francis Group, 2023).

6. An important exception is Haytham Bahoora's contribution to "The War We Lived: Remembering the Iran-Iraq War After 40 Years," an online panel hosted by The Iranian Studies Initiative of New York University, December 17, 2020,

https://www.youtube.com/watch?v=wuPBojWHIBw. Parts of this chapter were drafted before the talk, but I am indebted to his thoughts as I developed it.

7. Ahmad Saadawi, *Frankshtāyin fī Baghdād* (Beirut and Baghdad: Manshūrāt al-Jamal, 2013), 14. *Frankenstein in Baghdad,* Jonathan Wright, trans. (New York: Penguin Books, 2018), 8. Elishva is reminiscent of Munes, the mother of the MIA soldier in Amir Hasan Cheheltan's short story "Munes, Mother of Esfandiar," covered in Chapter 2.

8. Saadawi, *Frankenstein* 64 (A); 54 (T).

9. Ibid., 65 (A); 55 (T).

10. Ibid., 94 (A); 82 (T).

11. Bahoora, "The War We Lived."

12. Official Blog of Hassan Blasim, http://blasim.blogspot.com/2008/03/blog-post_5221.html March 18, 2012

13. Blasim's stories have been published in English, most notably in three collections all in Jonathan Wright's translation: *The Madman of Freedom Square* (2009), and *The Iraqi Christ* (2013) both with Comma Press, and *The Corpse Exhibition* (2013) with Penguin. The final collection consists of stories that appeared in the former two. The Arabic version of *Madman* was published in 2012 in Beirut by al-Muʾassasa al-ʿArabiyya lil-Dirāsāt wa-l-Nashr as *Majnūn Sāḥat al-Ḥurriya*. Even so, "several parts of the text were erased prior to its Arabic publication." See Marcia Lynx Qualey, "'Majnūn Sāḥat al-Ḥurriyya:' Mamnūʿ Lākin Mutāh," *Hiber*, February 6, 2014, https://www.7iber.com/2014/02/blasimban/.

14. Robin Yassin-Kassab, "*Beirut 39*: New Writing from the Arab World, edited by Samuel Shimo," *The Guardian*, June 11, 2010, https://www.theguardian.com/books/2010/jun/12/beirut-new-writing-arab-world. For a survey of reviews of Blasim's writings by critics writing in Arabic, see Khaled al-Masri, "The Politics and Poetics of Madness in Ḥasan Blāsim's *The Madman of Freedom Square*," *Journal of Arabic Literature*, vol. 49, no. 3 (2018): 272.

15. Joanna Sellman, *Arabic Exile Literature in Europe: Defamiliarizing Forced Migration* (Edinburgh: Edinburgh University Press, 2022), 83.

16. Hassan Blasim, *Majnūn Sāḥat al-Ḥurriyya* (Beirut: al-Muʾassasa al-ʿArabiyya lil-Dirāsāt wa-l-Nashr, 2012), 39; *The Madman of Freedom Square*, Jonathan Wright trans. (Manchester: Comma Press, 2009), 13.

17. Ibid., 41 (A); 14–15 (T).

18. It is worth noting that the Arabic original refers to these texts as *"riwāyāt"* (novels) while the English translation calls them "stories." Given the context, short stories are more plausible. See Chapter 1 for more on the short stories of Saddam's Qadisiyya.

19. Ibid., 42 (A); 16 (T).

20. Ibid., 46 (A); 18 (T).

21. Ibid., 19 (T), 48 (A).

22. Ibid., 20 (T), 49 (A)

23. Al-Masri, "The Politics and Poetics of Madness," 273.

24. *Al-'Arabī al-Jadīd*, "Ḥasan Blāsim…Tatwīj Adabī lil-Masīḥ al-'Irāqī," May 25, 2014, https://www.alaraby.co.uk/حسن-بلاسم-تتويج-أدبي-لـ"المسيح-العراقي".

25. Blasim, *The Madman of Freedom Square*, 13.

26. Masmoudi, "Literary Haunting and The Iran-Iraq War," *Michigan Quarterly Review* (published online accompanying MQR Issue 61:2, Spring 2022), https://sites.lsa.umich.edu/mqr/2022/04/literary-haunting-and-the-iran-iraq-war/

27. Nguyen, *Nothing Ever Dies*, 19.

28. Gordon, *Ghostly Matters*, xvi.

29. Al-Masri, "The Politics and Poetics of Madness," 275.

30. Diaa Jubaili, *Lā Ṭaḥāwīn fī al-Baṣra* (Baghdad: Dār Suṭūr lil-Nashr wa-l-Tawzī', 2018), 16 (A). *No Windmills in Basra*, Chip Rossetti, trans. (Dallas: Deep Vellum Publishing, 2022) 24 (T).

31. Ibid.

32. Ibid., 24 (A); 33 (T).

33. Ibid., 25 (A); 34–35 (T)

34. Sami A.A. Kubba and Mudhafar Salim, "The Wetlands Wildlife and Ecosystem" in *The Iraqi Marshlands and the Marsh Arabs: The Ma'dan, Their Culture, and the Environment* (Reading U.K.: Ithaca Press, 2010), 138.

35. Jubaili, *No Windmills in Basra*, 31 (A); 41 (T)

36. Ibid.

37. These battles are described by Hillawi's *Night* and Dehqan's *Journey* covered in Chapter 3. It is also possible that Dehqan's story "I Killed Your Son" (also covered in Chapter 3) took place during Karbala 4, although it is never explicitly stated.

38. This event was widely reported by news outlets in Iran, on Iranian social media, as well as on international news sites reporting on the region. There were massive processions organized in Tehran to accompany the return of the bodies and a slew of social media commentary about the divers, which continued for years fueled by conflicting comments made by high level politicians and military commanders about the incident. See for example, *Mehr News*, "Joz'iyāt-e Shahādat-e 175 Ghavās Khat-shekan / Mazlumiati keh dar Bāzi-ye Resāneh Bishtar Shod," June 3, 2015, (https://www.mehrnews.com/news/2769763/جزئیات-شهادت-۵۷۱-غواص-خط-شکن-مظلومیتی-که-در-بازی-رسانه-ای-بیشترشد) and "Operation Karbala-4 was not a military deception: General Soleimani," *Tehran*

Times, December 31, 2018, https://www.tehrantimes.com/news/431354/Operation-Karbala-4-was-not-a-military-deception-General-Soleimani.

39. International Society of the Red Cross, "Accounting for missing persons and exchanging human remains, Iran and Iraq: 2008–2015," Accessed February 1, 2024,

https://ihl-in-action.icrc.org/case-study/iraniraq-cooperation-search-and-repatriation-mortal-remains-after-iran-iraq-war-1980,

40. See, for example, "Vākonesh-hā beh Namāyesh-e Jasad-e Masnuʿi-ye Qorbāni-ye Jang dar Sedā va Sīmā," *Iran Wire*, May 29, 2023, https://iranwire.com/fa/news-1/118991-واکنشها-به-نمایش-جسد-مصنوعی-قربانی-جنگ-در-صدا-و-سیما/.

41. The Iraqi Red Crescent Society, "Al-Hilāl al-Aḥmar Yadʿū Dhawīhim l-Istislām Rafāt 629 Shahīdan fī al-Ḥarb al-ʿIrāqīyya al-Irānīyya," Accessed July 17, 2024, https://ircs.org.iq/الهلال-الأحمر-يدعو-ذويهم-لاستلام-رفات-62/.

42. *Pruning* is the literal title of the novel, but it might be more idiomatically translated as *Pruning the Palm Trees*.

43. Nasim Marashi, *Haras* (Tehran: Cheshmeh, 2017), 27.

44. Ibid., 28–29. A *hejleh* is a bridal chamber, but here it refers to the small, shrine-like structures that are placed on the streets where a deceased young unmarried man once lived. They were extremely common during the Iran-Iraq War and commemorated the deaths of bachelor soldiers who were considered martyrs. These *hejlehs* were "connected to the legend of the betrothal of Qasim b. Ḥasan to Imam Ḥusayn's daughter Zubayda (also called Faṭīma Kubrā) at Karbala, just before his martyrdom." See Jean Calmard, "Hejla," *Encyclopædia Iranica*, Last Updated: March 22, 2012, https://iranicaonline.org/articles/hejla. Jannat-Abad is a large cemetery outside of Khorramshahr.

45. See Tahir Hussain, *Kuwaiti Oil Fires: Regional Environmental Perspectives* (Oxford: Pergamon, 1995), 219–40.

46. The effort to put out the fires was international, with companies contracted from the United States, Canada, Kuwait, Iran, Hungary, Rumania, Russia, and China.

47. Youssef M. Ibrahim, "After the War: Another War Begins as Kuwaiti Oil-Well Fires Threaten Region's Ecology; Beyond Mideast, Black Rain and Acid-Filled Clouds," *The New York Times*, March 16, 1991. Section 1, page 4.

48. Marashi, *Haras*, 32.

49. Ibid., 95–6.

50. Ibid., 111–112.

51. Ibid., 39–40.

52. Rob Nixon, *Slow Violence, and the Environmentalism of the Poor* (Cambridge, MA: Harvard University Press, 2011), 2.

53. Hooshang Amirahmadi, "Iranian recovery from industrial devastation during war with Iraq" in Mitchell James, *The Long Road to Recovery: Community Responses to Industrial Disaster* (Tokyo: United Nations University Press, 1996) available online at: https://archive.unu.edu/unupress/unupbooks/uu21le/uu21leoe.htm#impacts%20of%20the%20war%20on%20human%20health%20and%20long%20term%20habitability%20of%20the%20region.

54. Ibid.

55. Islamic Republic News Agency, "Asarāt-e Zist-muhiti-e Jang-e Tahmili Hanuz Pābarjāst," September 20, 2020, https://www.irna.ir/news/84047085.

56. In this context, readers may see echoes of Moniro Ravanipour, *Ahl-e Gharq* (The Drowned) (Tehran: Khāneh-ye Āftāb, 1990); and Shahrnush Parsipour *Zanan Bedun-e* Mardan (Women Without Men) (Tehran: Nashr-e Nuqreh, 1989). Readers will notice an additional echo of *Women Without Men* in *Pruning* through the character of Zarrinkulah in the former, who for a period only sees men without heads.

57. Arabic does have a word to express this state: *thaklān*, and other variants of the root *th-k-l*, refer to one who is bereaved of a child or son and is especially used for mothers.

58. Arab fathers are often referred to as the father (*abū*) of their firstborn son. Likewise, Arab mothers are often referred to as the mother (*umm*) of their firstborn son (e.g., Umm 'Aqil is "Mother of Aqil"). *Pruning*'s dialogue is peppered with Arabic expressions reflecting the linguistic and ethnic diversity of Khuzestan.

59. Marashi, *Haras*, 161.

60. Ibid., 179.

61. Žižek, *The Parallax View* (Cambridge, MA: The MIT Press, 2006), 20–21. One could also consider Naval's state as a third category to Freud's bifurcated distinction between mourning and melancholia.

62. Gordon, *Ghostly Matters*, 64.

63. Marashi, *Haras*, 100.

64. Judith Butler, "Afterword: After Loss, What Then?" in *Loss*, Eng and Kazanjian, eds., 468.

65. Marashi, *Haras*, 181.

66. Ibid., 182.

67. This has not gone unnoticed by critics who have taken the novel to task for not celebrating any part of the defense of the country, see for example Sayyidah 'Azra Musavi, "Jahān Ingūneh beh Pāyān Mirisad: Naqdi bar Kitāb-e Haras," June 26, 2021, https://bookroom.ir/mag/content/336/هرس-کتاب-بر-نقدی-رسد-می-پایان-به-اینگونه-جهان.

Conclusion

1. Hassan Blasim has repeatedly complained about being unable to publish his stories in Iraq because of their perceived indecency. See, for example, Kholod Saghir, "Interview with the Iraqi author Hassan Blasim," Pen Sweden, June 10, 2021, http://www.penopp.org/articles/interview-iraqi-author-hassan-blasim?language_content_entity=en. Hanoosh also shows how these laws, which are based on the wording of Ba'thist censorship guidelines, have prevented writers from publishing in Iraq between 2008 and 2012. See Hanoosh, "Contempt," 397–398.

2. Laetitia Nanquette, *Iranian Literature after the Islamic Revolution: Production and Circulation in Iran and the World* (Edinburgh: Edinburgh University Press, 2021), 178.

3. See, for example, mhd4, "Bā Navā-ye Kāravān…Madiheh Sarāi-ye Hāj Sādeq-e Āhangarān," YouTube, Accessed July 18, 2024. https://www.youtube.com/watch?v=v4FdqvxFt2k.

4. YouTube and the Iranian video-hosting website Aparat contain numerous examples of these recitations.

5. Kevin L. Schwartz and Olmo Gölz, "Going to War with the Coronavirus and Maintaining the State of Resistance in Iran," Middle East Research and Information Project (MERIP), September 1, 2020, https://merip.org/2020/09/going-to-war-with-the-coronavirus-and-maintaining-the-state-of-resistance-in-iran.

6. "Chāp-e Tāzeh-ye Dā Montasher Shod," Iranian Student News Agency (ISNA), December 6, 2021, https://www.isna.ir/news/1400091511669. For more on the critique of this novel see Ghardashkhani, "*Da*;" Nanquette, "An Iranian Woman's Memoir on the Iran-Iraq War: The Production and Reception of *Da*," *Iranian Studies* 46.6, (2013): 943–957; Asad Seif, *Ketāb-e Dā: Yek Vāqe'iat va Sad-hā Dorugh*, DW News Persian Service, September 24, 2023, https://www.dw.com/fa/کتاب-دا-کی-واقعیت-و-صدها-دروغ/a-66909863-ir.

7. Marsin Alshamary, "Authoritarian Nostalgia Among Iraqi Youth: Roots and Repercussions," War on the Rocks, July 25, 2018, https://warontherocks.com/2018/07/authoritarian-nostalgia-among-iraqi-youth-roots-and-repercussions.

8. "'Yā Qā' Turābik Kāfūr, …' al-'Ughnīyya al-'Irāqīyya Wājihat Īrān fī 'Aṣrayn," *al-Ḥurra*, November 6, 2019, https://www.alhurra.com/iraq/2019/11/06/يا-قاع-ترابك-كافور-أغنية-عراقية-واجهت-إيران-في-عصرين.

9. See for example Ahmed Nawzad, "Yā Kā' Turābik Kāfūrī", Accessed July 20, 2024, https://www.youtube.com/watch?v=uqZntem4SS8.

10. Bint al-ʿIrāq, "Ughniyyat Yā Gā Turābich Kāfūrī: Ihdāʾ lil-Jaysh al-Ḥurr, Muhannad al-Munāwir," August 25, 2019, https://www.youtube.com/watch?v=mzHuXOI3q7A. See also Moosavi, *Dust*, 67.

11. See Rahma Hujja, "al-Marʾa fī Aghānī Intifāḍat Tishrīn: Thāʾira wa-Musʿifa wa Muhadida lil-ʿUrūsh al-Fisād," *al-Iḥtijāj*, March 11, 2020, https://alihtijaj.com/view.php?cat=1172.

12. Antoon, *The Corpse Washer*, 137 (A); 97–98 (T). This is also the title of a piece Antoon first published in the cultural supplement of the Lebanese newspaper *al-Nahār* (no. 200, September 7, 2003), after returning to Iraq for the first time since he left the country in 1991. It was reprinted on Jadaliyya, January 21, 2012, https://www.jadaliyya.com/Details/25159. It bears similarities to the short excerpt that appears in *The Corpse Washer* but is not the same piece.

13. "Iraq's perfect storm – a climate and environmental crisis amid the scars of war," The International Committee of the Red Cross, July 20, 2021, https://www.icrc.org/en/document/iraqs-perfect-storm-climate-and-environmental-crisis-amid-scars-war.

14. Mohammad Darvish (@darvish.mohammad), "Mohammad Darvish, Faʿāl va Konashgar-e Muhit-zist dar Goft-e-Gu bā Bāzār o Mā," Instagram, March 13, 2024, https://www.instagram.com/reel/C4dkDiKNtyR/?utm_source=ig_web_copy_link&igsh=MzRlODBiNWFlZA==

15. See "A War Not Forgotten" in this book's introduction.

Bibliography

'Abbas, Lu'ay Hamza. *'Alā Darāja fī al-Layl* [On a Bicycle at Night]. Amman: Azmina, 1997.

'Abbud, Salam. *Thaqāfat al-'Unf fī al-'Irāq* [The Culture of Violence in Iraq]. Cologne: Manshūrāt al-Jamal, 2002.

———. *Man Yaṣna' al-Dīktātūr?(Ṣaddām Namūdhijan)* [Who Creates the Dictator? (The Saddam Model)]. Cologne: Manshūrāt al-Jamal, 2008.

Abkenar, Hossein Mortezaeian. *'Aqrab ru-ye Pelleh-hā-ye Rāh-āhan-e Andimeshk, yā, Khun az in Qatar Michekeh, Qurbān!* [The Scorpion on the Steps of the Andimeshk Railroad, or, Blood is Dripping from this Train, Sir!]. Tehran: Nashr-e Nay, 2006.

———. "Dāstan-e Raḥmān" [Rahman's Story]. In *Konsert-e Tār-hā-ye Mamnu'eh* [A Concert of Forbidden Strings]. Tehran: Āgah, 1999.

Abrahamian, Ervand. *A History of Modern Iran*. Cambridge: Cambridge University Press, 2008.

———. *The Iranian Mojahedin*. New Haven, CT: Yale University Press, 1992.

———. *Tortured Confessions*. Oakland, CA: University of California Press, 1999.

'Abd al-Wahhab, Mahmud. *Rā'iḥat al-Shitā'* [The Scent of Winter]. Basra: Ittiḥād al-Udabā' wa-l-Kuttāb al-'Irāqīyyīn fī al-Baṣra, 2009

'Abd al-Wahid, 'Abd al-Razzaq. *al-'Amāl al-Shi'irīyya* [The Poetic Works of 'Abd al-Razzaq 'Abd al-Wahid]. Baghdad: Dār al-Shu'ūn al-Thaqāfa, 2001.

Abou Rached, Ruth. *Reading Iraqi Women's Novels in English Translation: Iraqi Women's Stories*. Abingdon, U.K.: Routledge, 2021.

"Accounting for missing persons and exchanging human remains, Iran and Iraq: 2008–2015." International Society of the Red Cross. Accessed July 17, 2024. https://ihl-in-action.icrc.org/case-study/iraniraq-cooperation-search-and-repatriation-mortal-remains-after-iran-iraq-war-1980.

Aghaie, Kamran Scot. *The Martyrs of Karbala: Shi'i Symbols and Rituals in Modern Iran.* Seattle: University of Washington Press, 2004.

Ahangaran, Sadeq. "Bahr-e Āzādi-ye Qods az Karbalā Bāyad Gozasht" [One Must Pass Through Karbala for the Liberation of Jerusalem]. Accessed: 08/17/2024. http://dl.aviny.com/voice/Defae_moghadas/21.mp3.

Ahmadzadeh, Habib, *Shatranj ba Māshin-e Qiāmat* [Chess with the Doomsday Machine]. Tehran: Sureh-ye Mehr, 2007.

———. *A City Under Siege: Tales of the Iran-Iraq War.* Translated by Paul Sprachman. Costa Mesa, CA: Mazda Publishers, 2010.

Ahmadi, Wali. *Modern Persian Literature in Afghanistan: Anomalous visions of history and form.* New York: Routledge, 2008.

Akbar, Kaveh. *Martyr!* New York: Alfred A. Knopf, 2024.

Al-Akhras, Muhammad Ghazi. *Kharīf al-Muthaqqaf fī al-'Irāq* [The Fall of the Iraqi Intellectual]. Beirut: Dār al-Tanwīr, 2011.

Alahamad, Nida and Arang Keshavarzian. "A War on Multiple Fronts." *Middle East Report in Print*, vol. 40, no. 4 (Winter 2010): 17–28.

Alavi, Samad. "The Poetics of Commitment in Modern Persian: A Case of Three Revolutionary Poets in Iran." PhD diss., University of California, Berkeley, 2013.

Albers, Yvonne, Georges Khalil, and Friederike Pannewick. *Commitment and Beyond: Reflections on/of the Political in Arabic Literature since the 1940s.* Wiesbaden: Reichert Verlag. 2015.

Al-Hassan, Harwaa. *Women, Writing and the Iraqi Ba'thist State: Contending Discourses of Resistance and Collaboration, 1968–2003.* Edinburgh: Edinburgh University Press, 2020.

Alipour, Farahmand. "Iraqi writer brings Persian literature to Arab world." Al-Monitor, July 16, 2015. http://www.al-monitor.com/pulse/originals/2015/07/iraqi-iranian-novels-arab-translation.html#ixzz3j4mYVDis.

Alshamary, Marsin. "Authoritarian Nostalgia Among Iraqi Youth: Roots and Repercussions." War on the Rocks, July 25, 2018. https://warontherocks.com/2018/07/authoritarian-nostalgia-among-iraqi-youth-roots-and-repercussions.

Antoon, Sinan. "Bending History." *Middle East Report* 257, (2010): 29–31.

———. "Debris and Diaspora: Iraqi Culture Now." In *Uncovering Iraq: Trajectories of Disintegration and Transformation,* edited by Christopher J. Toensing and Mimi

Kirk. Washington, D.C.: Center for Contemporary Arab Studies, Georgetown University, 2010.

———. *Iʻjām: Riwāya*. Beirut: Manshūrāt al-Jamal, 2013.

———. *Iʻjaam: An Iraqi Rhapsody*. Translated by Antoon and Rebecca Johnson. San Francisco: City Lights, 2007.

———. "*Iṭlāl al-Mushtāq ʻalā Aṭlāl al-ʻIrāq*" [A Lover Pauses before Iraq's Ruins]. Jadaliyya, January 21, 2012. https://www.jadaliyya.com/Details/25159

———. *Waḥdahā Shajarat al-Rummān* Beirut: al-Muʾassasa al-ʻArabīyya lil-Dirāsāt wa-l-Nashr, 2010.

———. *The Corpse Washer*. New Haven, CT: Yale University Press, 2013.

Al-Aqlām, "Mawqifuna" [Our Position]. No. 15 (1980): Front matter.

Allen, Roger. *An Introduction to Arabic Literature*. Cambridge: Cambridge University Press, 2000.

———. *The Arabic Novel: an Historical and Critical Introduction*. Syracuse, NY: Syracuse University Press, 1982.

Amanat, Abbas. *Iran: A Modern History*. New Haven, CT: Yale University Press, 2017.

Amirahmadi, Hooshang. "Iranian recovery from industrial devastation during war with Iraq." In *The Long Road to Recovery: Community Responses to Industrial Disaster*, edited by Mitchell James. Tokyo: United Nations University Press, 1996.

"*ʻAqrab Ru-ye Pelleh-hā-ye Rāh-āhan-e Adimeshk*: Negāhi-ye Motafāvet-e Defāʻ-e Moqaddas" [The Scorpion on the Steps of the Andimeshk Railroad: A Different Look at the Sacred Defense]. Iran Book News Agency (IBNA). Accessed July 17, 2024. http://www.ibna.ir/fa/doc/report/9755/عقرب-روی-پله-های-راه-آهن-اندیمشک-نگاهی-متفاوت-دفاع-مقدس.

Arns, Inke and Sylvia Sasse, "Subversive Affirmation. On Mimesis as Strategy of Resistance." In *Irwin: East Art Map*, edited by IRWIN Artists Group. London: Afterall, 2006. 444–455.

"Asārat-e Zist-muhiti-ye Jang-e Tahmili Hanuz Pābarjāst" [The Environmental Effects of the Imposed War are Ongoing]. *Islamic Republic News Agency (IRNA)*, September 20, 2020. https://www.irna.ir/news/84047085.

Ashcroft, Bill Gareth Griffiths, and Helen Tiffin. *The Empire Writes Back: Theory and Practice in Post-Colonial Literatures*, 2nd ed. New York and London: Routledge, 2002.

Al-Attabi, Qussay. "The Polemics of Iltizām: *Al-Ādāb's* Early Arguments for Commitment." *Journal of Arabic Literature*, vol 52, nos. 1–2 (2021): 124–146.

Atwood, Blake. *Underground: The Secret Life of Videocassettes in Iran*. Cambridge, MA: The MIT Press, 2021.

"Avvalin Kārbord-e Vāzheh-ye Defāʿ-e Moqaddas Tavassot-e cheh Kasi Bud?" [Who Was the First Person to Use the Term 'Sacred Defense']. Navid-e Shāhed, February 11, 2014. https://navideshahed.com/fa/news/315705/

Aviny.com. Official Website of the Shahid Aviny Foundation. Accessed July 17, 2024. www.aviny.com.

Bacevich, Andrew J. *America's War for the Greater Middle East: A Military History*. New York: Random House, 2016. Kindle edition.

Bajoghli, Narges. *Iran Reframed: Anxieties of Power in the Islamic Republic*. Stanford, CA: Stanford University Press, 2020.

———. "*The Outcasts*: The Start of 'New Entertainment' in Pro-Regime Filmmaking in the Islamic Republic of Iran." *Middle East Critique*, vol 27, no. 1 (February 2017): 61–77.

Bakhtin, Mikhail M. *Problems of Dostoevsky's Poetics*. Translated by Caryl Emerson. Minneapolis: University of Minnesota Press, 1984.

———. *The Dialogic Imagination: Four Essays*. Translated by Michael Holquist. Austin, TX: University of Texas Press, 1981.

Bahoora, Haytham. "Iraq." In *The Oxford Handbook of Arab Novelistic Traditions*, edited by Waïl S. Hassan. Oxford: Oxford University Press, 2017. 247–264.

———. "The War We Lived: Remembering the Iran-Iraq War After 40 Years." Online panel hosted by The Iranian Studies Initiative at New York University. Accessed July 17, 2024. https://www.youtube.com/watch?v=wuPBojWHIBw

———. "Writing the Dismembered Nation: The Aesthetics of Horror in Iraqi Narratives of War." *Arab Studies Journal*, (2015): 184–209.

Baram, Amatzia. *Culture, History, and Ideology in the Formation of Baʿthist Iraq, 1968–89*. New York: St. Martin's Press, 1991.

Baudrillard, Jean. *The Gulf War Did Not Take Place*. Bloomington, IN: Indiana University Press, 1991.

Bayat, Asef. *Life as Politics: How Ordinary People Change the Middle East*. Amsterdam: Amsterdam University Press, 2010.

Behrouzan, Orkideh. *Prozak Diaries: Psychiatry and Generational Memory in Iran*. Stanford, CA: Stanford University Press, 2016.

Bengio, Ofra. *Saddam's Word: Political Discourse in Iraq*. New York: Oxford University Press, 1998.

Blasim, Hasan. *Majnūn Sāḥat al-Ḥurrīyya*. Beirut: al-Muʾassasa al-ʿArabiyya lil-Dirāsāt wa-al-Nashr, 2009.

———. *The Madman of Freedom Square*. Translated by Jonathan Wright. Manchester: Comma Press, 2009.

———. Personal website: http://blasim.blogspot.com/2008/03/blog-post_5221.html

"Blood-Soaked Secrets." Amnesty International, 2017. https://www.amnesty.org/en/latest/campaigns/2018/10/blood-soaked-secrets.

Bocco, Riccardo, Hamit Bozarslan, Peter Sluglett, and Jordi Tejel, editors. *Writing the Modern History of Iraq: Historiographical and Political Challenges*. Singapore: World Scientific, 2012.

Bozarsalan, Hamit, "Revisiting the Middle East's 1979." *Economy and Society*, vol 41, no. 4 (2012): 158–167.

Brand, Laurie. *Official Stories: Politics and National Narratives in Egypt and Algeria*. Stanford, CA: Stanford University Press, 2014.

Brown, Ian. *Khomeini's Forgotten Sons: The Story of Iran's Boy Soldiers*. London: Grey Seal Books, 1990.

Byrne, Malcolm. *Iran-Contra: Reagan's Scandal and the Unchecked Abuse of Presidential Power*. Lawrence, KA: University Press of Kansas, 2014.

Calmard, Jean. "Hejla." *Encyclopædia Iranica*, March 22, 2012. https://iranicaonline.org/articles/hejla.

Calarco, Matthew, Zoographies: *The Question of the Animal from Heidegger to Derrida*. New York: Columbia University Press, 2008.

Carly, Christian. *Strange Rebels: 1979 and the Birth of the 21st Century*. New York: Basic Books, 2013.

Caiani, Fabio, and Catherine Cobham. *The Iraqi Novel: Key Writers, Key Texts*. Edinburgh: Edinburgh University Press, 2013.

———. "Autumn Visions: War and the Imagery of Muḥammad Khuḍayyir," *Journal of Arabic Literature*, 49 (2018): 243–270.

Chandler, Jennifer. "No Man's Land: Representations of Masculinities in Iran-Iraq War Fiction." PhD Diss., University of Manchester, 2012.

"Chāp-e Tāzeh-ye Dā Montasher Shod," [A New Edition of *Da* has been Published] Iranian Student News Agency (ISNA). December 6, 2021. https://www.isna.ir/news/1400091511669.

Cheheltan, Amir Hasan, "Bāzkhāni-ye Dāstān-e 'Naqqāsh-e Bāghāni' asar-e Hushang-e Golshiri" [Rereading Hushang Golshiri's 'Painter of Baghan']. BBC Persian. June 5, 2010. http://www.bbc.com/persian/arts/2010/06/100603_l41_golshiri_memory_cheheltan.shtml.

———. *Chizi beh Fardā Namāndeh Ast* [Nothing Left For Tomorrow]. Tehran: Negāh, 1998.

Chelkowski, Peter and Hamid Dabashi. *Staging a Revolution: The Art of Persuasion in the Islamic Republic of Iran*. New York: New York University Press, 1999.

Chelkowski, Peter. "Taʿzia." *Encyclopædia Iranica*, July 15, 2009. http://www.iranicaonline.org/articles/tazia.

Coker, Christopher. *Men at War*. London: Hurst & Company, 2014.

Cole, Sarah. *At the Violet Hour: Modernism and Violence in England and Ireland*. New York: Oxford University Press, 2012.

Colla, Elliot. "The Military-Literary Complex." Jadaliyya, July 8, 2014. http://www.jadaliyya.com/pages/index/18384/the-military-literary-complex.

"Constitution of the Islamic Republic of Iran." The Constitute Project. Accessed July 17, 2024. https://constituteproject.org/countries/Asia/Iran_Islamic_Rep_of_?lang=en

cooke, miriam. *War's Other Voices: Women Writers on the Lebanese Civil War*. New York: Cambridge University Press, 1988.

———. *Women and the War Story*. Berkeley, CA: University of California Press, 1996.

Dah Shab: Shab-hā-ye Shāʿerān va Nevisandegān dar Anjoman-e Farhang-e Irān-Ālmān [The Ten Nights: Evenings of Poets and Writers at the German-Iranian Cultural Association.] Tehran: Amir Kabir, 1978.

Dabashi, Hamid. *Makhmalbaf at Large: The Making of a Rebel Filmmaker*. London: I.B. Tauris, 2008.

———. *Theology of Discontent: The Ideological Foundation of the Islamic Revolution in Iran*. London: Routledge, 2017.

———. "The Poetics of Politics: Commitment in Modern Persian Literature." *Iranian Studies* 18, no. 2 (Spring–Autumn, 1985): 147–188.

Daftar-e Motālaʿāt-e Adabiyāt-e Dāstāni. Gozideh-ye Dāstān-hā-ye Kutāh dar Zamineh-ye Jang-e Tahmili va Defāʿ-e Moqaddas az Matbuʿat-e Iran [A Selection of Short Stories from the Imposed War and Sacred Defense]. Tehran: Markaz-e Motālaʿāt va Tahqiqāt-e Farhangi, Vezārat-e Farhang va Ershād-e Eslāmi, 1996.

Daryaee, Touraj. *Sasanian Persia: The Rise and Fall of an Empire*. London: I.B. Tauris, 2014.

Daughtry, Martin. *Listening to War: Sound, Music, Trauma and Survival in Wartime Iraq*. New York: Oxford University Press, 2015.

Davis, Eric. *Memories of State: Politics, History, and Collective Identity in Modern Iraq*. Berkeley, CA: University of California Press, 2005.

Deer, Patrick. *Culture in Camouflage: War, Empire and Modern British Literature*. New York: Oxford University Press, 2009.

Dawes, James. *The Language of War: Literature and Culture in the U.S. from the Civil War through World War II*. Cambridge: Harvard University Press, 2002.

Dehqan, Ahmad. *Man Qātel-e Pesar-e-tān Hastam* [I Killed Your Son]. Tehran: Ofoq, 2004.

———. *Safar beh Garā-ye Devist va Haftād Darajeh*. Tehran: Sureh-ye Mehr, 2005.

———. *Journey to Heading 270 Degrees.* Translated by Paul Sprachman. Costa Mesa, CA: Mazda Publishers, 2006.

"Dīn wa Dawla fī Īrān" [Religion and State in Iran]. *Āfāq ʿArabīyya*, no. 5, (1980): 4–6.

al-Dulaymi, Lutfıyya. *Budhūr al-Nār* [Seeds of Fire]. Baghdad: Dār al-Shu'ūn al-Thaqāqfıyya al-ʿĀmma, 1987.

Eagleton, Terry. *Criticism and Ideology: a Study in Marxist Literary Theory.* London: NLB: Humanities Press, 1976.

———. *Ideology: an Introduction.* London and New York: Verso, 1991.

Elling, Rasmus Christian. *Minorities in Iran: Nationalism and Ethnicity after Khomeini.* New York: Palgrave Macmillan, 2013.

Eng, David and David Kazanjian, editors. *Loss: The Politics of Mourning.* Berkeley, CA: University of California Press, 2003.

"Enteqād-e Shakeri az Dāvari-ye Ketāb-e Sāl-e Moqaddas" [Shakeri's Critique of the Judgement of the Sacred Defense Book of the Year]. Ketāb News, November 8, 2007. http://www.ketabnews.com/fa/news/ مقدس-دفاع-کتابسال-داوری-از-شاکری-انتقاد/1805.

"Enteshār-e Romān-e Toqif Shodeh-ye ʿAqrab dar Farānseh" [The Publication of the Banned Novel, *The Scorpion* in France]. Rādio Zamāneh, January 17, 2011. www.radiozamaneh.com/30387.

Escanilla, Ingrid Bejarano. "Al-Mirbad: un Festival de Poesía en Iraq." *Sharq Al-Andalus: Estudios Mudejares y Moriscos* 6, (1989): 207–239.

Fahimi, Sayyed Mehdi. *Farhang-e Jebheh: Shuʿār-hā va Rajaz-hā* [The Culture of the Front: Slogans and Battle Cries]. Tehran: Muʿāvenāt-e Farhangi va Tablighāt-e Jang, Sitād-e Farmāndeh-ye Kul Qovā, 1991.

Fakhraeirad, Armaghan, Laudan Nooshin, and Anna Rezaie. "A Sonic Tale of Two Cities: Memory, Trauma, and Auditory Scars in Tehran and Abadan-Khorramshahr." *City, University of London Research Online.* Accessed: July 17, 2024. https://openaccess.city.ac.uk/id/eprint/30089/.

Farasat, Qasem-ʿAli. *Nakhl-hā-ye bi Sar* [Headless Palms]. Tehran: Amir Kabir, 1988.

Faridani, H. *The Imposed War.* Tehran: Ministry of Islamic Guidance, 1983.

Farzaneh, Sam. *Shirāzeh: Ketāb-khāneh-ye Qarn (50): Man Qātel-e Pesar-e-tān Hastam* [Shirzeh Podcast: The Library of the Century, Episode 50, *I Killed Your Son*]. May 30, 2024. https://www.bbc.com/persian/arts-69075151.

Faust, Aaron. *The Baʿthification of Iraq: Saddam Hussein's Totalitarianism.* Austin, TX: University of Texas Press, 2015.

Fischer, Michael. *Iran: From Religious Dispute to Revolution.* Cambridge, MA: Harvard University Press, 1980.

Foucault, Michel. *Power/Knowledge: Selected Interviews and Other Writings, 1972–1977*. Translated and edited by Colin Gordon. New York: Pantheon Books, 1980.

"*Gelāyeh-hā-ye Ahmad Dehqan az Pedarkhāndeh-hā-ye Adabiyāt va Farhang / Barkhi bā Faryād-e Zed-e Jang Dokān-e Dunabash bar Pā Kardeh-and*" [Ahmad Dehqan's Complaints about the Godfathers of literature and Culture / Saying he can't have it both ways, some accuse him of being "Anti-War"]. *Mehr News*, September 25, 2013. http://www.mehrnews.com/news/2295361/گلایه-های-احمد-دهقان-از-پدرخوانده-های-ادبیات-و-فرهنگ-برخی-ب

Ghaffarzadegan, Davud. *Fāl-e Khun* [Fortune Told in Blood]. Tehran: Entesharāt-e Qadyāni, 1996.

Ghanoonparvar, M. R. "War Veterans Turned Writers of War Narratives." In *Moments of Silence: Authenticity in the Cultural Expressions of the Iran-Iraq War, 1980–1988*, edited by Arta Khakpour, Shouleh Vatanabadi, and Mohammad Mehdi Khorrami. New York: New York University Press, 2016. 88–102.

———. "Drama," *Encyclopædia Iranica*, November 29, 2011. http://www.iranicaonline.org/articles/drama.

———. *Iranian Film and Persian Fiction*. Costa Mesa, CA: Mazda, 2016.

Ghardashkhani, Goulia. "Narrative Geometry in 'Ali Reza Gholami's *Divar* (The Wall): New Developments in Iranian War Literature." *Iranian Studies*, vol 53, nos. 5–6 (2020): 873–892.

———. "*Da* and Its Mothers of the Martyred: Meaning and Contest in an Iranian War Memoir." *British Journal of Middle Eastern Studies*, vol. 51, no. 2 (2024): 264–79.

Ghattas, Kim. *Black Wave: Saudi Arabia Iran and the Forty-Year Rivalry That Unraveled Culture Religion and Collective Memory in the Middle East*. New York: Henry Holt and Company, 2020.

Ghazoul, Ferial. "Iraq." In *Arab Women Writers: A Critical Reference Guide, 1873–1999*, edited by Radwa 'Ashur, Ferial Ghazoul, and Hasna Reda-Mekdashi. Cairo: American University in Cairo Press, 2008. 178–203

Gheissari, Ali. *Iranian Intellectuals in the Twentieth Century*. Austin: University of Texas Press: 1997.

Gholami, 'Alireza. *Divār: Romān* [The Wall: A Novel]. Tehran: Entesharāt-e Morvārid, 2015.

Gieling, Saskia. *Religion and War in Revolutionary Iran*. London and New York: I.B. Tauris, 1999.

Seyed-Gohrab, Asghar. *Martyrdom Mysticism and Dissent: The Poetry of the 1979 Iranian Revolution and the Iran-Iraq War (1980–1988)*. Berlin: De Gruyter, 2021.

Golestan, Layla. *Hekāyat-e Hāl: Goftegu bā Ahmad-e Mahmud* [The Tale of the State of Things]. Tehran: Ketāb-e Mahnāz, 1995.

Golshiri, Hushang. "Naqqāsh-e Bāghāni" [The Painter of Baghan]. In *Nimeh-ye Tārik-e Māh: Dāstān-hā-ye Kutāh* [The Dark Half of the Moon: Short Stories]. Tehran: Entesharāt-e Nilufar, 2002.

Gölz, Olmo, "Ten Revolutionary Nights in Tehran: On the Significance of the Poetry at the *Dah Shab* for the '1979 Moment' in Iran." TRAFO: Blog for Transregional Research, November 30, 2022. https://trafo.hypotheses.org/23713.

Gordon, Avery. *Ghostly Matters: Haunting and the Sociological Imagination*. Minneapolis: University of Minnesota Press, 1997.

Gordon, Joy. *Invisible War: The United States and the Iraq Sanctions*. Cambridge, MA: Harvard University Press, 2010.

Gramsci, Antonio. *Selections from the Prison Notebooks of Antonio Gramsci*, edited and translated by Quintin Hoare and Geoffrey Nowell Smith. London: Lawrence and Wishart, 1971.

Hafez, Sabry. *The Genesis of Arabic Narrative Discourse*. London: Saqi Books, 1993.

Halim, Hala. "Lotus, the Afro-Asian Nexus, and Global South Comparatism." *Comparative Studies of South Asia, Africa and the Middle East*, vol. 32, no. 3 (2012): 563–583.

———. "The Pre-postcolonial and Its Enduring Relevance: Afro-Asian Variations in Edwar al-Kharrat's Texts." In *Postcolonialism Cross-Examined: Multidirectional Perspectives on Imperial and Colonial Pasts and the Neocolonial Present*, edited by Monika Albrecht. New York: Routledge, 2019. 79–95.

Hanoosh, Yasmeen. "Contempt: State Literati vs. Street Literati in Modern Iraq." *Journal of Arabic Literature*, vol. 43, no. 2–3 (2012): 372–408.

"Ḥasan Blāsim...Tatwīj Adabī lil-Masīḥ al-ʿIrāqī" [Hassan Blasim: A Literary Coronation for *The Iraqi Christ*]. al-ʿArabī al-Jadīd, May 25, 2014. www.alaraby.co.uk/"حسن-بلاسم-تتويج-أدبي-لـ-المسيح-العراقي".

Hasan, Husayn Sarmak. *Ighmāḍ al-ʿAynayn al-Mumīt: Dirāsāt fī Adab Luʾay Ḥamza ʿAbbās al-Qiṣaṣī* [The Deadly Closing of the Eyes: Studies on the Literature of Luʾay Hamza ʿAbbas]. Stockholm: Dār al-Yanābīyaʿ, 2010.

Hassan, Waïl S. "Arabic and the Paradigms of Comparison." In *The 2014–2015 Report on the State of the Discipline of Comparative Literature*. Website of the American Comparative Literature Association. February 28, 2015. http://stateofthediscipline.acla.org/entry/arabic-and-paradigms-comparison-1#_edn3.

Hassan, Kadhim Jihad. "Iraqi Literature: an Exemplary Multi-millennia Continuity." *Banipal*, (Summer 2003): 45.

———. *Le Roman arabe, (1834–2004)*. Arles, France: Sindbad, 2006.

Herr, Michael. *Dispatches*. New York: Knopf, 1977.

"Al-Hilāl al-Aḥmar Yadʿū Dhawīhim l-Istilām Rafāt 629 Shahīdan fī al-Ḥarb al-ʿIrāqīyya al-Irāniyya" [The Red Crescent calls on families of 629 Martyrs of the Iraq-Iran War to receive their remains], The Iraqi Red Crescent Society. Accessed July 17, 2024. https://ircs.org.iq/62-الهلال-الأحمر-يدعو-ذويهم-لاستلام-رفات.

Hillawi, Janan Jasim. *Kul yā Ṭāwūsī Ḥatta Takbar* [Eat, my Peacock, so That You May Grow]. Uddevalla, Sweden: Dār al-Manfā, 1999.

———. *Layl al-Bilād* [Night of the Country]. Beirut: Dār al-Ādāb, 2002.

Hiro, Dilip. *The Longest War: The Iran-Iraq Military Conflict*. New York: Routledge, 1991.

Hujja, Rahma. "al-Marʾa fī Aghānī Intifāḍat Tishrīn: Thāʾira wa-Musifa wa Muhadida lil-ʿUrūsh al-Fisād," [Woman in the Songs of the Tishreen Revolution: A Revolutionary, Assistant, and Threat to the Thrones of Power]. al-Iḥtijāj March 11, 2020. https://alihtijaj.com/view.php?cat=1172.

Husayni, Sayyed Vahid. *Bazm-e Razm* [The Feast of the Fight]. Tehran: Muʾassaseh-ye Revāyat-e Fath, 2016.

Hussain, Tahir. *Kuwaiti Oil Fires: Regional Environmental Perspectives*. Oxford: Pergamon, 1995.

Hynes, Samuel. *A War Imagined: The First World War and English Culture*. New York: Random House, 2011. Kindle Edition.

Ibrahim, Muhammad Hasan. *"Bayn al-ʿArabiyya wa-l-ʿIbriyya: al-Jānib al-Lughawī min al-Ṣirāʿ al-ʿArabī al-Suhīyūnī fī al-Filisṭīn"* [Between Arabic and Hebrew: the Linguistic Side of the Arab-Zionist Conflict in Palestine]. *al-Aqlām* 16 (1981): 61–72.

Ibrahim, Youssef M. "After the War: Another War Begins as Kuwaiti Oil-Well Fires Threaten Region's Ecology; Beyond Mideast, Black Rain and Acid-Filled Clouds," *The New York Times,* March 16, 1991, section 1, page 4.

"Iḍāʾāt" [Illuminations]. al-ʿArabīyya, January 12, 2012. Accessed: July 17, 2024. http://www.youtube.com/watch?v=t_DG-LfoXGo.

"Iran–Iraq War." Wikipedia. Accessed July 18, 2024. https://en.wikipedia.org/w/index.php?title=Iran%E2%80%93Iraq_War&oldid=1191040919

Iranian Ministry of Guidance. *The Imam and the Ommat*. Tehran: Ministry of Islamic Guidance, 1980.

Iranian Writers' Association. *Nāmeh-ye Kānun-e Nevisandegān* [The Journal of the Iranian Writers' Association]. no. 4 (1980). Tehran: Entesharāt-e Āgāh.

Ismael, Tareq Y. *The Rise and Fall of the Communist Party of Iraq*. Cambridge: Cambridge University Press, 2008.

Jabar, Faleh. "Why the Uprising Failed." *Middle East Research and Information Project,* 176 (May/June 1992): https://merip.org/1992/05/why-the-uprisings-failed.

Jameson, Frederic. *A Singular Modernity: Essay on the Ontology of the Present.* New York: Verso, 2002.

Jazini, Mohammad Javad. "*Romān-e* Nakhl-hā-ye bī Sar *Sarāghāz-e Neveshtan Barāye Jang ast*" [The Novel *Headless Palms* is the Beginning of War Writing], Iranian Book News Agency, August 2, 2010. http://www.ibna.ir/news/77041/رمان-نخل-هاي-بي-سر-سرآغاز-نوشتن-براي-جنگ-است.

"Joz'iyāt-e Shahādat-e 175 Ghavās Khat-shekan / Mazlumiati keh dar Bāzi-ye Resāneh Bishtar Shod" [Details of the Martyrdoms of the 175 Frontline Divers / The Injustice that Grew in the Media's Game]. Mehr News, June 3, 2015. https://www.mehrnews.com/news/2769763/جزئیات-شهادت-۱۷۵-غواص-خط-شکن-مظلومیتي-که-در-بازی-رسانه-ای-بیشترشد.

Jubaili, Diaa. *Lā Ṭahāwīn fī al-Baṣra.* Baghdad: Dār Suṭūr lil-Nashr wa-l-Tawzīʿ, 2018.

———. *No Windmills in Basra.* Translated by Chip Rossetti. Dallas: Deep Vellum Publishing, 2022.

al-Kamali, Shafıq. "al-Thaqāfa wa-l-Maʿraka" [Culture and the Battle]. *Āfāq ʿArabiyya*, no. 6, (1980): 138–141.

Karimi, Pamela. "Imagining Warfare, Imagining Welfare: Tehran's Post Iran-Iraq War Murals and their Legacy." *Persica* 22, (2008): 47–63.

Karimi-Hakkak, Ahmad, "Introduction: Iran's Literature 1977–1997." *Iranian Studies*, vol 30, no. 3 (Summer – Autumn, 1997): 193–213.

———. "Protest and Perish: A History of the Writers' Association of Iran." In *A Fire of Lilies*: Perspectives on Literature and Politics in Modern Iran. Leiden: Leiden University Press, 2020. 53–84.

———. "Censorship," *Encyclopaedia Iranica*, December 15, 1990. http://www.iranicaonline.org/articles/censorship-sansur-in-persia.

al-Khafaji, Isam. "War as a Vehicle for the Rise and Demise of a State-Controlled Society: The Case of Baʿthist Iraq." In *War, Institutions, and Social Change in the Middle East*, edited by Steven Heydemann. Berkeley, CA: University of California Press: 2000.

Khakpour, Arta. "Each into a World of His Own: Mimesis, Modernist Fiction, and the Iranian Avant-Garde." PhD diss., New York University, 2014.

Khasbak, ʿAʾid. "Ākhir al-Rijāl" [The Last Men]. In *Qādisiyyat Ṣaddām*: *Qiṣaṣ Taḥt Lahīb al-Nār*, vol. 9. Baghdad: Wizarāt al-Thaqāfa wa-l-ʿIlām. 167–178.

Khayyoun, ʿAli. "Mourning Does not Become the Martyrs." In *Battle Front Stories from Iraq*. Translated by A.W. Luʾluʾa. Baghdad: Dar al-Maʾmūn for Translation and Publishing, 1982. 167–177.

Khidr, ʿAbbas. *al-Khākiyya: min Awrāq al-Jarīma al-Thaqāfiyya fī al-ʿIrāq* [Khaki: From the Documents of Cultural Crime in Iraq]. Cologne: Manshūrat al-Jamal, 2005.

Khorrami, Mohammad Mehdi. *Literary Subterfuge and Contemporary Persian Fiction: Who Writes Iran?* New York and London: Routledge, 2014.

———. *Modern Reflections of Classical Traditions in Persian Fiction*. Lewiston, NY: Edwin Mellen Press, 2003.

———. Editor and translator. *Sohrab's Wars: Counter Discourses of Contemporary Persian Fiction*. Costa Mesa, CA: Mazda Publishers, 2008.

———. and Amir Moosavi, editors. *Losing Our Minds, Coming to Our Senses: Sensory Readings of Persian Literature and Culture*. Leiden: Leiden University Press, 2021.

Khosrokhavar, Farhad. *Suicide Bombers Allah's New Martyrs*. Translated by David Macey London: Pluto Press, 2005.

Khosronejad, Pedram, editor. *Iranian Sacred Defense Cinema: Religion, Martyrdom and National Identity*. Herefordshire, U.K.: Sean Kingston Publishing, 2012.

Khoury, Dina Rizk. *Iraq in Wartime: Soldiering, Martyrdom, and Remembrance*. Cambridge: Cambridge University Press, 2013.

Khudayyir, Muhammad. *Baṣrāyāthā: Ṣūrat al-Madīna*. Baghdad: al-Amad, 1993.

———. *Basrayatha: Story of a City*. Translated by William Hutchins. New York: Verso, 2008.

———. *Al-Mamlaka al-Sawdāʾ* [The Black Kingdom]. Cologne: Manshūrāt al-Jamal, 2005.

———. "Wasiyyat al-Jundī." [The Soldier's Testament]. *Asfār*, no. 2. (1985): 24–25.

Kiarostami, Abbas. *Mashq-e Shab* [Homework]. DVD. 1978.

Klemm, Verena, "Different Notions of Commitment (*iltizām*) and Committed Literature (*al-adab al-multazim*) in the Literary Circles of The Mashriq." *Arabic and Middle Eastern Literatures* 3.1 (2000): 51–62.

Kubba, Sami A.A., and Mudhafar Salim. "The Wetlands Wildlife and Ecosystem" in *The Iraqi Marshlands and the Marsh Arabs: The Maʿdan, Their Culture, and the Environment*, edited by Sami Kubba. Reading, U.K.: Ithaca Press, 2010.

Kubaysi, Tarrad. *Qaṣīdat al-Ḥarb al-Ḥaditha fī al-ʿIrāq* [The Modern War Poem in Iraq]. Baghdad: Dār al-Shʾūn al-Thaqāfiyya, 1986.

Kurzman, Charles. "Death Tolls of the Iran-Iraq War." Personal Website of the author. Accessed July 17, 2024. http://kurzman.unc.edu/death-tolls-of-the-iran-iraq-war/.

Lesch, David., *1979: The Year that Shaped the Modern Middle East*. Cambridge, MA: Westview Press, 2001.

Lionnet, Françoise. "Postcolonial studies, Creolizations, and Migrations." In *Postcolonialism Cross-Examined: Multidirectional Perspectives on Imperial and Colonial*

Pasts and the Neocolonial Present, edited by Monika Albrecht. London: Routledge, Taylor and Francis Group, 2020. 65–78.

Litvak, Meir. "Karbala." *Encyclopædia Iranica,* April 24, 2012. https://iranicaonline.org/articles/karbala.

Lu'lu'a, Abd al-Wahid. "Preface." In *Battle Front Stories from Iraq.* Baghdad: Dār al-Ma'mūn for Translation and Publishing, 1982.

Lockman, Zachary. *Contending Visions of the Middle East: The History and Politics of Orientalism.* Cambridge: Cambridge University Press, 2009.

Ma'rufi, 'Abbas. *Fereydun Seh Pesar Dāsht* [Fereydun Had Three Sons]. Berlin: Gardun, 2008.

Maghsoudlou, Bahman. *Ahmad Mahmoud: A Noble Novelist,* Venice, CA: Pathfinder Pictures, 2009.

Mahmud, Ahmad. *Zamin-e Sukhteh* [Scorched Earth]. Tehran: Nashr-e Now, 1982.

Makhmalbaf, Mohsen. *Bāgh-e Bolur* [The Crystal Garden]. Tehran: Nashr-e Nay, 1997.

———. "Qesseh-ye Maktabi" [The *Maktabi* Story]. *Jong-e Sureh,* no. 2 (Nov-Dec, 1981): 63–67.

Makiya, Kanan. *Cruelty and Silence: War, Tyranny, Uprising, and the Arab World.* New York: W.W. Norton, 1993.

———. *The Monument: Art, Vulgarity, and Responsibility in Iraq.* Berkeley, CA: University of California Press, 1991.

———. *Republic of Fear: The Politics of Modern Iraq.* Berkeley, CA: University of California Press, 1998.

Mamduh, 'Aliya. *al-Maḥbūbāt* [The Loved Ones]. Beirut: Dār al-Sāqi, 2003.

Mandanipur, Shahriyar. "Rang-e Ātash-e Nimruzi." In *Māh-e Nimruz* [Midday Moon]. Tehran: Nashr-e Markiz, 1997.

———. Translated by Mohammad Mehdi Khorrami. "The Color of Fire at Midday." In *Sohrab's Wars.* Costa Mesa, CA: Mazda, 2008. 68–82.

———.Translated by Sara Khalili. "The Color of Midday Fire." In *Seasons of Purgatory.* New York: Bellevue Literary Press, 2022.

Marashi, Nasim. *Haras* [Pruning]. Tehran: Cheshmeh, 2017.

Masmoudi, Ikram. *War and Occupation in Iraqi Fiction.* Edinburgh: Edinburgh University Press, 2015.

———. "Literary Haunting and The Iran-Iraq War," *Michigan Quarterly Review.* Published online accompanying MQR Issue 61:2, Spring 2022. https://sites.lsa.umich.edu/mqr/2022/04/literary-haunting-and-the-iran-iraq-war/

———. "Portraits of Iraqi Women: between testimony and fiction." *International Journal of Contemporary Iraqi Studies* vol. 4, nos. 1 & 2 (2010): 59–77.

Mason, Herbert. "Impressions of an Arabic Poetry Festival." *Religion & Literature*, 20 (Spring 1988): 157–161.

al-Masri, Khaled. "The Politics and Poetics of Madness in Ḥasan Blāsim's *The Madman of Freedom Square*." *Journal of Arabic Literature* vol. 49, no. 3 (2018): 271–295.

"Mawʿid fī al-Mahjar" [An Appointment in Exile]. *al-Jazeera*. Accessed July 17, 2024. http://www.aljazeera.net/programs/a-date-in-exile/2009/7/13/محسن-الرملي.

Mazlum, Muhammad. *Ḥaṭab Ibrāhīm aw al-Jīl al-Badawī: Shiʿr al-Thamānīnāt wa-Ajyāl al-Dawla al-ʿIrāqiyya* [Ibrahim's Forest or the Bedouin Generation: The Poetry of the 1980s and Generations of the Iraqi State]. Damascus: al-Takwīn lil-Taʾlīf wa-l-Tarjama wa-l-Nashr, 2007.

McLoughlin, Kate. *The Cambridge Companion to War Writing*. Cambridge: Cambridge University Press, 2009.

McHale, Brian. *Postmodernist Fiction*. London and New York: Routledge, 1987.

Meyer, Stefan. *The Experimental Arabic Novel: Postcolonial Literary Modernism in the Levant*. Albany, NY: State University of New York Press, 2001.

Milani, Farzaneh. *Words Not Swords: Iranian Women Writers and the Freedom of Movement*. Syracuse, NY: Syracuse University Press, 2011.

Milich, Stephan. "The Positioning from Baathist Intellectuals and Writers Before and After 2003: The Case of the Iraqi Poet Abd al-Razzaq Abd al-Wahid." *Middle East Journal of Culture and Communication*, no. 4 (2011): 298–319.

Milich, Stephan, Friederike Pannewick, and Leslie Tramotini, editors. *Conflicting Narratives: War, Trauma and Memory in Iraqi Culture*. Wiesbaden, Germany: Reichert Verlag, 2012.

Mir-ʿAbedini, Hasan. *Sad Sāl Dāstān Nevisi-ye Irān* [100 Years of Persian Fiction]. Tehran: Nashr-e Cheshmeh, 2004.

Mohsen, Fatima. "Cultural Authoritarianism." In *Iraq Since the Gulf War: Prospects for Democracy*, edited by Fran Hazelton. Atlantic Highlands, NJ: Zed Books. 1994.

———. "Debating Iraqi Culture: Intellectuals between the Inside and Outside." In *Conflicting Narratives: War, Trauma and Memory in Iraqi Culture*, edited by Stephan Milich, Friederike Pannewick, and Leslie Tramotini. Weisbaden: Reichert Verlag, 2012.

Moosavi, Amir. "Dark Corners and the Limits of Ahmad Dehqan's War Front Fiction." *Middle East Critique*, vol. 27, no. 1 (February 2017): 45–59.

———. "Desacralizing a Sacred Defense: The Iran-Iraq War in the fiction of Hossein Mortezaeian Abkenar." *Iran Namag* (Fall 2020): 158–175.

———. "Dust That Never Settled: Ideology Ambivalence and Disenchantment in Arabic and Persian Fiction of the Iran-Iraq War (1980–2003)." PhD Diss., New York University, 2016.

———. "Mourning Mothers and Wars That Never End: Reading Nasim Marashi's *Haras* (Pruning) in the Shadow of the Iran-Iraq War." *British Journal of Middle Eastern Studies* 51, no. 2 (2024): 249–63.

———. "How to Write Death: Resignifying Martyrdom in Two Novels of the Iran-Iraq War." *Alif: Journal of Comparative Poetics*, no. 35 (2015): 9–31.

———. "Sonic Triggers and Fiery Pools: The Senses at War in Hossein Mortezaeian Abkenar's *Scorpion*." In *Losing Our Minds, Coming to Our Senses*, edited by Mehdi Khorrami and Amir Moosavi, 171–194. Leiden: Leiden University Press, 2021.

Mufti, Aamir. Forget *English! Orientalisms and World Literatures*. Cambridge, MA: Harvard University Press, 2018.

al-Musawi, Muhsin. *Reading Iraq: Culture and Power in Conflict*. London: I.B. Tauris. 2006.

Mustafa, Shakir. "Genre Negotiations: Review of Muhammad Khudayyir, *Basriyatha: Sûrat Madina*. Baghdad: Manshûrat al-Amad, 1993." *Edebiyat: Journal of Middle Eastern Literatures*, vol. 13, no. 1 (2002): 105–109.

Naficy, Hamid. *A Social History of Iranian Cinema, Volume 3, The Islamicate Period, 1978–1984*. Durham, NC: Duke University Press, 2012.

———. *A Social History of Iranian Cinema, Volume 4, The Globalizing Era, 1984–2010*. Durham, NC: Duke University Press, 2012.

Nafisi, Azar. *Reading Lolita in Tehran*. New York: Random House, 2003.

al-Nahar, Muthana. "Maḥaṭāt fī Ḥayāt al-Adīb al-ʿIrāqī Muḥsin al-Ramlī...al-Ḥayāt wa-l-Barzakh wa-l-Jinna," [Stages in the Life of the Writer Muhsin al-Ramli: Life, Purgatory, and Heaven]. *Al-Jazeera*, December 16, 2022. https://www.aljazeera.net/culture/2022/12/16/محطات-في-حياة-الاديب-العراقي-محسن.

Nanquette, Laetitia. "An Iranian Woman's Memoir on the Iran-Iraq War: The Production and Reception of *Da*." *Iranian Studies* 46.6 (2013): 943–957.

———. *Iranian Literature after the Islamic Revolution: Production and Circulation in Iran and the World*. Edinburgh: Edinburgh University Press, 2021.

Nasir, ʿAbd al-Sattar. *al-Shahīd 1777* [Martyr 1,777]. Baghdad: Dār al-Ḥurriyya lil-Ṭabāʿa, 1981.

Nguyen, Viet Thanh. *Nothing Ever Dies: Vietnam and the Memory of War*. Cambridge, MA: Harvard University Press, 2016.

Nixon, Rob. *Slow Violence and the Environmentalism of the Poor*. Cambridge, MA: Harvard University Press, 2011.

O'Brien, Tim. *The Things They Carried*. New York: Penguin Books, 1991.

"Operation Karbala-4 Was Not a Military Deception: General Soleimani." *Tehran Times*, December 31, 2018. https://www.tehrantimes.com/news/431354/Operation-Karbala-4-was-not-a-military-deception-General-Soleimani

Paul, Drew. "Transmission and Transit in Contemporary Arabic Literature: *Naql* and Its Limits." *Journal of Arabic Literature* 53, 1–2 (2022): 100–131.

Partovi, Pedram. "Martyrdom and the 'Good Life' in the Iranian Cinema of Sacred Defense." *Comparative Studies of South Asia, Africa and the Middle East,* vol 22, no. 3 (2008): 513–532.

Perez de Cuellar, Javier. *A Pilgrimage for Peace: A Secretary General's Memoir.* New York: St. Martin's Press, 1997.

Plesu, Andrei. "Intellectual Life under Dictatorship." *Representations,* no. 49 (Winter 1995): 61–71.

Potter, Lawrence G. and Gary G. Sick, editors. *Iran, Iraq and the Legacies of War.* New York: Palgrave Macmillan, 2004.

Qualey, Marcia Lynx. "'Majnūn Sāḥat al-Ḥurriyya:' Mamnūʿ Lākin Mutāh" [The Madman of Freedom Square: Banned but Available]. Hiber. February 6, 2014. https://www.7iber.com/2014/02/blasimban

Rafaʿi, Sima. "Dāstān-e Jang 25 Sāleh Mīshavad: Negāhi beh Adabiyāt-e Dāstāni-ye Jang" [The War Story Turns 25: A Look at War Fiction]. BBC Persian, September 22, 2005. http://www.bbc.co.uk/persian/arts/story/2005/09/050913_pm-war-literature.shtml

Rahgozar, Reza. *Nim Negāhi beh Hasht Sāl-e Qeṣṣeh-ye Jang* [A Glance at Eight Years of War Stories]. Tehran: Howzeh-e Honari, 1991.

al-Ramli, Muhsin. *al-Fatīt al-Mubʿathir.* Cairo: Dār al-Markaz al-Ḥaḍāra al-ʿArabiyya, 2000.

———. *Scattered Crumbs.* Translated by Yasmeen Hanoosh. Fayetteville, AR: University of Arkansas Press, 2003.

Rastegar, Kamran. *Literary modernity between the Middle East and Europe: Textual Transactions in Nineteenth-century Arabic, English, and Persian literatures.* London: Routledge, 2007.

———. *Surviving Images: Cinema, War and Cultural Memory in the Middle East.* New York: Oxford University Press, 2015.

Rentzou, Efthymia. "Animal." In *A New Vocabulary for Global Modernism*, edited by Eric Hayot and Rebecca Walkowitz. New York: Columbia University Press, 2016.

Rohde, Achim. *State-Society Relations in Baʿthist Iraq: Facing Dictatorship.* New York: Routledge, 2010.

Rossetti, Chip. "A Shared Imaginary City: The Role of the Reader in the Fiction of Muḥammad Khuḍayyir." PhD Diss., University of Pennsylvania, 2017.

Rawlinson, Mark. "War and Civilians." In *War and Literary Studies*, edited by Anders Engberg-Pedersen and Neil Ramsey, 201–15. Cambridge: Cambridge University Press, 2023.

Saʿad al-Din, Kazim. "Min Shiʿr al-Ḥarb wa-l-Muqāwama fī al-ʿĀlam" [On War and Resistance Poetry in the World]. *al-Aqlām* 16 (1981): 86–101.

Saadawi, Ahmad. *Frankstayn fi Baghdad*. Beirut and Baghdad: Manshūrāt al-Jamal, 2013.

———. *Frankenstein in Baghdad*. Translated by Jonathan Wright. New York: Penguin Books, 2018.

Saeed, Hend. "Recommendations: On the New Wave of Memoirs from Iraq." Arablit, May 24, 2024. https://arablit.org/2024/05/14/recommendations-on-the-new-wave-of-memoirs-from-iraq/.

Saʿidi, Mehdi. *Adabiyāt-e Dāstāni-ye Jang dar Irān*.[War Fiction in Iran]. Tehran: Pazhoheshgāh-e ʿOlum-e Ensāni va Motāleʿāt-e Ejtemāʿi-ye Jahād Dāneshgāhi, 2016.

Saghir, Kholod. "Interview with the Iraqi author Hassan Blasim." Pen Sweden, June 10, 2021. http://www.penopp.org/articles/interview-iraqi-author-hassan-blasim?language_content_entity=en.

al-Salim, Warid Badr, Hamza Mustafa, and Muhammad Hayyawi, editors. *Dhākirat al-Ghad: Shahādāt wa-Ruʾā wa-Tajārib* [Memory for Tomorrow: Testimonials, Visions and Experiences]. Baghdad: Wizārat al-Thaqāfa wa-al-Iʿlām, Dār al-Shuʾūn al-Thaqāfiyya al-ʿĀmma "Āfāq ʿArabiyya," 1989.

Saleh, Zainab. *Return to Ruin: Iraqi Narratives of Exile and Nostalgia*. Stanford, CA: Stanford University Press, 2020.

Santora, Marc. "Aftereffects: Basra; Near the Border with Iran, Memories of War Blend with Hope for Better Relations." *New York Times*, May 5, 2003. http://www.nytimes.com/2003/05/05/world/aftereffects-basra-near-border-with-iran-memories-war-blend-with-hope-for-better.html

Saghafi, Morad. "Crossing the Desert: Iranian Intellectuals after the Revolution," *Critique*, no. 18 (Spring 2001): 15–45.

Sassoon, Joseph. *Saddam Hussein's Baʿth Party: Inside an Authoritarian Regime*. Cambridge and New York: Cambridge University Press, 2012.

Said, Edward. *Orientalism*. New York: Vintage Books, 1978.

Saeed, Haider. "How Small the State, How Grand the Idea." In *Shahadat: Witnessing Iraq's Transformation After 2003*, edited by Angela Wollenberg. Berlin: Friedrich Ebert Foundation, 2007. 92–97.

al-Samarraʾi, ʿAbd al-Jabbar Mahmud. "Ḥawl Mafhūm al-Istishhād" [On the Concept of Martyrdom]. In *Qādisiyyat Ṣaddam wa-l-Khiyār al-Qawmī* [Saddam's Qadisiyya and the National Choice]. Baghdad: Dār al-Shuʾūn al-Thaqāfiyya al-ʿĀmma, 1986.

Samarraʾi, Salim. "al-Muqaddama." [Introduction] In *Qādisiyyat Saddam: Qiṣaṣ Taḥt Lahīb al-Nār* [Saddam's Qadisiyya: Stories from the Blaze], vol. 1, edited by Salim Samarraʾi. Baghdad: Manshūrāt Wizārat al-Thaqāfa wa-l-ʿIlām, 1981.

Sarkuhi, Faraj. "'Arseh-ye Ketāb: az *Zamin-e Sukhteh* ta Khāterāt-e Clisheh-ye *Dā*" [A Book Review: From *Scorched Earth* to the Clichéd memoir *Da*], *Radio Farda*, September 22, 2010. http://www.radiofarda.com/content/f35_Literature_and_War_II/2155297.htm.

Sarshar, Reza (see also: Reza Rahgozar). *Khodā-hāfez, Barādar* [Goodbye, Brother]. Tehran: Nashr-e Barg, 1989.

———. Telegram site of Mohammad-Reza Sarshar. Accessed July 18, 2024. https://t.me/s/Mrsarshar?before=1658

Satrapi, Marjane. *Persepolis*. New York: Pantheon, 2003.

Schwartz, Kevin L. "Citizen Martyrs": The Afghan Fatemiyoun Brigade in Iran." *Afghanistan*, vol. 5, no. 1 (2022): 93–121.

Schwartz, Kevin L. and Olmo Gölz. "Going to War with the Coronavirus and Maintaining the State of Resistance in Iran." *Middle East Research and Information Project*. September 1, 2020. https://merip.org/2020/09/going-to-war-with-the-coronavirus-and-maintaining-the-state-of-resistance-in-iran.

———. "Visual Propaganda at a Crossroads: New Techniques at Iran's Vali Asr Billboard," *Visual Studies* 36, 4–5 (2021): 476–490.

Seif, Asad. "Ketāb-e *Dā*: Yek Vāqeʿiat va Sad-hā Dorugh" [The Book *Dā:* One Truth and Hundreds of Lies]. DW News Persian Service, September 24, 2023. https://www.dw.com/fa-ir/کتاب-دا-یک-واقعیت-و-صدها-دروغ/a-66909863

Sellman, Joanna. *Arabic Exile Literature in Europe: Defamiliarizing Forced Migration*. Edinburgh: Edinburgh University Press, 2022.

Sepanlu, Mohammad. *Sargozasht-e Kānun-e Nevisandagān-e Irān* [The Story of The Iranian Writer's Association]. Spanga, Sweden: Bārān, 2002.

Shahnahpur, Saeedeh. *Writing War in Contemporary Iran: The Case of Esmāʿil Fasih's Zemestān-e 62*. New York: Peter Lang, 2019.

Shahidi, Hossein. *Journalism in Iran: From Mission to Profession*. New York: Routledge, 2007.

"Shakeri: Majmuʿeh-ye 'Man Qātel-e Pesar-e-tān Hastam" *Māteriyālisti ast*." [Shakeri: 'The short story collection, *I Killed Your Son*, is Materialistic], *Fars News Agency* September 24, 2006. Accessed May 13, 2015. http://farsnews.com/newstext.php?nn=8507020264.

Shams, Fatemeh. *A Revolution in Rhyme: Poetic Co-Option Under the Islamic Republic.* Oxford: Oxford University Press, 2021.

———. "Literature, art, and ideology under the Islamic Republic: An extended history of the Center for Islamic Art and Thought." In *Persian Language, Literature and Culture: New Leaves, Fresh Looks*, ed. Kamran Talattof. New York: Routledge, 2015.

"Shaping Saddam: How the Media Mythologized A Monster," *The Yale Review of International Studies*, June 2018. http://yris.yira.org/acheson-prize/2473.

Shirazi, Mohammad 'Ali Sadr. *'Amaliyāt-e Mersād va sarnevesht-e munāfiqin* [Operation Mersad and the Fate of the Hypocrites]. Tehran: Markaz-e Asnād-e Enqelāb-e Eslāmi, 2013.

Siamdoust, Nahid. *Soundtrack of the Revolution: The Politics of Music in Iran.* Stanford, CA: Stanford University Press, 2017.

Siavoshi, Sussan. "Cultural Policies and The Islamic Republic: Cinema and Book Publication." *International Journal of Middle East Studies* 29, (1997): 509–530.

Sluglett, Marion Farouk and Peter Sluglett. *Iraq Since 1958: From Revolution to Dictatorship.* London: I.B. Tauris, 2001.

Stanton, Anna Ziajka. *The Worlding of Arabic Literature: Language, Affect, and the Ethics of Translatability.* New York: Fordham University Press, 2023.

Spivak, Gayatri Chakravorty. *Death of a Discipline.* New York, 2003.

Tahmasebi, Azim. "Romān-e Mo'āser-e 'Arabi: Sa'ud-e al-San'usi va Sāqeh-ye Bāmbu." [The Modern Arabic Novel; Sa'ud al-San'usi and *The Bamboo Stalk*], *'Etemad*, July 28, 2015. http://www.etemadnewspaper.ir/1394/05/06/Main/PDF/13940506-3302-9-69.pdf.

Talattof, Kamran. *The Politics of Writing in Iran: a History of Modern Persian Literature.* Syracuse, NY: Syracuse University Press, 2000.

Talebi, Shahla. "An Iranian Martyr's Dilemma: The Finite Subject's Infinite Responsibility." *Comparative Studies of South Asia, Africa, and the Middle East* 33, (2) (2013): 177–96.

———. *Ghosts of Revolution: Rekindled Memories of Imprisonment in Iran.* Stanford, CA: Stanford University Press, 2011.

Terdiman, Richard. *Discourse / Counter-Discourse: The Theory and Practice of Symbolic Resistance in Nineteenth-Century France.* Ithaca, NY: Cornell University Press, 1985.

Thornber, Karen. "Comparative Literature, World Literature, Asia." In *The 2014–2015 Report on the State of the Discipline of Comparative Literature.* Website of the American Comparative Literature Association. March 3, 2014. http://stateofthediscipline.acla.org/entry/comparative-literature-world-literature-and-asia#sthash.JJFkOJmo.dpuf.

Thompson, Levi. *Reorienting Modernism in Arabic and Persian Poetry.* Cambridge: Cambridge University Press, 2022.

Toumaj, Amir, Candace Rondeaux, and Arif Ammar. "Soleimani's Shadow: The Fatemiyoun Division & Iran's Proxy Warfare Propaganda." New America, July 2021. https://www.newamerica.org/international-security/reports/soleimanis-shadow.

Trabulsi, Fawwaz. "On Being Silent: A Response to Kanan Makiya." *Middle East Report*, no. 187/188. (March-June 1994): 61–63.

"Vākonesh-hā beh Namāyesh-e Jasad-e Masnuʻi-ye Qorbāni-ye Jang dar Sedā va Simā" [Reactions to the Display of an Artificial Body of a War Victim on Islamic Republic of Iran Broadcasting]. Iran Wire, May 29, 2023. https://iranwire.com/fa/news-1/118991-واکنشها-به-نمایش-جسد-مصنوعی-قربانی-جنگ-در-صدا-و-سیما

Vanzan, Anna. "The Holy Defense Museum in Tehran, or How to Aestheticize War." *Middle East Journal of Culture and Communication* 13, 1 (2020): 63–77.

Varzi, Roxanne. *Warring Souls: Youth, Media and Martyrdom in Post-Revolutionary Iran.* Durham, NC: Duke University Press: 2006.

Webster, Annie. "Writing Urban Warfare: Pedestrian Perspectives in Post-2003 Baghdad." In *The Routledge Companion to Literary Urban Studies,* edited by Lieven Ameel. London: Routledge, 2023.

Weeden, Lisa. *Ambiguities of Domination: Politics, Rhetoric and Symbols in Contemporary Syria.* Chicago and London: University of Chicago Press, 1999.

Winter, Jay. *Sites of Memory, Sites of Mourning.* Cambridge: Cambridge University Press, 1995.

"'Yā Qāʻ Turābik Kāfūr, …' al-Ughniyya al-ʻIrāqiyya Wājihat Īran fī ʻAṣrayn" [Oh Land, Your Earth is my Camphor'…The Iraqi Song Confronting Iran During Two Periods], al-Ḥurra, November 6, 2019. https://www.alhurra.com/iraq/2019/11/06/يا-قاع-ترابك-كافور-أغنية-عراقية-واجهت-إيران-في-عصرين"

Yassin-Kassab, Robin. "*Beirut 39*: New Writing from the Arab World, edited by Samuel Shimo." *The Guardian*, June 11, 2010. https://www.theguardian.com/books/2010/jun/12/beirut-new-writing-arab-world.

Yousefi, Hamed. *Sanʻat-e Farhang-e Jang* [Manufacturing the Culture of War]. *BBC Persian*, 2013.

Žižek, Slavoj. *The Parallax View.* Cambridge, MA: The MIT Press, 2006.

———. *Violence.* New York: Picador, 2008.

Index

1968 Coup, 17, 18
2003 invasion of Iraq, 8, 20; madness and, 162

Abadan, Iran, 5, 6, 39, 168
'Abbas, Lu'ay Hamza, 22, 63–64, 79–80, 90–91
'Abbud, Salam, 31, 48, 49; Khalaf and, 55
'Abdollahi, Asghar, 43
Abkenar, Hossein Mortezaeian, 1–2, 21–22, 93; depictions of soldiers and, 107; *Scorpion*, 113–15, 119–20; *Shahnameh* and, 215n71
Abrahamian, Ervand, 150, 203n53, 209n60
absence, 90–91
abstraction, 71
al-Ādāb (journal), 16
Adabiyāt-e Dāstāni (journal), 30
Āfāq 'Arabiyya (journal), 12, 44–46, 53
afterlives, 26–29, 29, 154–57, 166, 173–77; "An Army Newspaper" and, 160–64; *Frankenstein in Baghdad* and 158–60; ghosts and, 157–58, 160, 164, 168, 176–77, 180; haunting and, 156–57; Jubaili and, 164–68; panoramic optics and, 179; post-1979 literature and, 190–92; *Pruning* and, 168–72, 178–79
Agamben, Giorgio, 71
Ahangaran, Sadeq, 33, 185
Ahmadzadeh, Habib, 119, 218n61; *Chess with the Doomsday Machine*, 120
Ahvaz, Iran, 42–43, 168, 171, 178, 199n13
al-Akhras, Muhammad Ghazi, 37
Alavi, Bozorg, 18
al-'Alim, Mahmud Amin, 16
Allah, 'Ali 'Abd, 187
American Granddaughter, The (al-Ḥafīda al-Amrīkiyya) (Kachachi), 156
Aminpour, Qaysar, 41
Anfal Campaign, 85, 103
animal motifs, Judaili's frogs, 166-167; Khudayyir and 68–69, 71;

INDEX

animal motifs, Judaili's frogs (*cont.*) Mandanipour's leopard, 76–79; Marashi's water buffaloes, 174, 176; modernist use of, 78

Anis, 'Abd al-'Azim, 16

Antoon, Sinan, 1–2, 48, 125, 220n17, 228n12; caricaturing official war discourse and, 129; *Corpse Washer*, 1–2, 156, 188–89; direct criticism and, 152; Hussein's fall and, 153; *I'jaam*, 138–43, 220n33, 221n35; subversive affirmation and, 148

apocryphal history, 119, 121; war front and, 93

al-Aqlām (journal), 46

Arab League, 5

Arabic literature, 3–4, 182

Arabs, 5, 12–13, 39; Ba'thist Revolution and, 54; contemporary wars and, 68; liberation of, 46; loyalty to Iran of, 9; nationalism and, 51–55; Saddam's Qadisiyya and, 45

"Army Newspaper, An" (Blasim), 160–64, 179–80

Arns, Inke, 111, 148

art, 143, 151–52; impossibility of creating, 140; *Sky So Close* and, 129–31; social function of, 135–37; *See also* "Painter of Baghan, The" (Golshiri).

Ashura, 11

al-Assad, Bashar, 185

Autumn Visions (*Ru'yā Kharīf*) (Khudayyir), 61, 64-65

Avini, Morteza, 33

Azarm, M., 39

Babylonian history, 52

Badr, 'Ali, 107

Baghdad-Basra train, 80–81

Baghdad Clock, The (*Sā'at Baghdad*) (al-Rawi), 156

Bahman, Kaveh, 30

Bahoora, Haytham, 156, 157, 222n6

Bani-Ameri, Hasan, 119

Basra, Iraq, 6; Baghdad-Basra train and, 80–81; decimation of, 102–3

Basrayatha: Portrait of a City (*Baṣrāyāthā: Ṣūrat Madīna*) (Khudayyir), 61, 64–65, 70–71; "War Diary," 65–70; Baghdad-Basra train in, 81

Baudrillard, Jean, 132

Baygi, Ebrahim Hasan, 56

Ba'th Party, 182–83; afterlives and, 161–62; criticism from exile of, 106–7; dissent against, 110; exile and, 121–23, 153; fall of, 155; Hillawi and, 102–4; *I'jaam* and, 139–43; al-Kamali purged by, 208n47; Kurdish resistance to, 216n18; literature of Saddam's Qadisiyya and, 24; martyrdom and, 50, 51, 54; nationalist caricature and, 111; Operation *Beyt ol-Moqaddas*, 59; palm tree symbol and, 189; *Scattered Crumbs* and, 112; Sh'ia expulsion by, 198n11; *Sky So Close* and, 133, 138, 152; tolerance of literary critical stances by, 48; undead and, 164

Ba'thification, 13–14, 15, 17; Baghdad-Basra train and, 81; means of, 201n33; *Sky So Close* and, 127

al-Bitar, Astrid Ottosson, 105

Black Kingdom, The (*al-Mamlaka al-Sawdā'*) (Khudayyir), 65

Blasim, Hassan, 154, 157; inability to publish and, 227n1; uncanniness and, 166

Blind Owl, The (Buf-e Kur) (Hedayat), 23
bloody palm image, 88, 90
bombing campaigns, 124–25; Iraqi bombardment of Tehran and, 134, 136–37; US and, 129, 132, 166
Butler, Judith, 177

Caiani, Fabio, 71
censorship, 31–32, 36–37, 37, 41; abstraction and, 71; cultural resistance and, 131; direct criticism and, 152; indirection and, 130; Islamic Republic and, 183; morality police and, 190; post-Saddam era and, 182; Sacred Defense literature and, 56; war fatigue and, 49
Cheheltan, Amir Hasan, 22, 63–64, 91; Golshiri and, 134; "Munes, Mother of Esfandiar," 86–90
chemical weapons, 172, 175
Chess with the Doomsday Machine (Shatranj bā Māshin-e Qiāmat) (Ahmadzadeh), 120
Chopin, Fredric, 67
Christ on the cross imagery, 101
Chronicles of Victory (Revāyat-e Fath) (television program), 33
Chubak, Sadeq, 18
CIA (United States Central Intelligence Agency), 8
cinema, 19, 205n8
civilians, 24–26, 28–29; Antoon and, 140–43; art and, 136; depictions of suffering among, 55; *Sky So Close* and, 129–31, 133; war culture and, 32–33; *See also* home front narratives.
climate change, 189
Cobham, Catherine, 71

Cold War, 7, 39
Cole, Sarah, 94–95, 98
"Color of Fire at Midday, The" ("*Rang-e Ātash-e Nimruzi*") (Mandanipour): duality with animals in, 76–79; Mandanipour, Shahriar, 72–76
commitment, 15–19, 201n40; pan-Arabism and, 55; state-sponsored rhetoric of, 36
comparative literary studies, 3–4
Coronavirus pandemic, 185
Corpse Washer, The (Waḥdahā Shajarat al-Rummān) (Antoon), 1–2, 156, 188–89, 228n12; alternative translation of, 197n3
"Counting the Dead" ('Abbas), 80–82, 84
Crystal Garden (Bāgh-e Bolur) (Makhmalbaf), 42
cultural production, 10, 13, 19, 21, 23, 27; contemporary Iran and, 184–86; early postwar period and, 61; Islamic Republic and, 184; literature and, 34; mobilization and, 34–37; official vs. real war representations and, 98–99; post-1979 literature and, 191–92; post-2003 Iraq and, 186–87; resistance to, 129; Saddam's Qadisiyya collections as, 49; subversive affirmation and, 148; truth and, 93; war culture and, 31; writing and, 137–38; *See also* Sacred Defense; Saddam's Qadisiyya.
Cultural Revolution (1980–83), 15, 40

"Dark Hand, Light Hand" (*Dast-e Tārik, Dast-e Roshan*) (Golshiri), 134
darkness, 78
Darvish, Mohammad, 189–90

Davis, Eric, 21
"days of plenty" (*ayyām al-khayr*), 126–27
death, 79–81; 1988 dead and, 82–86; corporeality of, 94, 97–98, 101, 104–6
Deer, Patrick, 32
Dehnamaki, Mahsoud, 98
Dehqan, Ahmad, 93, 218n61, 221n49; dark areas of official narratives and, 119–20; "I Killed Your Son," 99–102; insider status and, 122; *Journey to Heading 270 Degrees*, 95–99
demonization, 35
desertification, 190
desertion, 28, 85, 107, 109–13
diaspora, 183–84, 219n64
digital publishing, 182–83
disenchantment, 93–95, 98, 101
distance, 26, 72; anachronism and, 71; exile and, 91
Dowlatabadi, Mahmud, 18
duality, 72, 77–79
al-Dulaymi, Lutfiyya, 48
dystopia, 93, 110–13; *Scorpion* and, 114–15, 116, 120; state-sponsored literature and, 121

Egypt, 22
Eng, David, 90–91
environmental damage, 29, 168, 173–75, 178, 188–90
Ettelāʿāt (*Information*) (newspaper), 51
exile, 48, 91, 121–23, 153; Hillawi and, 106–7; internal publishing and, 182–84; *Scattered Crumbs* and, 108, 112–13

Falak, Nasif, 107
"Falconer, The" ('Abbas), 82

"Familiar Serpents" ("*Al-Thaʿābīn al-Alīfa*") (Khudayyir), 68–69, 70–71
Farasat, Qasem-ʿAli, 41–42, 56; Dehqan compared to, 98; *Headless Palms*, 58–59
Farman, Ghaʾib Tuʿma, 17, 22
Faslnāmeh-ye Honar (Arts Quarterly), 42, 207n38
Fassih, Esmail, 61
Ferdowsi (Abu al-Qasem Ferdowsi Tusi), 89
Fī al-Thaqāfa al-Miṣriyya (*On Egyptian Culture*) (Amin and Anis), 16
Fī al-Thaqāfa wa-l-Ḥarb (*On Culture and War*) (Iraqi Ministry of Culture), 53
Five Treasures (*Panj Ganj*) (Golshiri), 137
Five Voices (*Khamsat Aṣwāt*) (Farman), 22
First Iranian Writers' Congress (*Nokhostin Kongereh-ye Nevisande-gān-e Irān*), 15
First World War, 6; modernism's rejection of propaganda and, 90
formal antonyms (*aḍādd nawʿiyya*), 37, 122
Foucault, Michel, 21, 92
Foundation for the Preservation and Publication of Sacred Defense Works and Values (*Bonyād-e Hefz-e Āsār va Nashr-e Arzesh-hā-ye Defāʿ-e Moqaddas*), 95
Frankenstein (Shelley), 158
Frankenstein in Baghdad (Saadawi), 158–60; panoramic optics and, 179
freedom of expression, 28
friendship, 72, 75, 77–78
"Frog, The" (Jubaili), 166–67
futility-power debate, 28

Garden of the Martyrs, The (*Rawzat al-Shohadāʾ*) (Kashefi), 11
generational difference, 180
Ghaffarzadegan, Davud, 120
Gholami, Alireza, 148–50, 221n49; *Wall*, 125, 138, 144–47, 152–53
Gieling, Saskia, 51
Golshiri, Hushang, 23, 125; direct criticism and, 151, 152; *I'jaam* and, 143; "Painter of Baghan," 133–37; *Sky So Close* and, 137–38
Gordon, Avery, 156, 177
Gramsci, Antonio, 21
Grand Mosque, siege of (Mecca), 5
Great Harvest, 96, 167
Gulf War (1990–91), 7, 20, 126; environmental effects of, 175; oil fires and, 172–73; Operation Desert Storm and, 131–32; *Pruning* and, 179; revocation of martyr status and, 50; US bombing of Iraq in, 129

Hammudi, Basim ʿAbd al-Hamid, 46
Hanoosh, Yasmeen, 21
Hasan, Kadhim Jihad, 30, 48
Hashemi-Rafsanjani, Ali-Akbar, 62
al-Hassan, Hawraa, 47–48, 55
al-Hattab, Jawad, 65
headless palm trees motif, 174, 177, 180, 188–89
Headless Palms (*Nakhl-hā-ye bī Sar*) (Farasat), 42, 58–59, 98
Hedayat, Sadeq, 18, 23
heroism, 35; Mandanipour and, 74; *See also* martyrdom.
Hillawi, Jinan Jasim, 21, 93; Dehqan compared to, 105–7; disenchantment and, 95; exile and, 121–22, 153; *Night of the Lands*, 102–5; *Scattered Crumbs* and, 113
historical fiction, 119
Hizballah, 8, 185
home front narratives, 27, 28, 124–26, 126–28; direct criticism and, 152; dystopia and, 108, 111, 113; *I'jaam* and, 138–40; "Painter of Baghan" and, 133, 137–38; *Pruning* and, 180
Hoseini, Hasan, 41
Hoseyni, Seyyedeh Zahra, 186
"How to Tell a True War Story" (O'Brien), 25–26
Howzeh-ye Honari (Center for Islamic Art and Thought), 30, 40, 95, 102; Dehqan and, 107; war narratives and, 108
Human Rights Watch, 85
Hussein bin ʿAli, 10–11, 11; bloody palm image and, 90; *hejlehs* and, 225n44; martyrdom and, 51–52, 58–59
Hussein, Saddam, 5–6, 7–9; ʿAbbas and, 79; Baʿthification and, 11–14; censorship and, 182; direct criticism and, 152; dominating certainty of, 84; draining of marshlands by, 189; exile resistance to, 121–23; fall of, 155; *I'jaam* and, 140, 142–43; Karbala Five campaign and, 96; literary critiques under, 31; martyrdom and, 142; Nebuchadnezzar and, 52; nostalgia for, 186–87; *Scattered Crumbs* and, 109–10; secularizing Shiʿi martyrology by, 53; *Sky So Close* and, 131; Tikriti ruling cadre and, 201n37; war until victory slogan and, 2; writers after fall of, 153; *See also* Saddam's Qadisiyya.
Hussein, Taha, 16

Ibrahim, Sonallah, 22
I'jaam: An Iraqi Rhapsody (*I'jām*) (Antoon), 125, 138–43, 220n33, 221n35; caricaturing official war discourse and, 129; direct criticism and, 152; Hussein's fall and, 153; subversive affirmation and, 148
I Killed Your Son (*Man Qātel-e Pesar-e-tān Hastam*) (Dehqan), 99
"I Killed Your Son" (Dehqan), 99–102, 105; criticisms of, 107
iltizām (commitment), 15–16
Images from the Battlefield (*Ṣuwar min al-Maʿrika*) (television program), 33
imperialism, 36
Imposed War, 9, 24, 39; mutual framing of, 35
intellectuals, 34, 36, 37
Iran Air Flight 655, 8
Iran Hostage Crisis, 7
Iran-Contra scandal, 7–8
Iranian Revolution of 1979, 14–15; Battle of Karbala and, 11; bloody palm image and, 90; commitment and, 19; diaspora and, 184; exile and, 122; Iranian Writers' Association and, 38; land reform and, 212n26; post-1979 literature and, 190–92; *Scorched Earth* and, 43
Iranian Writers' Association, 38–40, 44
Iraqi Christ, The (Blasim), 157
Iraqi Communist Party (ICP), 14, 17, 216n18
Iraqi Martyrs' Foundation, 50–51
Iraqi Monarchy, 17
"I Should Erase and Draw" ("*Amḥū wa-Arsim*") (Khudayyir), 70

Islam, 10–13, 36; original Islamic Revolution in Iraqi history and, 54
Islamic Republic of Iran, 21, 183; contemporary cultural production and, 184–85; formation of, 4–5, 9, 14–15, 19; influence of, 187; as martyrs' welfare state, 209n60; rapprochement with Saudi Arabia and, 200n22; Sacred Defense and, 24; televised confessions and, 149–50
Islamic revolution, 56, 58–59; original Islamic revolution and, 54; secular Arab resistance to, 51
Islamic State (IS or Daesh), 185
Islamification, 15
Islamism, 18; left wing of, 39–40
Israel, 6; anti-imperialism and, 36; Palestinian literature and, 16; Saddam's Qadisiyya and, 45

Jahan-Ara, Mohammad, 59
Jerusalem, Karbala as route to, 35
Johnson, Rebecca, 139
Journey to Heading 270 Degrees (*Safar beh Garā-ye Devist va Haftād Darajeh*) (Dehqan), 95–99, 101–2; Hillawi compared to, 105–7
Jubaili, Diaa, 154, 157, 180; environment and, 168; "Frog, The," 166–67; *No Windmills in Basra*, 158, 164–68; "Saltworks, The," 165; slow violence and, 189; "Taste of Death, The," 165–66
July 1958 Revolution, 17, 18

Kachachi, Inaam, 132
al-Kamali, Shafiq, 45, 208n47
Kanafani, Ghassan, 16, 22

Karbala 4 Operation, 167
Karbala Five campaign, 96, 167
Karbala, Battle of, 10–12; *hejlehs* and, 225n44; Husayn's martyrdom at, 51; Khorramshahr likened to, 59; slogans invoking, 35; *See also* Sacred Defense.
Kashefi, Husayn Vaiz, 11
al-Kati', Kazim al-Isma'il, 187
Kazanjian, David, 90–91
Kazim, Salam, 37
Khalaf, Ahmad, 55
Khamenei, Ali, 185
Khansa' (mother of the modern martyrs), 52
al-Kharrat, Edwar, 22
Khatami, Mohammad, 63
Khedairi, Betool, 125, 129–31; 220n17; Ba'th and, 152; indirect criticism and, 151; *I'jaam* and, 143; media and, 140; "Painter of Baghan" and, 137–38; *Sky So Close*, 126–30, 132–33, 140, 143
Khidr, 'Abbas, 48
Khomeini, Ayatollah Ruhollah, 14; ceasefire and, 5–6, 8; *Headless Palms* and, 58; Iraqi literary journals and, 45; Karbala and, 11; liberalization after, 63; martyrdom and, 51; "Qomified" style of rule and, 201n37; Sacred Defense and, 36; war until victory slogan and, 2
Khorrami, M. M., 21, postmodernism and, 218n60
Khorramshahr, Iran, 58–59; *Pruning* and, 168–71, 173, 175–77
Khoury, Dina, 62, 85
Khoury, Elias, 16, 48; *I'jaam* introduction by, 139

Khudayyir, Muhammad, 48, 61, 63–64; "War Diary," 65–70; animals and, 78; *Basrayatha*, 64–65, 70–71; influence on 'Abbas of, 79–80; Saddam's Qadisiyya and, 211n5
Khuzestan, Iran, 5, 6, 45, 226n58
Kissinger, Henry, 7, 199n6
al-Kubaysi, Tarrad, 46
Kurds, 102–3, 105, 216n18; massacres of, 85
Kuwait, 49; occupation of, 7; oil fires in, 172–73; Saddam's Qadisiyya and, 46–47

Lebanon, 5, 6; United States hostages in, 8
leftists, 36, 39–40, 203n53
legitimacy, 36–37
literary criticism, 24, 30–31, 44, 46–49; Gorky-inspired fiction and, 41; martyrdom and, 52; mobilization and, 35; Persian war literature and, 115; postcolonialism and, 22; postmodernism and, 218n60; Sacred Defense and, 56–58; *Scorpion* and, 115; state imperatives and, 48
literary culture, 34–37
literary journals, 44–47; Saddam's Qadisiyya collections and, 47–49
Littérature engagée, 16
loss, 27, 63–64; Butler on, 177–78; *Pruning* and, 168, 170, 173, 175, 179
Lukonin, Mikhail, 68

Madman of Freedom Square, The (Blasim), 157
madness, 162–64
Mahfouz, Naguib, 22–23

Mahmud, Ahmad, 18, 42–44, 222n49; *Scorched Earth*, 61
al-Majidi, Khazal, 37
Makhmalbaf, Mohsen, 41–42
maktabi fiction, 41–42
Mandanipour, Shahriar, 63–64; "Color of Fire at Midday, The," 72–76; duality with animals in, 76–79; publication and, 86; works of, 71–72
Marashi, Nasim, 180; environmental damage and, 168, 173–75, 189; *Pruning*, 155–58, 169–72, 176–79
Marriage of the Blessed (Arusi-ye Khubān) (film), 42
"Marsh, The" ("*Māndāb*") (Sarshar / Rahgozar), 56–57
marshlands, 166, 168–69, 174, 177
Martyr 1777 (al-Shahīd 1777) (Nasir), 54
Martyr's Day (*Yawm al-Shahīd*), 52
Martyr's Monument (*Nuṣb al-Shahīd*), 33, 52, 205n10
martyrdom, 2, 9, 10–11, 27, 28, 35, 50–53; Behesht-e Zahra cemetery and, 215n69; devalorization of, 104, 105–6; disenchantment and, 94–95; dystopia and, 111–12; *hejleh*s and, 225n44; *I'jaam* and, 141–42; "I Killed Your Son" and, 99–102;Islamic Republic of Iran and, 209n60; *Journey to Heading 270 Degrees* and, 95–99; missing dead and, 84; "Munes, Mother of Esfandiar" and, 89–90; murals and posters of, 33; Sacred Defense literature and, 56–59; Saddam's Qadisiyya collections and, 53–56; *Scorched Earth* and, 43; state-sanctioned war narratives and, 20; *Sureh* and, 40; truth and, 92–93
Martyrs' Foundation (*Bonyād-e Shahid*), 50
Marxism, 18, 38
masculinity, 74
Masmoudi, Ikram, 132
McHale, Brian, 93, 119
memorialization narratives, 62
Men in the Sun (Rijāl fī al-Shams) (Kanafani), 22
Middle Eastern literature, 4, 192, 198n6
Ministry of Culture and Islamic Guidance (MCIG), 30, 40, 86, 144; Sacred Defense and, 153
Miramar (Mīrāmār) (Mahfouz), 23
Mir-'Abedini, Hasan, 52, 57
missing persons, 167, 180; *Frankenstein in Baghdad*, 159–60
mobilization, 35, 57; martyrdom and, 141
modernism, 22–23, 28, 63; animals in, 78; distance and, 91; self-questioning style and, 72; toothless opposition and, 37; wartime propaganda and, 90
Mohsen, Fatima, 17, 48, 182; martyrdom and, 52
Mosaddeq, Mohammed, 15; CIA coup of, 18
"Mother of All Battles" (*Umm al-Ma'ārik*), 9
mothers, 66–67; death of children and, 175–76; martyrdom and, 141; *thaklān* and, 226n57
mourning, 80, 89, 90–91, 168, 177; *See also* afterlives; loss; *Pruning*.
"Munes, Mother of Esfandiar" (Cheheltan), 86–90

al-Musawi, Muhsin, 47, 53, 208n49; indirection and, 130
Muʿawiya, Yazid ibn, 11

Nanquette, Laetitia, 183
Nasir, ʿAbd al-Sattar, 54, 210n74
nationalism, 43–44; Baʿthist ideology and, 111; "*nashinan*" as, 109–10; NKN and, 38–39; Ṣaddam's Qadisiyya collections and, 56; secularized readings of martyrdom and, 51
Nebuchadnezzar, 52
Neighbors (*Hamsāyeh-hā*) (Mahmud), 42
neoliberalism, 7
Nguyen, Viet Thanh, 25–26; haunting memory and, 164; panoramic optics and, 151, 179
Night of the Lands (*Layl al-Bilād*) (Hillawi), 21, 102–5; Dehqan compared to, 105–7; exile and, 153
nightmare imagery, 114, 116–18
Nixon, Rob, 174
NKN (*Nāmeh-ye Kānun-e Nevisande-gān*) (Journal of the Iranian Writers' Association), 38–40, 42, 43; *Sureh* and, 41
No Windmills in Basra (Jubaili), 158, 164
normalization, 33, 67
Not Much Time Until Tomorrow (*Chizi beh Fardā Namāndeh Ast*) (Che-heltan), 86

O'Brien, Tim, 25–26
"Oh Homeland, Your Earth is my Camphor" ("*Yā Gāʿ, Turābich Kāfūrī*") (song), 187
"On a Bicycle at Night" (ʿAbbas), 79–80, 82–86

"On the Concept of Martyrdom" ("*Ḥawla Mafhūm al-Istishhād*") (al-Samarraʾi), 53
"On True War Stories" (Nguyen), 25
Operation Desert Storm, 7, 79, 129, 131–32
Organization for Islamic Propaganda (*Sāzmān-e Tablighāt-e Eslāmi*), 40
Organization of Islamic States, 5
otherness, 69, 77; duality and, 72
"Our Position" ("*Mawqifunā*") (al-Hamid and Tarrad), 46
Outcasts, The (*Ekhrāji-hā*) (film), 98

Pahlavi, Mohammed Reza, 14, 15
"Painter of Baghan, The" ("*Naqqāsh-e Bāghāni*") (Golshiri), 125, 133–37; direct criticism and, 151, 152; *Iʿjaam* and, 143; *Sky So Close* and, 137–38
Palestine, 16; Iraqi literary journals and, 46–47; modernism and, 22; war narratives and, 36
pan-Arabism, 16; committed literature and, 55
Pannewick, Fredericke, 148
panoramic optics, 26, 151, 179
Persian literature, 3–4, 183–84; ; postmodernism and, 218n60; use of name "Naser" in, 210n87
Persians, 12–13
PMOI (*Mojahedin-e Khalq*), 18, 85–86
poetry, 35; of commitment, 18
"Point of Contact" ("*Nuqṭat Tamās*") (Khalaf), 55
post-2003 Iraq, 155–57, 155–57; *Frankenstein in Baghdad* and, 158–59, 160; historical scope and, 152; *Iʿjaam* and, 222n58; Iraqi cinema and, 19;

post-2003 Iraq *(cont.)*
  panoramic optics and, 179; violent landscape of, 160; visionary style and, 71
postcolonial literary criticism, 22, 203n64
postmodern historical novels, 119, 218n60
President's Garden, The (al-Ramli), 156
prisoners, 87, 102–5; Antoon and, 138–43
propaganda, 30–32; literary criticism and, 48
Pruning (Haras) (Marashi), 155–58, 169–72, 176–79; environmental damage and, 168, 173–75, 189; home front narratives and, 180; literary influences on, 226n56

Qadisiyya, Battle of, 10, 12, 24, 27, 51–52; *See also* Saddam's Qadisiyya.
Qādisiyyat Ṣaddām wa-l-Khiyār al-Qawmī (Saddam's Qadisiyya and the National Choice) (Iraq Ministry of Culture), 53
Qādisiyyat Ṣaddām: Qiṣaṣ Taḥt Lahīb al-Nār (Saddam's Qadisiyya: Stories from the Fire's Blaze) (book series), 47–49

Rabihavi, Qazi, 39, 43
Rafsanjani, Akbar Hashemi, 120
"Rahman's Story" ("Dāstān-e Rahmān") (Abkenar), 1–2
Al-Ramli, Muhsin, 93; art in, 151; caricaturing official war discourse and, 129; dystopia and, 108; exile and, 121–22; *I'jaam* and, 143; *President's Garden*, 156; *Scattered Crumbs*, 109–10, 110–13; subversive affirmation and, 148
al-Rasif, Jasim, 55
realism, 71, 91; generational differences and, 180; surrealistic depictions of war as, 115, 117; uncanniness and, 162–63
relational comparison, 4
Rentzou, Efthymia, 78
resistance, 9, 16, 24; Antoon and, 138, 142–43; cultural forms of, 131; Islamic Republic and, 184; over-identification as, 111; *Sureh* and, 40; world literature and, 47
revisionism, 119
revolution, 36; Ba'thist Socialist Movement and, 54; *komitehs* and, 207n31; *See also* Iranian Revolution of 1979.
Revolutionary Guard Corps (IRGC), 5
Rohde, Achim, 48

Saadawi, Ahmed, 154, 157, 180; uncanniness and, 166
Sacred Defense Garden Museum (Tehran), 34
Sacred Defense, the (Defāʿ-e Moqaddas), 10, 20, 40–42, 56–59; Abkenar's representation of, 119; contemporary cultural production and, 184–85; Dehqan and, 95–96, 99, 107; disenchantment and, 98; duality of friend and enemy and, 77; dystopia and, 108; Khomeini's first use of, 36; legitimacy and, 29; literature of, 24, 27, 30–31; MCIG and, 153; "Munes, Mother of Esfandiar" and, 89–90;

nonconforming depictions of, 60–61; postwar narratives of, 60–61; *Pruning* and, 178–79; resistance and, 184; *Scorpion* and, 115, 119–20; subversive affirmation and, 148; *Sureh* and, 40–42; truth and, 92–93; war culture and, 32

Saddam's Qadisiyya, 9–10, 10, 12, 20, 32–33; *Basrayatha* and, 66; direct criticism and, 152; dystopia and, 108, 110–13; early war literature of, 55; *Headless Palms* and, 58; *I'jaam* and, 140; Khudayyir and, 71, 211n5; Kuwait invasion and, 62; literary journals and, 44–46; literature of, 30–31; lost interest in, 186; madness and, 163; martyrdom and, 50, 54, 53–56; mothers and, 67; mourning and, 142; Nasir and, 210n74; nationalist pop songs of, 33; nonconforming depictions of, 60–61; nostalgia for, 187; postwar narratives of, 60–61; silence compared to discourse of, 80; *Sky So Close* and, 127, 129, 131; truth and, 92–93; wild beasts passage and, 69; writing and, 161

Sadeqi, Bahram, 23
Saeed, Haidar, 17
"Saltworks, The" (Jubaili), 165
al-Samarra'i, 'Abd al-Jabbar Mahmud, 53
sanctions, 131–32, 183
al-Saqr, Mahdi 'Isa, 17
Sarir (publishing house), 95, 98
Sarshar, Mohamed-Reza (Reza Rahgozar), 41, 56–58
Sartre, Jean Paul, 15–16
Sassanian Empire, 12, 52, 200n30

Sasse, Sylvia, 111, 148
Scattered Crumbs (Fatīt alMuba'thir) (Al-Ramli), 109–10; art in, 151; caricaturing official war discourse and, 129; dystopia and, 108, 110–13; *I'jaam* and, 143; subversive affirmation and, 148
Scorched Earth (Zamin-e Sukhteh) (Mahmud), 42–44, 61
Scorpion on the Steps of the Andimeshk Railroad, or, Blood is Dripping from this Train, Sir! (Abkenar), 22, 113–15, 119–20; nightmare imagery and, 116–18, 116–18; postmodernism and, 218n60
second-person narration, 118
self-sacrifice (*isār*), 40
Shahnameh (Ferdowsi), 89, 215n71
Shakeri, Ahmed, 107
Shamlu, Ahmad, 18
Shams, Fatemeh, 19
Shariati, Ali, 40, 207n33
Shelley, Mary, 158
Shih, Shu-mei, 4
Shi'a Islam, 10–11; Abuzar Brigade and, 199n14; Ba'thist expulsion of, 198n11; loyalty to Iraq of, 9; martyrology of, 52, 53; paramilitary organizations and, 185; repatriation to Iraq of, 6
Shoja'i, Mehdi, 41, 56
silence, 80, 83, 86, 91
Six Day War (1967), 16
Sky So Close, A (Kam Badat al-Samā' Qarība) (Khedairi), 126–30, 132–33; artistic life and, 125, 129–31; Ba'ths and, 152; indirect criticism and, 151; *I'jaam* and, 143; media and, 140; "Painter of Baghan" and, 137–38

slow violence, 29, 168, 174, 180, 189
social media, 185, 187
social realism, 17, 18
socialist realism, 16, 18, 50
Soleimani, Qasim, 185
South-South cultural studies, 3–4, 191
Soviet Union, 7, 39
Soviet-Afghan War, 5, 6
specters, 157, 168, 179–80; *See also* afterlives.
Sprachman, Paul, 96
Stanton, Anna Ziajka, 143
state ideology, 57
state-sponsored culture, 17, 19–23, 25, 26–27; contemporary Iran and, 184; Dehqan and, 107; depictions of war front and, 120–23; early postwar period and, 28; failure of representations of, 63–64; financial opportunities and, 181; home front and, 125; literary criticism and, 48; literary culture and, 34–37; mass production of, 163; realism and, 115; Sureh-ye Mehr and, 98; war culture and, 31–34; *See also* Sacred Defense; Saddam's Qadisiyya.
Story of a City, The (*Dāstān-e yek Shahr*) (Mahmud), 42
struggle, sites of, 19–23, 90, 95, 120
subversive affirmation, 111, 148–50
Sureh (journal), 40–42, 56
Sureh-ye Mehr (publishing house), 95, 98–99, 120
surrealism, 115
survival, 63–64, 66–68
symbolic valorization, 95, 106; *See also* martyrdom.
Syria, 185, 187

al-Tabari, Muhammad ibn Jarir al, 11
tahyij (encouragement, excitement), 35
al-Tarkarli, Fu'ad, 17
takhassos (professionalism), 19
Talebi, Shaleh, 108
Talib, 'Ali ibn Abi, 52
Talib, 'Umar Talib, 47–48
"Tanker War, The," 8
al-Tarkarli, Fu'ad, 81
"Taste of Death, The" (Jubaili), 165–66
ta'ahhod (commitment), 15
ta'bi'a (to mobilize or call to arms), 35
Ten Nights readings (*Dah Shab*), 38
"The Tenth Night" ("*al-Layla al-ʿĀshira*") (Khudayyir), 66
Thawrat Tishrīn (demonstrations), 187
Things They Carried, The (O'Brien), 25–26
"To That Shore of the Arvand River" (Azarm), 39
train motifs, 80–81
"Train Going Up to Baghdad, The" (al-Wahab), 81
transnational exchange, 172, 183
truth, 92–94, 120; representation and, 121
Tudeh Party (Iranian Communist *Tudeh* Party), 18, 44; leftism and, 203n53

Umayyad Caliphate, 11
uncanniness, 158, 162–63, 165, 166, 171, 180; *See also* afterlives.
undead, 29, 154, 157, 164, 166–67, 179; *Frankenstein in Baghdad*, 158–60; *See also* afterlives.
United Nations (UN), 5, 8
United States (US), 6–9; anti-imperialism and, 36; invasion by, 158; post-2003 literature and, 155

"*'urs al-gā'* ("The Land's Wedding") (song), 141

Victory Arch (*Qaws al-Naṣr*), 33
violence, 98; disenchantment and, 94–95; slow violence as, 174
visual commemorations of war, 33–34

al-Wahab, Mahmud 'Abd, 65, 81
al-Wahid, 'Abd al-Razzaq 'Abd, 45
Wall, The (*Divār*) (Gholami), 125, 138, 144–47, 152–53, 221n49; subversive affirmation and, 148–50
war culture, 31–32, 34; early postwar period and, 62; literary production and, 34–37
war front narratives, 120–23; "I Killed Your Son" and, 99–102; *Basrayatha* and, 67–68; desertion and, 109; dystopia and, 108, 113–15, 116; Hillawi and, 102, 104–5; *Journey to Heading 270 Degrees* and, 95–99; nightmare imagery and, 117–19
War in the Iraqi Short Story (*al-Ḥarb fī al-Qiṣṣa al-'Irāqiyya*) (Talib), 47–48
war narratives, 3, 20–23, 24–26, 106–8, 182; cultural narratives as, 13–15; dark areas of, 119–20; declarations of victory and, 9; Iraqi journals and, 44; Islam and, 10–13; Islamic Republic and, 184; literary production and, 36–37; official narratives and, 31; postwar changes in, 62–64; *Sky So Close* and, 133; state controlled opposition and, 37; state tolerance of criticism and, 49; subversive affirmation and, 148; *Wall* and, 152; *See also* Sacred Defense; Saddam's Qadisiyya.
"War Diary" (Khudayyir), 78
"War of the Cities," 6
"war until victory" (slogan), 2
witness, 106
writing, 140–41, 152–53; difficulty of, 134–38
"writing back," 21–22, 22, 190

"yearning for martyrdom" (*shahādat-talabi*), 51
Yushij, Nima, 18

Zemestān-e 62 (*The Winter of '83*) (Fassih), 61
Žižek, Slavoj, 177

Stanford Studies in Middle Eastern and
Islamic Societies and Cultures

Lara Deeb and Sherene Seikaly, editors

The Revolution Within: Islamic Media and the Struggle for a New Egypt   2025
YASMIN MOLL

Unruly Labor: A History of Oil in the Arabian Sea   2024
ANDREA WRIGHT

The Incarcerated Modern: Prisons and Public Life in Iran   2024
GOLNAR NIKPOUR

Elastic Empire: Refashioning War Through Aid in Palestine   2023
LISA BHUNGALIA

Colonizing Palestine: The Zionist Left and the Making of the Palestinian Nakba   2023
AREEJ SABBAGH-KHOURY

On Salafism: Concepts and Contexts   2023
AZMI BISHARA

Revolutions Aesthetic: A Cultural History of Ba'thist Syria   2022
MAX WEISS

Street-Level Governing: Negotiating the State in Urban Turkey   2022
ELISE MASSICARD

Protesting Jordan: Geographies of Power and Dissent   2022
JILLIAN SCHWEDLER

Media of the Masses: Cassette Culture in Modern Egypt   2022
ANDREW SIMON

States of Subsistence: The Politics of Bread in Contemporary Jordan   2022
JOSÉ CIRO MARTÍNEZ

Between Dreams and Ghosts: Indian Migration and Middle Eastern Oil   2021
ANDREA WRIGHT

Bread and Freedom: Egypt's Revolutionary Situation   2021
   MONA EL-GHOBASHY

Paradoxes of Care: Children and Global Medical Aid in Egypt   2021
   RANIA KASSAB SWEIS

The Politics of Art: Dissent and Cultural Diplomacy in Lebanon, Palestine, and Jordan   2021
   HANAN TOUKAN

The Paranoid Style in American Diplomacy: Oil and Arab Nationalism in Iraq   2021
   BRANDON WOLFE-HUNNICUTT

Screen Shots: State Violence on Camera in Israel and Palestine   2021
   REBECCA L. STEIN

Dear Palestine: A Social History of the 1948 War   2021
   SHAY HAZKANI

A Critical Political Economy of the Middle East and North Africa   2020
   JOEL BEININ, BASSAM HADDAD, AND SHERENE SEIKALY, EDITORS

Showpiece City: How Architecture Made Dubai   2020
   TODD REISZ

Archive Wars: The Politics of History in Saudi Arabia   2020
   ROSIE BSHEER

Between Muslims: Religious Difference in Iraqi Kurdistan   2020
   J. ANDREW BUSH

The Optimist: A Social Biography of Tawfiq Zayyad   2020
   TAMIR SOREK

Graveyard of Clerics: Everyday Activism in Saudi Arabia   2020
   PASCAL MENORET

Cleft Capitalism: The Social Origins of Failed Market Making in Egypt   2020
   AMR ADLY

The Universal Enemy: Jihad, Empire, and the Challenge of Solidarity   2019
   DARRYL LI

For a complete listing of titles in this series, visit the Stanford University Press website, www.sup.org.

The authorized representative in the EU for product safety and compliance is:
Mare Nostrum Group
B.V Doelen 72
4831 GR Breda
The Netherlands

www.ingramcontent.com/pod-product-compliance
Lightning Source LLC
Chambersburg PA
CBHW022003220426
43663CB00007B/943